A WEEKLY GUIDE TO BEING A MODEL LAW STUDENT

Third Edition

Alex Ruskell
Director of Academic Success and Bar Preparation
University of South Carolina Joseph F. Rice School of Law

WEST ACADEMIC

860 Blue Gentian Road, Suite 350
Eagan, MN 55121
1-877-888-1330

Published in the United States of America

ISBN: 979-8-88786-445-7

This book is dedicated to Kerry Egan, noted author and ice cream aficionado.

ACKNOWLEDGMENTS

My sincerest gratitude to those who graciously lent a hand in the writing of this book: Professor Jennifer Carr, Kerry Egan, Professor Lisa Eichhorn, Professor Jacqueline Fox, Professor Ami Leventis, Professor Colin Miller, Dean Eboni Nelson, and Dean Ned Snow.

SUMMARY OF CONTENTS

TABLE OF CONTENTS

A Weekly Guide to Being a Model Law Student

Third Edition

INTRODUCTION

1. YOU KNOW MORE THAN YOU THINK YOU KNOW, BUT YOU NEED DIRECTION

Welcome to law school!

First, congratulations! Not everyone who wants to go to law school gets to do so.

Second, remember that fact and try to approach law school with joy. There will be some rough days and some things you don't really want to do, and there will be a lot of work, but ultimately law is really interesting and can lead you to a pretty interesting life. On those days when you're tired and have 100 pages of reading in a class you're not particularly jazzed about, remind yourself about how good you really have it.

You might be nervous. But you know more about how to do well in law school than you think you do. I'm going to use a real federal court case to prove it. It's my favorite case of all time. I think you'll be surprised at how much you already know about thinking like a lawyer, even if you have little or no legal experience.

In the early 1970s, Gerald Mayo was having a pretty rough life. So he did the only sensible thing: he sued Satan and his staff in a class action lawsuit in United States federal court in Pennsylvania. I'm not kidding that this case is real. It can be found at *Mayo v. Satan and His Staff*, 54 F.R.D. 282 (1971). My favorite part is the inclusion of "His Staff." I imagine Hell has a lot of soul-selling contracts to file, pitchforks to sharpen, and ironic forms of torture to research and develop. One of the things you'll need to know to really understand this case is that a class action is a case in which one person sues on behalf of a large group of people. For example, imagine a case where one person sues on behalf of all people injured by a company's defective lawnmowers. Mayo claimed that Satan was personally behind all of the bad things that happened in everyone's lives and should be liable for damages. The federal court took Mayo seriously and decided that the rules of civil procedure could not allow Mayo's case to go forward.

Why do you think Mayo couldn't sue Satan in federal court? The court came up with three reasons. Take a minute to think about this before you continue reading. Thinking about the answer on your own before jumping to the model answer is important in law school. In fact, developing your ability to think on your own is the entire point of all of your classes. Let me repeat that: Thinking about and puzzling out the answer on your own before checking the correct answer will, in large part, determine your success. Students often find their grades suffer because they are used to looking for an immediate answer to a question instead of spending time pondering the possibilities.

So, embrace the joy in this ridiculous situation and try to come up with at least two reasons Mayo could not bring a class action in federal court against Satan and his staff for his life being terrible. Remember, Satan is real in this scenario. What do you know about Satan? What do you know about people having trouble in their lives? Use what you know to answer the question.

Ultimately, the court held that Mayo could not bring a class action in federal court against Satan because:

1. There is no indication that Satan is actually subject to the laws of the United States. After all, he is the "Prince of Darkness": a foreign prince. For English majors, the court does make an allusion to "The Devil and Daniel Webster," but notes that the story isn't exactly the final rule on whether Satan is bound by United States law.

2. A class action is inappropriate because everyone's life has different struggles (that is, Satan doesn't mess up our lives in the same ways). For some, it might be a broken down car. For others, a broken heart. For some, it could be foreclosure and homelessness. For others, male pattern baldness. Consequently, a court couldn't really make a decision that addresses the millions of varying ways people have been adversely affected by Satan. It's not like everyone bought the same lawnmower and got injured mowing the grass.

3. There is no way to serve Satan with notice of the lawsuit. How would you find him to give him the papers? Where would the person delivering the papers go? How would he or she get there? Whom would he or she give the papers to? Would you just hand someone a Ouija board?

Without a day of law school, you could probably guess at least one of these reasons why Mayo couldn't sue Satan in a class action in federal court.

What you did when you used what you know and considered reasons why Mayo couldn't sue Satan is called legal analysis. It's the key part of law school, and what professors mean when they say "think like a lawyer." Law school's goal is not for you to memorize a thousand laws. A computer can do that better than a human ever will. A law school's goal is to teach you how to think in a particular way. To do this, professors often use the unfairly maligned "Socratic Method." But here's a little hint—if you fully engage in class and your casebooks with as much joy as you can muster, and really give yourself the room to think, you'll do fantastic in law school. You need to foster the attitude that thinking through problems is the most important skill of law school, even when you aren't absolutely positive of the answer, and even when you are unexpectedly called on in class and your brain falls out (more on this later).

Professors LOVE students who are thoughtful and engaged, and following this book will help you be the kind of student professors love. These are the students that earn the good grades.

2. WHY STUDENTS DO POORLY THEIR FIRST YEAR

For over 20 years, I have worked in Academic Success. Academic Success (sometimes called "Academic Support") is the office tasked with helping students learn the necessary skills for doing their best in law school. At the start of the second semester, I ask students who have performed below their expectations to meet with me. At that meeting, I begin by asking them what they felt they did wrong. I get the same answers every time:

1. They didn't stick to a study schedule.
2. They didn't go to tutoring or Academic Success Workshops.
3. They spent all of their time reading for class and didn't start preparing for exams until the end of the semester.
4. They made bad outlines late in the semester.
5. They didn't do enough practice questions throughout the semester (THIS IS THE BIG ONE).

Most law school classes come down to one high-stakes test at the end. Many professors don't provide any practice quizzes or midterms along the way, so it is up to you to practice and evaluate your progress as you go. A big part of success in law school and success in law practice is learning how to honestly evaluate your own work. Because many students overestimate how well they understand or underestimate how much is expected of them, there's a famous saying: "Everyone in law school has an A until the exam." Use this book to make sure you actually get an A on the exam.

Students who do poorly simply read, attend class, perhaps answer a professor's question here and there, and feel like they are doing well. But if they haven't done the work suggested in this book, they are likely in for a big disappointment at the end of the semester. I've seen it happen again and again and again over my career.

3. STOP WORRYING WHAT TO DO AND USE THIS BOOK AS A CHECKLIST

This book is set up as a week-by-week checklist of the things you should do to succeed as a law student. When an important new concept is introduced, this book will explain the concept and provide examples. In the second semester, there will be less explanation, but the checklist format will remain to keep you on track. Consequently, this book is not meant to be read in one sitting, but is meant for you to read as you go through your first year. If your school has more or less than 13 weeks of instruction, cut or repeat the tasks from Weeks Five and Six. There may be material you'll want to read at different times or more than once (for example, the suggested meditation in Week 10 in the Second Semester). If something comes up and you want to check out what this book has to say about it, just jump right to that section. You can use the table of contents to figure out where everything is.

This book should take a little pressure off, in that you won't waste time sitting around wondering what you should do, which usually leads to procrastination, worry, and goofing off on the Internet. Your studying will be as effective as it can be, and your time away from law school will actually be fun and restorative.

There will be a checkbox (☐) after the title of everything you should do in a particular week. Just like items on a grocery or chore list, checking them off every week will make sure they get done and give you a sense of accomplishment. The goal is to check off every one of them.

4. THINGS YOU DON'T NEED TO WORRY ABOUT

A. Law School Static

Law school is stressful, and because you are in the same classes, doing the same things, with the same group of people, there tends to be a "feedback loop" of people making each other crazy. This dynamic will come out in several classic ways. Rumors will fly around regarding the "best" outlines, the amount of studying everyone is doing, the genius who isn't doing anything but knows everything, the class romances, the best study group, etc.

There is no way to avoid this static, so you should just accept it for what it is: a byproduct of a large group of successful, high-achieving people thrown into an intense situation together. Many people compare this situation to fifth grade. Don't let it get you down or affect what you do. It will all magically dissipate by second year, and you will honestly wonder what all the weirdness was about.

B. The Grading Curve

Many new students worry a lot about the grading curve. If anything, the curve will help you and your classmates. In over two decades of teaching, I have never heard of a professor grading a student poorly simply because of the curve.

Here's a secret: your professors very much want you to succeed. They want their students to be successful, have good grades, and do good work—but they are not going to simply hand good grades to their students. If they did, their students would pay either on the bar exam or when they are in practice.

When a student does poorly in a class, there is usually no question that the student has made some mistake in studying or exam-taking that led directly to that grade. Consequently, sitting around worrying about the class curve is an absolute waste of time. Focus on getting your work done and learning the material.

C. Class Participation

You must speak up in class. This is how lawyers learn. Law school teaching is based entirely on a student's engagement, and if you don't try to actively wrestle with the material in class, you're not going to get much out of it. Even if it's not in your nature to do so, you should ask and answer questions in class. This book will keep reminding you to do so.

No matter how gruff your professors may act, so long as you are trying, they are happy that you are attempting to engage with the material. If they didn't like students, they'd be doing something else. In fact, the most common complaint I hear from my colleagues is how quiet a particular class is. I feel the same way. The worst thing in the world is to ask a question and have 70 blank faces stare back at you. I like students. I like the law. I'd like my students to like it too. No one wants to spend all day lecturing to a roomful of mannequins.

The only time a professor will be truly angry with you is if you are unprepared. Being "prepared" does not mean that you understand everything from the reading. In fact, if you understand everything from the reading, you might throw off my lecture. As an example, when I teach Constitutional Law, I have a bit about close reading where I ask, "What did Eve offer Adam in the Garden of Eden?" I expect someone to say "apple." When they do, I can point out that the Bible doesn't actually say "apple." Then I can go into a whole explanation of why knowing the actual words of the Constitution is important and how people sometimes believe that there are things in the Constitution that aren't actually there (like an express right to privacy). If someone says the right answer, which is "fruit," then it doesn't work out as well because it blows up my whole "gotcha" moment. Ultimately, "unprepared" just means you didn't do the reading at all or you weren't paying attention in class because you were messing around on your computer.

Exams are graded anonymously, and your professor is not standing in front of the class deciding who gets the "A" based on what students say in class. When you do speak in class, not one of your classmates is thinking, "What a bozo" or "What a genius." All they are thinking is, "Wow, I'm glad I wasn't called on." When you get called on, it's natural to feel like your brain just fell out. Keep calm, have your briefs ready (more on briefs later), and do your best. Your professor wants to see you think—both what you think and how you think.

D. Your Intelligence

You are now in a group of people as smart or smarter than you are. They might be as driven or even more driven. They might know more important people than you do. They might come from a family of lawyers.

There is no reason to compare yourself to your classmates. It's natural to compare, but keep reminding yourself that it is a terrible habit that will probably only make you sad—unless you are a swaggering egomaniac, then go nuts and revel in your feelings of superiority (although I imagine you won't be super popular with your professors and colleagues). At the end of the day, you will be getting the same degree as your classmates. If you can make yourself follow the plan of this book, you will likely do better than many of them.

E. Accommodations

If you have been diagnosed with a learning disability or received accommodations in undergrad (for an ADHD diagnosis, for example), you should apply for accommodations with the school. This is usually done through the Dean of Students or another Academic Dean.

If you have received accommodations in the past, your first year of law school is not the time to experiment with changing accommodations, although many students try to do so. Usually, this experiment does not end well because law school has a much larger workload than undergrad. Please reflect on whatever your reason is for not seeking accommodations if you have received them in the past and reconsider. Also, if you haven't received accommodations in the past but believe you might be eligible, the sooner you get them squared away, the better. Ask your

Academic Success Director or Dean of Students for more information on how to go about this.

So, with these preliminaries out of the way, let's start law school!

First Semester

WEEK ONE

You're going to have to do a lot of new things in the first few weeks. Consequently, the first few chapters of this book will be a lot longer than the chapters that come later. Simply follow the steps below (and remember to check the boxes so you have a visual record of all of the stuff you are accomplishing):

1. MAKE A SET SCHEDULE EVERY WEEK ❑

Making a set schedule every week means taking out a piece of paper, a whiteboard, or your phone or computer and writing down exactly what you are doing for that week. The biggest mistake students make is not making a schedule. The second biggest mistake is not making that schedule a detailed one that includes all the things one needs to do to perform well in law school.

Most students, if they make a schedule at all, simply write "study" or "read" or "torts" to cover a big chunk of time in their day. Because of this generalization, they usually end up just reading cases and preparing for that day's class during their study time.

The problem with this strategy is that the final exam is going to be more than a reading test. Just reading in order to prepare for the exam would be like getting into a boxing ring when all you have ever done is read about how to box. No sane person would do that. If you wanted to box and not get beaten to a pulp, you might read about boxing, but you would also exercise, do boxing drills, spar a little, etc.

A. The Goals of a Schedule

A schedule is designed to do three things: keep you on track, keep you studying enough, and make sure you use your time effectively and actually get things done.

We live in an amazing age of ubiquitous time-sucks. We have constant access to the Internet, TikToks, apps, video games, and pictures of people's delicious salads. If you don't keep yourself on track, you may easily spend an hour playing around on Instagram when you should be studying. If you wait to do the fun stuff until after you've studied, the fun stuff will be a lot more fun. Additionally, if you have a schedule that you have actually written down, it is one less thing you have to remember.

i. Keeping on Track

To do well in law school, you must do four primary things: participate in class, read and brief cases, write an outline, and do practice questions. Your weekly schedule should have each of these tasks listed specifically, so you are sure to do them. You want to be sure that you don't inadvertently take away time from outlining to give yourself more time to read, for example. Both tasks are equally necessary.

A set schedule works because it provides both a carrot and a stick for every task. Instead of thinking you have 20 pages to read over some nebulous time period, your schedule will tell you that you have two hours to read and brief 20 pages of contracts before you need to move on to your next task in torts. The carrot is that you know you only have to do this for two hours; the stick is that you know you only have two hours to get the work done or you may find yourself unprepared.

A schedule can help you create a little internal pressure to get work done. Pressure motivates. For example, imagine telling yourself on Friday night, "I should clean my apartment this weekend." You might get around to it Sunday night, since other stuff is going to get in the way and you're probably not psyched to do it in the first place. But if the Dean of the law school is coming over to your apartment in an hour, you will focus and clean your apartment in an hour. A weekly schedule can help you create this kind of motivation for yourself and make your studying much more effective.

ii. Keep You Studying Enough

If you want to do your best, you should treat law school like a job. Come to school at the same time every day, leave at the same time every day, and make sure you put those hours in. Many first year law students make the mistake of studying like they did in undergrad, which is likely nowhere near enough for law school because of the increased difficulty and workload. Treating law school like a job will make your life a lot easier even if you've never had a full-time job before. You'll get used to the routine and you'll be a lot more effective with the use of your time. Treating law school like a job will also prepare you for the demands of law practice.

iii. Using Your Time Effectively

As stated above, you must be able to do four things during the course of the semester: participate in class, read and brief, outline, and do practice questions. The amount of time you take per week on each activity will vary from week to week. For example, you will read more in the first two weeks than you will do practice questions because you don't know enough law yet to make practice questions worthwhile. Consequently, for Week One, your schedule will only include going to class, going to Academic Success events or tutoring hours, going over notes, and reading and briefing. Things will be added, subtracted, or changed as the weeks progress.

Many students feel overwhelmed by the amount of work in law school. They are tempted to skip voluntary things, like Academic Success Workshops and tutoring. But one of the things that has become very apparent to me over the years is that the best-performing students take advantage of Academic Success Programs and tutoring, and the worst-performing students rarely go. It's a good idea to incorporate these programs into your set schedule.

You also need to sleep enough. Lack of sleep impairs your cognitive and emotional strength. Keep the same bedtime and wakeup time every day. Your mind will be spinning from information and stress, so you want to train yourself to relax and sleep soundly.

Finally, you need to get at least three hours of exercise a week because there is a huge link between mind, memory, mood, and exercise. Pick something fun, and don't look at it as a chance to drop the 20 pounds that have been bothering you, because you don't need any more stressors in your life. A lot of people run. Walking, dance classes, weight-lifting—whatever is a release for you. I try to swim every day. In law school, I boxed, which was good because I could hit people when I was in a bad mood.

Play to your strengths on your schedule. If you are not a morning person, don't schedule your most difficult tasks in the morning. If you have to go to sleep at nine, don't schedule your reading at night.

Finally, you may find a schedule this full a little bit constricting. Don't worry: you will be evaluating your schedule every week as the semester goes on, so you can make adjustments. Once you commit to following a weekly schedule, you'll likely discover that a detailed schedule actually frees up more time because you won't be wasting time procrastinating or wondering what you should do next.

Week One's schedule might break out like this, depending on what classes you are taking, when you want your free time to be, your sleeping habits, and when you most feel like doing work:

3 credit Criminal Law—four hours reading and briefing, 1 hour on notes, 1/2 hour tutoring session (if your school has tutoring)

3 credit Torts Law—four hours reading and briefing, 1/2 hour on notes, 1 hour tutoring session (if your school has tutoring)

3 credit Contracts Law—four hours reading and briefing, 1/2 hour on notes, 1 hour tutoring session (if your school has tutoring)

2 credit Legal Writing—two hours on assigned tasks*

First Week Academic Success Workshop

Three hours exercise

Bed by 11, up at 7

B. How to Put Your Schedule Together

1. Start with a blank schedule.

2. Fill in your school's hourly breakdowns on the side (some schools start every class on the hour, some provide 10 minute breaks—the included sample schedule has a school day that begins at 9:10 a.m. with 10-minute breaks between classes).

3. Fill in the times of your class meetings, the time of that week's Academic Success Workshop, and the times of tutoring (and any other mandatory things your school might have in Week One).

4. Fill in the time you want to get up everyday.

5. Fill in the time you want to go to bed everyday.

---

* This schedule assumes your work in Legal Writing is more hands-on research and writing, and that you won't need to be putting together an outline for a final exam in that course. Consequently, specific time to review your notes is not set aside. You also want to specifically note when Legal Writing assignments are due. By setting time aside to work on Legal Writing each week, you shouldn't need to do an immense amount of work right before an assignment is due. Pulling all-nighters the night before might be how you wrote your papers in undergraduate, but trying to pull this off in law school is a stressful mistake.

6. Fill in your three hours of exercise.

7. Fill in your study times. Look at your syllabus to estimate how much time you might need for each class each week. In general, you may want to have some cushion between your class reading and the class itself. For example, if you have a 10 o'clock civil procedure class and you are planning to do your reading for that specific class day from 8–10 that morning, what happens if your car breaks down or your alarm doesn't go off? You need to try to insulate yourself from the consequences of this kind of mishap, because it will happen eventually. Set up your schedule so problems don't turn into calamities. Week One will only include Reading, Briefing, and Reviewing Your Notes. Other tasks will be added as the semester goes on.

8. All the blank time is your time. Do laundry, relax, etc. However, make sure you separate your necessities from your relaxing, or your relaxing is unlikely to occur in any meaningful way.

9. Mark out a set time for any catch-up you need to do in case you have a particularly heavy class one week or get behind in your reading or practice questions.

Here's what a sample Week One schedule might look like (a blank schedule is provided at the end of the book, so you can make photocopies to fill out). The study times do not add up exactly to any set time. However, all classes are given equivalent coverage, and the student is basically treating law school like a job:

	MON	TUES	WED	THURS	FRI	SAT	SUN
7:00 to 9:00	Breakfast and exercise	Breakfast	Breakfast and exercise	Breakfast	Breakfast and exercise		
9:10 to 10:10	Torts Class	Torts Class	Torts Class	Torts Class	Read and Brief Contracts		Read and Brief Contracts
10:20 to 11:20	15 min. Go Over Torts Notes/Read and Brief Torts	Legal Writing Class	15 min. go over Torts Notes/Read and Brief Torts	Legal Writing Class	Legal Writing Class		Read and Brief Contracts
11:30 to 12:30	Read and Brief Criminal Law	15 min. Go over Torts Notes/Read and Brief Torts	Read and Brief Criminal Law	15 min. go over Torts Notes/Read and Brief Torts	Legal Writing Homework		Read and Brief Contracts
12:40 to 1:40	Read and Brief Criminal Law/Lunch	Academic Success Meeting/Lunch	Read and Brief Criminal Law/Lunch	Club Meeting/Lunch	Legal Writing Homework/Lunch		
2:00 to 3:00	Contracts Class	Contracts Class	Contracts Class	Contracts Class	Read and Brief Torts		
3:10 to 4:10	Criminal Law Class	Criminal Law Class	Criminal Law Class	Criminal Law Class	Read and Brief Torts		
4:20 to 5:20	Tutoring for Contracts	15 min. Go over Contracts Notes/Read and Brief Contracts	Tutoring for Torts	Tutoring for Criminal Law	Read and Brief Torts		
5:30 to 8:00	15 min. Go over Contracts Notes/Read and Brief Contracts	15 min. Go over Criminal Law Notes/Read and Brief Criminal Law	15 min. Go over Torts Notes/Read and Brief Torts	15 min. Go over Contracts Notes/Read and Brief Contracts			Catch-Up
8:00 to 11:00	Go Home/Relax/Eat Dinner/Go to Bed						Catch-Up/Read Weekly Guide Chapter/Make Schedule for Week

C. Now Try to Follow the Schedule to the Letter (You Will Evaluate How Effective It Was Next Week)

Don't panic if you get off schedule, but try to stick to it as much as possible so you can see if it actually works for you. To keep on track, a good idea is to use the stopwatch on your phone or computer to set an alarm at the beginning of each set task (for example, a 15-minute alarm when you sit down for "15 minutes of going over Contract notes"). The alarm will help you stay focused and remind you to move on. Many people I know actually invest in a cooking timer for this purpose.

D. Alternative Schedule Idea

There is enough stress in law school without your schedule adding to it, so if the above scheduling suggestion is too intimidating, you can try a "To-Do List" Schedule. I believe the set schedule suggested above is actually the most effective, so at least give it a shot before you try another version.

For the "To-Do List" Schedule, simply make a list every day of all the tasks that should be completed that day and the amount of time that should be allotted to it. Then scratch out each task as you complete it. Do the tasks in the amounts of free time you have. For example, if you have a 30-minute break, you might be able to read a case. If you've allotted two hours to reading that day, you can cross out the "two hours" and replace it with "1.5."

Importantly, in making a "To-Do List" Schedule, you still have to make sure you divide your time up in the same way as a set schedule, with time specifically set aside for reading and briefing, outlining, practice questions, and reviewing your notes. A lot of people get through life with lists, and there is something very satisfying about scratching something off a to-do list.

The upsides to the "To-Do List" Schedule are that it's more flexible, it's probably less imposing, and it's a good way of using all the little breaks that come up during the day. The downsides are that you don't have a clear structure set for your days and it is a lot easier to procrastinate and end up having to do 30 things at night when you should be sleeping. However, if the set schedule doesn't work for you, you should give the "To-Do List" Schedule a try. Some people end up doing both, depending on the semester or week.

2. SOCIAL EVENTS ❒

In Week One, there are likely a bunch of social events. You should schedule these as well. It's important to feel socially connected at law school, and those students who do feel socially connected to their law school tend to have higher grades than those who do not.

A. You Need Friends

Friends in law school can help you keep on track, provide you notes when you are sick, and laugh with you at whatever goofy thing happened in class that day. They are invaluable for your success and make the entire process much easier.

B. Significant Others

"Significant others" includes romantic significant others, friends, and family. If you have a significant other who is not in law school, he or she will likely find you and your law school friends hard to be around. He or she won't get your jokes about criminal law or know who you are talking about when you reference someone from school. He or she might not share your interest in the law.

Most law schools have several events at the beginning of law school where significant others who are not in law school can meet. Some schools even have societies or clubs. Especially if he or she is a romantic significant other or family member who travelled with you to a new city so you can go to school, helping him or her find some non-law student friends of his or her own can make the whole experience easier for both of you.

C. You'll Get Weird

Law school is stressful. You see the same people every day, go to the same classes, and wrestle with the same difficult concepts. You need to blow off some steam and bond with others going through the same process.

D. These People Will Know You in Practice

You will likely know many people in your law school class for the rest of your life. They will be judges, partners, defenders, corporate counsel, and professors in your area, and you want to make sure you are on good terms with all of them. Later in your career, you want to make sure you have a good reputation with them and you might even be looking to them for a job or a referral.

E. A Caveat—Don't Overdo It

You can't do well in law school if you socialize like you did your senior year of college. Many students who do poorly in their first year go into law school as if law school were Senior Year 2.0. Or, some students believe that the most important part of law school is extracurricular activities and networking. It's not. Be reasonable with your time. Realize you can't get wrecked on Wednesday night and understand the Erie Doctrine on Thursday morning. Whether or not you are the president of every society at your law school, you'll still need to know the Erie Doctrine to do well and get a job. Complete your law school responsibilities first (this is where your schedule is key).

3. HOW TO READ A CASE ❒

A casebook is primarily made up of court opinions, which are primary sources. Unlike information in the textbooks you may have had in undergrad, the information in your casebooks is not already interpreted. The meaning and importance of the case is not explained. It might be edited for emphasis or cut up for space, but that's about it. Consequently, you can't read a case like a short story or magazine article.

First, make sure you read when you are actually feeling awake. Otherwise, it will take you twice as long. This might seem obvious, but in practice it's not. Many times, students schedule their reading at night like they were reading a book for fun instead of trying to learn information for a class.

Also, think seriously about where you are doing your reading. Avoid reading on your bed, because your brain is going to start equating your bed with study time, which is not going to allow you to relax and sleep. The law library is OK for some, but terrible for others. All your new friends are there—how distracting do you think they will be? Coffee shops can be good, as are other libraries on campus where you don't know anyone. It really depends on finding the place where it's easiest for you to focus.

Second, before you read the case, notice where it is in the casebook or syllabus because its location will tell you what concept the case represents in your class. When professors decide to teach a class, they go through all the available casebooks (there are usually a lot) and determine which casebook does the best job of clearly showing examples of all the concepts they want to cover. You should use this selection to your advantage. For example, if *McGilliguddy v. Mackadoodle* is listed in the section titled "BATTERY," that case is probably there to either give you the definition of battery, an exception to battery, an example of battery, a historical view of battery, or a tweak to the primary rule for battery.

Third, figure out who the parties are and what they want. These are real people with real problems who want something. Whatever it is they want is the point of the case.

Fourth, go to the end of the case and scan up from the bottom until you find the line that says "we hold" or "the holding is" or "the best rule is" or something to that effect. It may not always be clearly marked, but you will get better at finding it as you read more cases. This line or text is the holding of the case. The holding is the court's decision regarding the question posed by the case. You can read much faster and more effectively if you already know what the holding is from the beginning. You can also simply Google the case and see what it stands for. There's likely a Wikipedia or Oyez article telling you exactly what the holding is. Get the holding from there and then read the case.

When you are reading cases, you need to keep your reading within the time you scheduled for it. Consequently, you need to learn the most efficient way to pull a case apart and get to the parts you are going to use in class and on the exam. Poor-performing students often tell me that they read each case "three or four times." Don't do that. You don't have time for it. You'll get better and faster at reading as the semester progresses, so if the reading is slow now, don't worry.

Here is an example of a case in a casebook with notes. Although it is based on a real case, I made up a fictional example for illustrative purposes. Throughout this book I will use made-up cases to make sure you are writing your own briefs and outlines and using this book primarily as a model for your own work.

EXAMPLE OF A CASE IN A CASEBOOK

Chapter 1—Intentional Interference with Person or Chattels[1]

A. Mistake[2]

Morriss v. West,[3] 35 S.C.App. 250 (1886)[4]

STIPE, J.[5] delivered the opinion of the court.

West was out hunting for wolves. As he was hunting, he crossed onto Morriss's land. Morriss had a dog who bore a striking resemblance to a wolf. West, absolutely believing the dog was a wolf, shot the dog. Morriss sued for damages. At trial, the court ruled in favor of Morriss, finding that West intentionally shot the dog whether he was acting under a mistake or not. West appealed to the South Carolina Court of Appeals, arguing his good faith mistake meant he could not be liable for shooting Morriss's dog.[6]

FACTS

West rode his horse, Babe, to Edisto Island. He was accompanied by Magnum, a local banker of good standing, and Tweedy, a ne'er-do-well from Chicago. The three men also had five hunting dogs. The men intended to hunt and kill wolves that had been spotted near several local farms. Several goats and sheep had gone missing, and a calf had been severely injured. The men crossed through private property until they reached a beach. The beach was owned by Morriss, although the men believed they were on unowned land. While the men were eating a dinner of crab legs and beer, a large animal broke out of the scrub and started running down the beach toward them. The sun was behind the animal, but the men could still make out the shape of something that looked very much like a wolf. The men released their dogs, and the dogs ran toward the animal, chasing it. The animal

---

1 From the title of the chapter, you should infer this case is likely to deal with issues of intent. Also, if you don't know what a "chattel" is, you should look it up—the professor will certainly ask in class. Look up any word you don't know. It's fair for a professor to be annoyed that you didn't.

2 Mistake will be the focus of the case, so pay particular attention to anything that has to do with mistakes or the reasons someone made a mistake.

3 You will only need to know the name of the case on your exam if your professor says he or she wants to see case names on the exam or if it is a very important case and you spent a lot of time on it in class. Also, if the case is famous, like *Brown v. Board of Education* or *Marbury v. Madison*, you should probably know the name as well.

4 On the exam, you won't need to know the case cites. It would be unimaginably cruel if professors expected you to memorize them.

5 In class, you might be asked who delivered the opinion of the court—especially at the beginning, when your professors are making sure you can find your way around a case. But you won't need to know it on the exam (except in Con Law or in the case of special tests such as the Learned Hand test—your professor will note these).

6 This is the procedural history, or how the case ended up in this particular court. At the beginning of the semester, or in civil procedure, you'll be asked about this a lot.

turned around and Tweedy yelled, "That's a wolf, by golly!" West managed to get on his horse first and pursued the dogs and the "wolf" for a mile along the beach. The dogs eventually cornered the "wolf" in a briar bramble, and West shot it with his rifle. At that moment, Morriss arrived on his horse and declared that West had actually shot his dog, Petunia. Petunia was a very large (120-pound) mixed-breed animal that looked very much like a wolf. Morriss sued West for damages.[7]

DISCUSSION

The question submitted to us is whether West, because of his true but mistaken belief that he was shooting a wolf, could be found liable for shooting Morriss's dog.[8] If we take refuge in the ancient writers who wrote upon general principles of law, the judgment should be affirmed. Learned commentators have made several learned statements in this area. Judge Huffle[9] notes good faith mistakes do not insulate one from liability. *See Malk v. Brown,* 345 S.C. 23 (1883) (man accidentally euthanized the wrong horse). But Judge Slyth notes that *actus non facit reum nisis mens sit rea.*[10] Importantly, we are also concerned about the dangerous nature of wolves, and would like to encourage their eradication. However, we want to make sure that society's clear and justified zeal in eradicating such dangerous beasts does not encourage hunters to shoot, trap, or hunt without the necessary care. Under these circumstances, a clear rule that is not dependent upon the unknown depths of a man's heart is preferable. Otherwise, men could escape all types of liability simply by claiming they made a mistake, when it may be impossible to tell whether that mistake was made in good faith.[11] Consequently, we hold[12] that a person is liable for the

---

7 Because we looked at the holding first, we know the only facts we care about are those facts that could influence that decision—hunting wolf, seeing dog that looks like wolf, shooting dog, what West was thinking when he shot dog, how justified he may have been, etc.

8 Nice sentence to use in class if called on—"The issue here is whether West, because of his true but mistaken belief that he was shooting a wolf, could be found liable for shooting Morriss's dog." The case holding will be the answer to this.

9 Cases, in explaining their reasoning, will likely refer to older commentators and cases.

10 If you don't understand a Latin word or phrase, make sure you look it up. The most expedient thing would be to Google it, although a standard law dictionary will have any terms you need.

11 The past few sentences gave reasons for the court's ultimate rule. In class, it will be important to be able to explain why the court chose a certain rule.

12 The first thing you should do when you read a case is see where it is in the case book (here, Intentional Interference with Persons or Chattel). The second thing you should do, before you read anything else, is find the holding, which will usually be denoted by some version of the word "hold." This text will be the rule provided by the case. If you know this first, you can be much quicker when you read through the rest of the facts and discussion because you know you primarily care about language relevant to this decision (for example, the fact West shot the dog with a rifle is immaterial, unless

damages caused by his mistake, notwithstanding the fact he was acting in good faith. Thus, West is liable for the value of the dog.

DISSENT

BOWE, J.

I must respectfully dissent with my colleagues. In shooting the dog, West believed he was doing God's work and protecting the local populace. He should not be penalized because a local landowner chose to have a pet that looked very much like a wolf. In choosing to have a dog that looked like a wolf, *in an area known for wolf attacks,* Morriss invited West's actions upon himself and put the local populace, himself, and West unnecessarily at risk. A better rule would be to allow a person to escape liability in situations such as here where the mistake was reasonable and in good faith.[13]

NOTES

1. Here, the majority noted that the dog closely resembled a wolf. Would it have changed their decision if the dog didn't look much like a wolf?[14]

2. In situations where a party is claiming self-defense or other privilege, courts look at the reasonableness of the belief under the totality of the circumstances. *See Murp v. Mighte,* 345 U.S. 34 (1977) (landowner thought plaintiff was a home invader who had broken into his property).[15]

4. BRIEF EACH CASE ❐

A. What's the Point of a Case Brief?

A case brief is a short document you create that allows you to tear apart the case into something manageable and useful. Many people might tell you they don't brief for class. However, especially at the beginning of the school year, not briefing is a

the holding had said something regarding shooting the animal with a particular type of weapon). Here, the rule and the holding are the same, but in other instances, a student may need to distinguish between a generally applicable rule and a fact-specific holding.

[13] You should always read dissents if included. In class, a professor will often ask questions about why the case's rule might not work. You'll want to know the potential reasons why. Also, for some difficult cases, the dissent may do a better job of explaining the case holding than the main decision. Finally, the dissent in one case often becomes the rule in a later case.

[14] Always read the case notes and answer any questions you find there. These are possible hypotheticals or questions for a professor to pose—make a reasoned decision about all of them before you get to class and write your decision in the margins. Things included in notes might also be used on the exam.

[15] This note has provided you with an alternative situation that you should know—basically, what happens when someone makes a mistake and still claims self-defense or privilege.

major mistake. As you get more comfortable, you might move to book-briefing, which will be discussed in Week 11.

There are three purposes for making a case brief. First, it is a nice "cheat sheet" you can read if you get called on so you aren't in a panic flipping through your casebook pages. Second, it's a page you can mark up as you're following the class discussion. For example, you might find that your idea of the case's holding was wrong. If so, you can easily fix it on the brief, creating a record of the areas you may have to do more work in. Third, it forces you to test yourself to see if you actually understand what is going on. If the case brief is in front of you, you will know if your idea of the holding was wrong, or if you failed to note relevant facts, or if you didn't follow the court's reasoning. Without having done the case brief, it is too easy to sit in class, listen to the lecture, and feel like you "got" the case when you really didn't. Remember the famous saying, "Everyone has an 'A' until the final." Doing your case briefs can alert you to any problems early, which is essential if you want to do your best in law school.

B. What Parts You'll Need for Class

Especially at the beginning, you would do well to use the "classic" elements of a case brief. If you are required to write a brief for Legal Writing or another class to turn in, your professor might require different elements, but they should have many core similarities. Here's a brief based on the case above that uses the classic elements. As you will notice, it is brief. Remember, this case is fictional.

SAMPLE BRIEF OF EXAMPLE CASE

Case Name[1]**:** *Morriss v. West,* Page 35 of casebook (1886).

Facts[2]**:** West mistakenly shot Morriss's dog because he believed it was a wolf.

Procedural History[3]**:** At trial, the court ruled in favor of Morriss, finding that West intentionally shot the dog whether he was acting under a mistake or not. West appealed to the South Carolina Court of Appeals, arguing his good faith mistake meant he could not be liable for shooting Morriss's dog.

Issue[4]**:** Is a person liable for loss of a dog if that person shoots it under the mistaken but good faith belief that it is a wolf?

Holding[5]**:** Yes. Even if the person shoots the dog under the mistaken but good faith belief that it was a wolf, he or she is still liable because he or she intended to shoot the animal.

Reasoning[6]**:** Majority rule points out it would be impossible to know if someone really made a good faith mistake. Also, it could be too easy to avoid liability by claiming mistake. Finally, we want hunters to be careful. LATIN: The act does not make a person guilty unless the mind should be guilty. CHATTEL: a personal possession.

Dissent/Concurrence[7]**:** Dissent concerned that majority rule fails to take into account reasonableness and social utility of West's actions. Also feels that Morriss took unnecessary risk of having a dog that looked like a wolf in an area known for wolf attacks.

C. Parts You'll Need for Exam

When you start creating your outlines to study for exams, you will usually only need to know three things about the above case:

---

1 The name of the case.

2 The facts important to the court's decision.

3 How the case got to be in this court.

4 What question is the court trying to answer?

5 The court's answer to that question.

6 Why did the court think this was a good answer?

7 Commentary from other judges involved in the case.

1. The Specific Legal Rule from the Case—A person is still liable for damaging someone else's person or property even if he or she made a good faith mistake in doing so.

2. The Court's Considerations in Making That Decision—Impossible to know what people are thinking, too easy to avoid liability, want people to be careful.

3. A One-Sentence Explanation of the Facts of the Case—Man shoots dog because of good faith belief it was a wolf.

Week 12's explanation of how to write a good exam will show you where these three parts fit in your exam answers.

5. HOW TO TAKE NOTES ❒

A. Taking Your Notes

Because law school is intimidating and students are unsure of what they are going to need to know on an exam, many students take notes like stenographers. They try to write down absolutely everything anyone says in class. Often, this means they are spending more time typing or writing than actually listening to the discussion in class. However, it is important that you listen and follow along with the discussion.

Whether you type your notes or write them is up to you, although some professors do not allow computers in the classroom because of how distracting they can be. Do whatever is most comfortable, although I would recommend handwriting your notes. There are several reasons for this: because you physically can't write fast enough to write every word, it forces you to listen more critically so you can discern what to keep; you won't have the computer's temptation to instant message or look at baseball scores; you can more easily draw arrows and diagrams; and you honestly don't want to be writing down absolutely every word. But if you aren't accustomed to handwriting your notes or you can't read your handwriting, you're probably better off typing them.

B. Reviewing Your Notes

The most important thing to do for your law school success is to review your notes after class. As set out in the sample schedule, immediately after class you should spend 10–15 minutes going over your notes. If you don't go over them immediately after class, you're likely to forget which things you wanted to mark or clarify. Human memory breaks down fairly quickly over 24 hours, so you cannot wait until the end of the week or when you are working on outlines to check and annotate your notes. Think about how many mornings you may have woken up saying, "Wow, that was a cool dream!" and forgotten what the dream was about by lunchtime.

When you go over notes, you want to do a few things. First, fill in any places where you might have zoned out during the lecture. Everyone zones out sometimes. So, if there was a moment where your professor said, "There are four elements to burglary," and you spaced out on elements two and three, make sure you ask a friend, ask the professor, or check some other resource to fill that space in. If you wait until later in the semester, it will be a lot harder to remember that you missed something.

Second, highlight and mark anything the professor indicated as important. A professor might be clear about this. He or she might say, "This is really important" or write it up on the board. A professor might specifically tell you how he or she wants to see answers on the exam.

A professor might indicate what is important in other ways. For example, you can figure out a lot of what is coming on the exam by "figuring out" your professor. When I was in law school, I got an "A" in one class because I noticed that every time the professor got really excited about something, he would jump like he'd suddenly fallen into an imaginary pothole. In my notes, I put stars next to everything he was saying whenever he did this. The "stuff he said in the hole" turned out to be the majority of the exam. If your professor gets really animated when talking about alienage and public functions or the parol evidence rule, you can bet it is coming on the exam. Mark this kind of thing when you go over your notes as well.

Third, make sure you mark clearly anything that you wrote down that was said by a fellow student and whether it was praised by the professor. You want to keep this stuff straight, and any arguments or thoughts that a professor praised are something you probably want to use on the exam.

Fourth, highlight the main ideas of the lecture and highlight any hypos given. "Hypos" are the hypothetical situations a professor might ask about in class. For example, "What if instead of cigar smoke, a person blew stinky tuna breath in someone else's face? Would that be offensive?" Hypos are likely previews of questions on the exam. Going through your notes will be the first step in your studying, and will be really helpful when you start your Outlines in Week Three.

Here's an example of what your notes might look like after you've gone over them (the bolded sections are things I marked or underlined while reviewing my notes after class). Remember this case is fictional:

> Date: August 15
>
> Reading today: ***Morriss***
>
> **Good faith mistake—does it insulate from liability—how does this relate to Intent?**
>
> Reflects importance of intent in law (generally don't punish people for unavoidable outcomes)—**POLICY**
>
> ****Study Hint (from prof)**—memorize rules/don't need to know case names/cites
>
> What if a doctor operated on wrong arm? Same analysis? What if it actually helped arm? What if mistake fixed by the doctor's mistake (for example, the intake nurse marked wrong arm and doctor's mistake led to operating on right one)?—**HYPO**
>
> **Student comment**—what about wrongful profit?—no wrongful profit in this case **(prof liked this)**
>
> **Prof hypo**—what if Morriss intended to trick West? What if he was using dog as decoy to protect wolves?
>
> West still intended to shoot dog—majority's concerns still apply
>
> What if social good extremely high?
>
> How does this affect issues of privilege, like self-defense?
>
> **In NOTES in Casebook**
>
> Social issue—how important is what wrongdoer was attempting to do?

Student Comment—Police officers who reasonably believe guy has gun can arrest

Student Comment—If guy hunting turkeys and shot pet one, would minority even care—turkeys aren't dangerous

****Exam Hint (from prof)**—make sure you use **SPECIFIC FACTS** in answer—reasonableness/type of animal could make difference

Dog—not situation where a human being is hurt

Intent can be broken down into: **SPACED OUT—ask friend for notes**

Many old citations in this case—old area of law—**Professor Bill's Guide to Tort Law** not bad to look at **LOOK FOR THIS IN LIBRARY/ASK ACADEMIC SUCCESS—STUDENT ALSO SAID THE EVERYDAY EXAMPLES by PROF TRISSLER was worth getting practice questions from—check out**

6. HOW TO APPROACH LEGAL WRITING ❒

First, while working on a paper the day before it is due may have worked for you in undergrad, it's a horrible habit in Legal Writing. The penalty for blowing a deadline is likely much worse, which mirrors what a judge would do to you for missing a deadline. Start your assignments early.

Second, the writing habits you might have gotten away with in your undergrad career might really hurt you now. It is fairly likely you are going to have to radically change your writing organization from "English assignment" to IRAC, CREAC, or whatever legal form you learn in class. This transition takes time, and you need to give yourself enough time for it.

Third, good writing (in any form, whether it be a memo or a poem) is really about good editing. Thus, you MUST do multiple drafts. If you turn in a first draft for an assignment, you are likely to be at the bottom of the grading curve.

Fourth, you need to take advantage of the opportunities for someone else to look at your drafts. Most schools only allow certain people to look at your drafts, or you could face an honor code violation. Consequently, you need to plan ahead so you can show it to your professor, your tutor, or whomever you are allowed to show it to. You can't do this if you run right up to the deadline.

Fifth, you'll have a much better product if you do it over a long period of time. By working over a period of time, you'll get a chance to think about what you write, look at it with new eyes, and protect your schedule and sanity. Also, it will be less "painful" if you write a paper in small chunks of a few hours at a time over a couple of weeks rather than try to write it in a 18-hour binge in a weekend. The more you put it off, and the bigger the task is, the more you will procrastinate.

Finally, Legal Writing can take over your life to the detriment of your other classes if you don't manage your time wisely. It can also be the knife in your GPA if you do poorly. Your professor's feedback will show you what you need to do to earn a good grade. Legal Writing is the one class that is guaranteed not to have a single cumulative exam at the end, and there is no reason you shouldn't do well.

Week Two

1. MAKE SCHEDULE ☐

Students who evaluate their schedules weekly and adjust accordingly perform significantly better than those who do not. Figuring out what works best for you is going to take some trial and error. You'll probably discover that it takes longer to get from home to school and back again. You might discover that you're more of a morning person than you thought you were. You might find you work better in a coffee shop than at a library. You might learn that going to the gym at 5 p.m. means you're going to waste 30 minutes waiting for a machine. Consequently, at the end of every week, you need to take a hard look at your schedule and see if it is working. If something doesn't work, fix it.

People are generally terrible judges of time. Time speeds up or slows down depending on a person's perception of the task at hand—fun things fly by, while boring things slog. The Internet compounds this problem.

The Internet is the most amazing time-suck ever created. A quick glance at a random listicle about the "10 Things That Are in Your Refrigerator That Can Kill You Right Now!" usually turns into a 30-minute trip down the rabbit hole of news, sports, Twitter, Instagram, Facebook, LOLcats, a "Which Vice President Are You?" quiz, and a video of stampeding golden retrievers. Websites are specifically designed to do this to you so they can get more clicks, so you need to be proactive in protecting yourself. If you take your notes on your computer, the Internet is always right there tempting you. Consider using a program to lock you out of the Internet when you are taking notes or studying.

I once had a student who told me she was horribly behind, working absolutely every minute of every day, and could see no way that she could keep up without giving up sleep. I asked her to use the method described below to keep track of what she was doing for a few days. It turned out that she checked Facebook three times a day—once in the morning, once at lunch, and once at night. She thought this would only amount to about 15 minutes a day, but it turned out that each Facebook visit was closer to 20 minutes—resulting in an hour a day on Facebook. There is nothing inherently wrong with playing around on the Internet for an hour, but when you are in law school and trying to do your best, spending an hour on something like Facebook is not doing you any favors.

Even if the Internet is not your poison of choice, plenty of other things can take up more time than you think—reading the news, watching television, working out, talking on the phone, or texting friends can all take up time you could be using to make your law school experience as successful as possible. I'm going to guess that, compared to law school, these are all "fun things," and your perception of how long you are spending on them is going to be really skewed. You need to do all these things to remain happy, but you need to keep them within reasonable time limits.

This is not to say that you need to give up "time-wasting" things cold turkey. In fact, you shouldn't or you'll have a nervous breakdown. But, much like a diet, there's a difference between allowing yourself one cookie after dinner and eating cookies all day long whenever you feel like it. You want to control your cookies.

A. How to Figure out Where Your Time Is Going

If you feel like your schedule isn't working, track your time like an attorney would for a few days.

Take a notebook and keep track of what you are doing in six-minute increments. For example, .1 is six minutes, .3 is 18 minutes, .7 is 42 minutes, and 1.0 is an hour. Your tracked day might look something like this:

.5—wake-up, brush teeth, get dressed

.5—coffee and bagel in kitchen/read HuffPo/Facebook/Twitter/Instagram

.6—drive to school/park

.3—wait for class to start/review notes

1.2—Torts

.3—fill in holes in Torts notes

.2—ESPN.com/Instagram/Stereogum

.2—walk to library/talk to mom on phone

.2—check email/get books out/settle down

.5—read *Miev v. Gaim*

.3—bathroom, go to vending machine

.2—check Salon.com, NYTimes

.6—read *Burr v. Ker*

.3—check Facebook, article on best Beatles records

.7—read *Mak v. Alar*

.3—walk to class/check briefs

1.2—Criminal law

(and so on and so forth through the day)

Lawyers do this in practice because each six minutes, while seemingly inconsequential, adds up. The example above tracks 8.1 hours of the student's time. Imagine this student is having trouble finding time to do practice questions during the day, and when he leaves it until after school to do, he never gets around to it because he is tired. But when you looked at his tracked day, he spends almost an hour goofing around on the Internet. If he was diligent and kept himself from "quick glances" at the Internet during the day, he could spend an hour doing practice questions and then have time at night to either look at the Internet or watch television or just go to bed. A lot of people tend to break up studying during the day by "glancing" at the Internet, but this takes up more time than you might think. Especially if you have children and/or a significant other, it makes more sense to get everything done during the day and have free time at home than to stretch your work out unnecessarily.

I am in no way saying that your day should be a breathless race without any breaks, but if you find yourself in need of time and track what you do for a few days, you may be able to find that extra time fairly easily. You won't be able to keep up a schedule where you consistently feel behind and stressed.

B. What to Do if You Get off Schedule

Unless you are extremely together and lucky, you are going to get off schedule your first year. Work may take longer than you expect (although as the semester progresses, you'll get faster). You'll probably get sick at least once. Your car might explode. You might have a day where you really just need to take a break. The important thing, if you get off schedule, is that you get back onto it as soon as you can. Unfortunately, students sometimes get off schedule and then just throw the entire thing out. This is a mistake.

i. Getting Sick

Unless you have the immune system of a Viking, you are going to get sick at some point in law school. This is a simple fact. If you get sick, just stay home, be sick, and get it over as quickly as possible. Get notes from good note-takers in the class, and be a good note-taker so you can pay it back. Once you are well, adjust your schedule to take out your free time and do whatever reading is required for your outline and the exam. Don't worry about reading at the same level as you would if you were worrying about getting called on. Just take out what you need for your outline and get back on schedule.

ii. Children

I know several people whose marriages suffered while they were in law school. For the majority of them, the issue was that the partner at home felt like the partner in law school had completely given up his or her childcare or domestic duties. Even if the partner not in law school agrees with or comes up with the idea himself or herself, it is a terrible idea to say "You concentrate on law school—I will do everything with the kids."

Kids don't understand what's going on—they just miss you. I have two children and I have learned to get absolutely everything I need to do done before I go home. That way, I am not playing Legos and worrying about a book or work project at the same time.

Kids also double or triple or quadruple the amount of things that can throw you off schedule. If they get sick, that might be a sick day for you. They have plays and baseball games and scout meetings you don't want to miss. They have school projects and hurt knees and nightmares.

Kids are going to take up a lot more time than you may have thought. Depending on how old they are, you could do homework or read together, but I have learned this is usually pretty futile. Consequently, the best way to deal with having kids in law school is the same way you would deal with law school if you didn't have kids—treat law school like a job, keep to a schedule as close as you can, and let your home time be your home time.

2. CONTINUE TO BRIEF ❒

While you might hear people talk about "book-briefing" (covered later in this book) or not briefing at all, you should continue to write out your briefs. The workload at this point is much less than it will be at the end of the semester, and you need to make briefing skills second nature. It will pay off in the long run.

3. ASK AND ANSWER RELEVANT QUESTIONS IN CLASS ❒

While many students have no problem participating in class, many students are intimidated by it. If you are someone who doesn't like participating in class, you should keep in mind a few things.

First, one of the worst feelings in the world for a law professor is posing a question to the class and being met with silent faces, so you should not fear a professor's questions. He or she genuinely wants to see you attack and struggle with the material so he or she won't view your "bad" answers too harshly. Now, if a professor asks a question like "What is the name of the case from the reading today" or "What is today's case about?" and you have no idea, the professor is going to be annoyed. But if you brief your cases, there is no way this can happen to you. Importantly, if the professor asks a less obvious question with no clear answer in the case, like "How might the court apply the rule in *Mayo* (*Mayo v. Satan and his Staff*, from this book's introduction) to Superman, if someone wants to bring a class action against Superman for destroying Metropolis during a fight with Lex Luthor?," the professor simply wants you to take what you do know and put together some kind of logical answer. For example, "Well, like Satan, Superman might not be subject to federal court jurisdiction because he is an alien from the planet Krypton. Serving him at the Fortress of Solitude might be just as impractical as serving Satan in Hell. Finally, Superman's wrecking of Metropolis likely affected everyone in completely different ways, so a class action is likely inappropriate." Something like this is a great answer.

Second, when you are a practicing attorney, no one is expecting you to be a perfect public speaker. The first time I went to court I was shocked at how "bad" the attorneys sounded while speaking. I don't mean to imply these were "bad" attorneys—they were hugely respected in the city, were working on complex cases for big time clients, and were doing great work. But from television and movies, I thought attorneys in court were flawless. These attorneys said "ummm," looked at legal pads, lost track, and stumbled here and there. The judges said "umm," looked at legal pads, lost track, and stumbled right back at them. After a steady diet of *Law and Order* and *To Kill a Mockingbird*, I couldn't believe it. My discovery was incredibly liberating. I had walked into court thinking I needed to sound like Gregory Peck when all I needed to do was make sense and sound like myself. The same is true in law school.

A. The Importance of Participation

Law school is about thinking like a lawyer, and you need as much practice in doing this as you can get. Speaking in class gives you practice expressing yourself in the law. Expressing yourself in the law is the skill that will make the difference on your exams and your professional career. Take as much advantage of practice as you can. Let your professors help you refine your understanding and communication skills. Otherwise, you might find yourself trying to express yourself in the law for the first time on your final exam, under time pressure and stress without any guidance or feedback.

B. How to Approach a Professor's Office Hours

Most law students don't take advantage of office hours. For years, I have heard my colleagues complain about students not coming to them with questions. If you don't understand a concept, go to office hours and talk with your professor. This way, you'll get to know him or her, and he or she will get to know you. You'll clear up confusion as soon as it comes up instead of waiting until the end of the semester when you might forget you had the question in the first place. You'll also be letting your professor know which concepts the class as a whole might be struggling with. Legal concepts build upon each other, and if you have some wonky understanding in the foundation, you will have trouble understanding the later, likely more difficult concepts.

If your professor gives a quiz or other assignment and you do poorly, you MUST go to office hours or schedule a meeting so you can learn how to correct the mistakes that caused your poor performance. Many times students fail to do this. In my experience, failure to do this seems to have a direct correlation with failing out or being put on academic probation.

C. Preparing to Meet Your Professor During Office Hours

You will get more out of meeting with your professor if you do a little planning. First, try to figure out the answer to whatever question you were planning to ask you professor on your own, either from commercial legal products, other students, or Google. In my experience, students vastly underuse Google. Many times, a quick Google search can give you the context you need to figure out the answer yourself. You might discover your confusion on an issue is simply the result of mishearing your professor or missing some context clue from the reading. For example, you might be confused as to why everyone is bringing up the time of day in common law burglary cases. If you look up burglary, you'll see that "at night" is one of the elements of the crime. You probably don't need your professor to explain things like that to you.

But, if after some searching you can't figure it out, go ahead and ask. Most professors I know just get a little annoyed when they feel like the student could have spent two seconds on Google and was just coming to ask because he or she didn't feel like doing it themselves. For example, I get annoyed when a student emails me to ask what days the bar exam is on. In that case, it probably took the student longer to write the email than it would to check the state bar website himself or herself.

I do not want to dissuade you from asking questions, but do take some time to think about them. For example, if you bomb a quiz and simply go in and ask the professor, "How could I do better?", you might get an answer like "I don't know—study harder?" That's not going to help you. You want to look at your work and ask the professor things like: "Was this a clear enough statement of the rule?" "Did I spot all the issues caused by the car wreck in the man's front yard?" "Do you have an example of an 'A' answer I can look at for comparison?" "Was my writing structure clear enough?" or "Did I adequately attach the facts to the law?"

4. REVIEW YOUR NOTES ❏

Make sure you take the time you've set aside in your schedule to go through your notes, fill in note-holes, and mark them up in preparation for your outline.

5. CONSIDER A STUDY GROUP ❏

A study group is not for everyone, but a study group can help keep you on task, give you practice explaining legal concepts to another person, and help you sort out difficult points of law. A study group should be small—no more than five people. Once you get bigger than that, you're basically having a party. The ideal size is probably three—you can fit around a small café table, everyone will need to talk, and you have a third person to break any impasses when two people are stuck on a point.

A. What a Study Group Is for, and How to Avoid Conflicts

The best way to use a study group is to go over practice questions and hypotheticals (these should be available from your professors, commercial materials, the law library, or your school's Academic Success Office). The absolute worst way to use a study group is to try to divide up the work. Why? Well, if you have one person making the torts outline, one person making the contracts outline, and one person making the criminal law outline with plans to swap outlines at the end, you'll only succeed in making yourself weaker in the two subject areas you did not outline yourself.

On the other hand, if you use the study group to do practice questions and hypotheticals, you can work on explaining points to others and you can get counterarguments you may not have thought of from the other members of your group. You can also help each other figure out what is coming on the exam. Finally, you'll get tons of practice answering law questions. Consequently, you'll do a lot better on exams.

B. Study Group Contract

Trying to keep any group together can involve stress. Over the years, I have heard a lot of student complaints about study group behavior. A member might never be prepared. A member might spend the entire time staring at their phone. A member might be "cheating" on his or her study group by also meeting with another. Since you do not need any more stress in your life as a first-year law student, I encourage you to have all of your study group members sign the contract below. It should help keep study group strife down to a minimum.

Although it may seem goofy, I am absolutely serious about photocopying this contract and having everyone sign it:

STUDY GROUP CONTRACT

This Study Group is made up of: ______________, ______________, ______________, ______________, and ______________, and all of us agree to abide by the rules below.

1. New members will be added only if _____ members agree.
2. A member may/may not belong to more than one study group. If a member belongs to more than one group, he or she must notify other group members.
3. A member will not be asked to leave the study group unless:
   a. The member is told what the problem behavior is (*e.g.*, consistently being late, rudeness, violating the other rules of this contract, failure to do work, etc.);
   b. The member has had ___ chances to change the problem behavior; and,
   c. After the member fails to change his or her behavior, the group unanimously votes to ask the member to leave.
4. A member who decides to leave the study group on his or her own must tell the other members that he or she intends to do so.
5. The study group will have a rotating leader who is responsible for setting the agenda and keeping the group on track each week. The order will be: ______________, ______________, ______________, ______________, and ______________.
6. The study group will meet _______ times per week at ________________ in/at ______________.
7. Study group members may/may not bring food.
8. Any materials developed by the study group together are not to be shared outside the group unless _______ of the members agree.
9. Study aids purchased jointly will be shared by: ______________________ (how will you share the aids?).
10. When not meeting, study group members will communicate with each other by text/phone call/email __________ (choose one).

Signed: __________________ __________________ __________________

__________________ __________________

WEEK THREE

1. MAKE SCHEDULE ❑

A. Add Study Group Time to Your Schedule (if You Join One)

B. Add Outlining Time to Your Schedule (Discussed Below)

2. CONTINUE TO BRIEF ❑

3. START YOUR OUTLINES ❑

Some sources may tell you to start outlines around Thanksgiving. This is terrible advice. You need to start now. There are several reasons why.

First, you are still in the first few weeks of law school. You should learn to outline now before your workload grows. Second, legal concepts build on each other, and creating an outline will help you see those connections. Third, in class, a professor provides you with "trees"—individual cases. To succeed, you need to take these "trees" and make a "forest." On the exam, you will not need to know case names unless your professor specifically asks for them. What you will need to know is how legal concepts interact and play off each other so you can take the "tree" of an exam issue (which is similar to getting a new case) and figure out where it belongs in that "forest." Writing an outline is basically making a map of the forest.

Your outline will be your primary study tool, ultimately becoming your personal guidebook to the class. You'll create your primary one, and then as you study later in the semester, you'll cut the outline down into an "attack outline" (discussed later in Week 13). Keep in mind the outline is a tool you will use to do well on your exam. No one will ever see your outline or grade it, although I do recommend showing drafts of your outline to your school's Academic Success person for tips. Sometimes, students spend far too many brain cells making the outline as if they will be turning it in for a grade, and this is clearly not the case.

This is important: **YOU MUST CREATE YOUR OWN OUTLINE.** This does not mean you should not look at commercial outlines or law school outline banks or outlines from other law students. In fact, you should look at commercial outlines and outlines made by other students. Doing so will likely make your life a lot easier and law school a lot less confusing. However, those things should only be used as tools to make your own outline better. You should use them to make sure you are not miswriting a rule of law in your outline or as an aid in figuring out your outline's structure. But the value of the outline is in making it, not reading it or memorizing it.

There is no set guideline in how long an outline should be. It has to be long enough to cover the class, but a 100-page outline is not going to do anyone any good because an outline that long would be impossible to memorize or use during an open-book exam. I would shoot for a ballpark figure of 20–30 pages for each class. That's absolutely manageable, and should allow it to fulfill everything you need it to do.

You can base the structure of your outline off your course syllabus, your casebook, or a commercial or student outline. Use the chapter or section headings as a basic framework and build from there.

Under no circumstances should you simply copy briefs into your outline. The weakest students line up one brief after another. On the exam, these students tend to see a question and write an answer like "*Johns v. Trissler* said that battery requires an intentional harmful touching of another. *Maya v. Alina* said consent is an absolute defense. In *Cathcart v. Palmer,* the plaintiff said, 'I dare you to hit me.' Here, the actions of the defendant clearly constituted a battery." This is an absolutely terrible answer on an exam because it doesn't explain how anything connects, why any particular law is implicated by the facts, or why a court may rule one way or another. This would be like a client coming into your office with a problem and you answering by handing them a stack of cases and saying "This should explain things." If you do something like this in practice, you will be on the phone with your malpractice insurance carrier a lot. Ideally, because you want to show your professors that you understand how the law works on your exams, and not that you simply know how to list a bunch of cases, you will be building your outlines around the law and using very little of the facts of the cases you read in class.

You need to make sure the Black Letter Law is precise on your outline. "Black Letter Law" refers to commonly understood legal rules. While close may count in horseshoes and hand grenades, it doesn't count on a law school exam. For example, if common law burglary is "The breaking and entering into the dwelling of another at night with the intent to commit a felony therein," then anything less is not common law burglary. On an exam, if you write "Burglary is going into the home of another with the intent to commit a crime," you would be wrong. Some professors may tell you what the Black Letter Law is. Some may not. Professors actually debate whether they should tell you. Some professors believe telling you the Black Letter Law does a disservice because it doesn't allow you to learn how to figure out legal concepts on your own. If a professor doesn't tell you what the Black Letter Law is, a commercial outline or other study aid will help you figure it out.

A. What Is the Point of an Outline?

You should write an outline because it is, in essence, the chance to plan and write 50 percent of your exam answer now. A good outline allows you to pre-think and pre-write your answers. You will be under a lot of time pressure during the exam, and you don't want to waste time then trying to figure out how you want to express the law. On the exam, you will be writing as if you were explaining things to a client, not your professor, so you want to plan a clear way of explaining things now. Your goal is explaining difficult legal concepts simply. In a nutshell, you'll do much better if you plan your answers for weeks than if you plan your answers for 10 minutes while you are taking your exam.

B. What Should You Include in Your Outline?

Remember, the outline is for you, but there are some basic things you should include:

i. What Your Instructor Communicates as Important

Anything your professor writes on the board or tells you is important should go into your outline. Your professor might also communicate these things in more subtle ways, like the professor I mentioned who kept falling into the imaginary "pothole."

ii. Black Letter Law with Elements and Exceptions

You need to have clear and precise statements of the Black Letter Law and any relevant exceptions to that law. On the exam, you will likely need to state the basic Black Letter Law and then explain why a particular exception applies. For example, you might need to write the rule for battery and then explain that the exception of consent applies.

iii. Any Instructions About Analysis Skills

A few years ago, a colleague of mine told his students repeatedly that they should start their analysis of negligence with "duty." On the exam, at least a quarter of the class didn't do this. Basically, these students were telling him on the exam that they weren't listening to him, which went over about as well as you would expect.

iv. Examples and Non-Examples of Each Concept

This is probably where the cases you read will fit in, and you'll want to use this as a pre-written part of your exam analysis. You might read a case showing an example of a contract offer and another showing where a contract offer wasn't made. You might want to use these examples on the exam. For example:

Offer—"I will sell you my guitar for $50."

Non-offer—"I would like to sell you my guitar for $50."

On the exam, you could use these two examples as parameters in explaining why "I could sell you my guitar for $50" is not a definite enough statement to create an offer.

v. Question Checklists

A question checklist is a list of the elements or considerations a court uses when deciding whether a particular Black Letter Law applies. These are really helpful to make sure you don't miss something on the exam. For some classes, if you are a visual learner, you might even consider turning these checklists into flowcharts. Your question checklists should also be the place where you write out the analysis skills highlighted by your professors (for example, always starting your negligence analysis with "duty").

Here's an example of what a question checklist might look like. This one goes through the thought process a student should use in evaluating a hypothetical regarding the Best Evidence

Rule, which is a rule requiring that an original document be presented at trial in certain circumstances:

1. Is the party presenting evidence concerning a writing, recording, or photograph?
2. Is the party seeking to prove the content?
3. Does the witness have personal knowledge?
4. Has the party produced the original?
5. Does the party have a "duplicate"?
6. Is there a genuine question as to authenticity or would it be unfair to admit it?
7. Is the original lost or destroyed in the absence of bad faith, unobtainable by judicial process, in the possession of the other party, or not closely related to a controlling issue?

As you will notice, you can't get to Point 7 without starting at Point 1. To get the most points possible on an exam answer involving the Best Evidence Rule, you would need to go through each of these points of Black Letter Law. Poor-performing students often jump to Point 7 without showing the professor the thought process of how they got there. Importantly, if you do not know all these points, you are going to miss potential issues on the exam.

vi. How to Memorize the Black Letter Law

You need to have the Black Letter Law of your class memorized whether or not you have a class with an open-book exam. This is especially important if your exam has multiple-choice questions (more on that later).

To memorize something, you want to engage in long term memory encoding. This is why advertising exists. In advertising, the idea is that you will see an advertisement and then remember that product when you go to the store. People don't usually buy products that they have never heard of.

The key to long term memory encoding is to make as many connections as you can in your mind between the thing you are trying to remember and other things you already know. For example, in advertising, you'll see a picture of something you know and understand like a beach or sun or friends and then the advertiser will shove a soda can in there. Pretty soon you'll connect that soda can with those things you already know and remember it the next time you think about the beach or sun or friends.

It's the same reason commercial jingles work. Honest to God, three mornings out of seven, I wake up with the Kit Kat jingle in my head ("give me a break . . ."). I don't really like candy, but I do like music a lot. When I actually do get the urge to buy a candy bar, it's always a Kit Kat. For all I know, I might like something else better, but Kit Kat is what pops up in my head when I think "candy bar."

Do you still sing the alphabet song when going through the alphabet? I do.

These are the kinds of stuff that you remember long term: the words to your favorite song; in the old days, the phone numbers of your friends (I can still tell you 10 phone numbers that I remember from when I was 12 years old); scenes from books and movies; jokes or funny lines; how to drive home; how things taste or smell; and long time acquaintances. The reason it's easy to remember those things is that they are connected to so many other things in your mind: happiness, fun, friends, comfort, etc.

As I've already mentioned, one of my favorite things in the world is music. Consequently, when I had to memorize a bunch of Emily Dickinson poems for school I used the fact that you can sing any Emily Dickinson poem to the tune of "The Yellow Rose of Texas." I'm from Houston, so I already knew the song really well. When I had to memorize the poems, I simply grafted " 'Hope' is a thing with feathers . . ." onto it. As I wrote this paragraph, I tested whether I could still do it. After 40-something years, I still could do six poems. I don't normally read Emily Dickinson poems.

Everything you've ever learned is in your head somewhere, it's just a recall issue.

a. Low Tech Encodes

1. Flash Cards

Make your own or buy commercial ones. Either way, instead of just reading the Black Letter Law, that moment of having to think before flipping over the card will help burn the Black Letter Law into your memory.

2. Memorize a Page or So of Your Outline

After you memorize the page, put it away and write it from memory. Keep going a little further each day. Eventually, you should be able to nail down the entire thing.

3. Practice Questions

Do a set of practice questions, go over them, and write your reason for getting any question wrong in a list of "Things I Do Not Know." Read the list every night. Wait a few days and do the practice questions again to see if you get them all correct. This is the best way to prepare for multiple-choice questions.

b. My Favorite Low Tech Encode

My favorite memory trick for memorizing Black Letter Law is to make up acronyms or sentences that include the elements you need to remember. A non-legal example of this is "Every Good Boy Does Fine" to memorize notes on a musical staff or "My Very Educated Mother Just Served Us Nachos" to memorize the planets in our solar system. I am a huge fan of using this trick on outlines. There are companies and books that will do it for you, and there are some classics you will probably learn from your professors in class, but I think making up your own is probably the best way to go. When I was in law school, I used to make up words and sentences that either made me laugh or reminded me of the particular legal issue. They come in handy when you are trying to remember the elements of a particular law, since they will remind you how many elements you actually need to remember.

c. *You Can Make up a Sentence to Remember the Elements of a Law*

For example, as a way to memorize the elements of the best evidence rule mentioned above, I might use this:

Writing

Content

Duplicate

Authenticity

Unfair

Unobtainable

***W**ill the **C**ourt **D**ig **A**lex's **U**ltimate **U**nderwear?*

For me, I can imagine the court needing to see this really cool underwear—plus, it's a little funny to me because I have the comedic taste of an eight-year-old.

d. *You Can Remember the Necessary Elements with a Word*

In property law, there is a concept called adverse possession where a person can gain title to a property even if he or she doesn't own it. The elements of this are Open and Continuous use that is Exclusive, Adverse, and Non-permissive. A great acronym for this is OCEAN. For me, I visualize a great wave coming along and sweeping someone's property away, which helps me remember it.

e. *Mind Maps*

Mind maps started in the 1960s and are good for people who like laying out information in a visual way. Think about police shows where they put all the information about a case on a wall and connect everything together with strings. To make a mind map, draw a box with the main concept in the middle. Then, draw lines to the subparts and then from those subparts draw lines to other subparts. The connections to help you remember will all be within the subject instead of bringing in outside things like songs or underwear jokes. You should end up with something that looks like this:

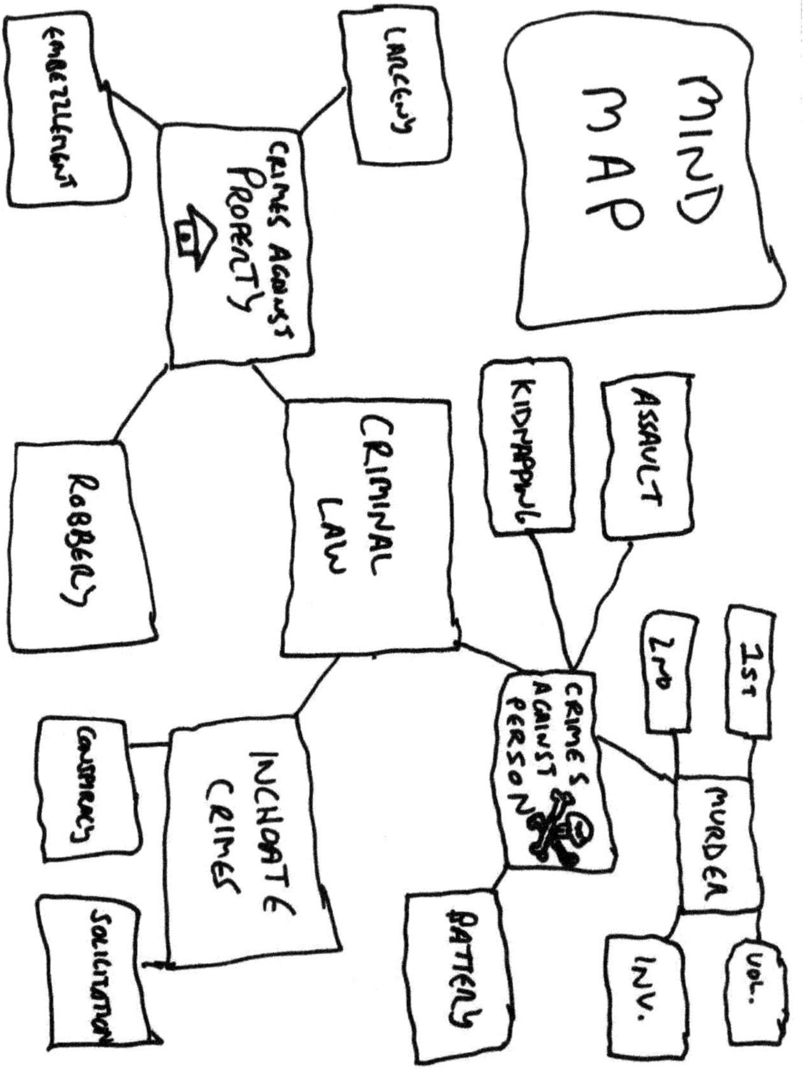

f. Spaced Repetition

Spaced repetition is probably the most popular learning tool in education. There are several computer programs that can do it for you, but you can also make your own with three boxes and some flashcards. I like actual boxes because I feel like I stare at computers enough as it is. If you don't use a computer program, this is how it works: Get or make a set of flashcards and get five boxes that you label Box 1, Box 2, Box 3, Box 4, and Box 5. Put all of the cards in Box 1 and review them 30 minutes per day. When you feel like you know a card, move it to Box 2. The cards in Box 2 are only reviewed every other day. Once you know a Box 2 card, move it to Box 3, which is reviewed once per week. If you know a Box 3 card, it goes to Box 4, which you review bi-weekly. If you know a Box 4 card, it goes to Box 5, which you review just before your exams.

If you are reviewing your cards and get one wrong, that card goes back to the lower box. So, for example, if you miss a Box 3 card, it goes to Box 2. When you get it right again, it moves back up. Your cards will move back and forth between the boxes throughout the semester depending on whether you are able to recall the information correctly. Spaced repetition is the hippest thing in education at the moment and it really works.

g. Memory Palace (Method of Loci)

People use this for extreme memory contests, which are actually a thing. How it works: first, imagine your house or a common path that you use. Visualize the rooms and their contents or the landmarks along the way. Then associate a concept with that landmark.

So, as an example, imagine that I am trying to remember the common law elements of burglary: (1) breaking and entering, (2) at night, (3) dwelling house of another, (4) with the intent to commit a felony therein.

To use a memory palace to remember this, I might visualize my walk to work. First, I visualize this one student house on the corner that has had a broken window blocked with cardboard for about six months. I visualize the window and think "breaking and entering." Then, I visualize the house where three baby raccoons were sitting in the middle of the road at night and almost got hit. I visualize that and think "night." Then, I visualize another house on the way where the homeowner once asked me to spray a big spider for her with cooking spray because she "just wanted to annoy it to make it go away." I visualize that and think "dwelling house of another." Finally, I picture a CBD and marijuana-smoking device store at the bottom of the hill and think "intent to commit a felony" (not that the store is doing anything illegal—I'm just old enough to remember when that kind of thing didn't fly so it still seems weird to me). When I want to remember the elements of burglary, I can just imagine my walk to work (which I do everyday) and all of the elements pop right up in my mind. A memory palace is the most complicated memory device, but you can memorize a dictionary with it.

C. What Information Do You Need from the Cases for the Outline?

While you might not necessarily put this information in this order, here is an example of all you need from any particular case. Below is an imaginary case regarding the legality of a confession:

> **Case Title—Stetson v. Carey**
>
> **Rule:** A confession must be made voluntarily to be lawful.
>
> **Short Summary:** In a case where five uniformed police officers stood over the 10-year-old suspect with Uzis while the suspect was in a county jail cell, the court held that the suspect's confession to burglary was not voluntarily given.
>
> **Court's Considerations:** Court looked at how many officers were present, if they had weapons drawn, if the suspect was in custody, if the suspect was a child, if a reasonable person would be placed in fear by police action, and if the suspect understood he or she was making a confession that could lead to further prosecution.

On the exam, you'll use the rule and then perhaps the facts of *Stetson v. Carey* to explain that rule. Then you would go through the court's considerations in answering the hypothetical. For example, imagine your question on the exam was something like this:

> Officer Casey was on vacation with his family in Big Foot Park when he saw Chad running across a field with a big sack with a dollar sign on it. Believing Chad

> might have just robbed a bank, Officer Casey chased him. Chad saw Officer Casey, who was wearing shorts and a Myrtle Beach t-shirt, running after him and shouting. Chad was 45 years old and very out of shape, so he only ran for a few hundred yards before getting tired. Chad sat down in the middle of the field. Officer Casey caught up with him and picked a stick off the ground. He poked Chad with the stick and yelled, "Did you rob the bank?" Chad replied that he had and started crying and asking for his mother.

Your answer to that question might look something like this:

> The issue is whether Chad's confession was lawful. A confession must be voluntarily made to be lawful. In determining voluntariness, courts look at how many officers were present, if they had weapons drawn, if the suspect was in custody, if the suspect was a child, if a reasonable person would be placed in fear by police action, and if the suspect understood he or she was making a confession that could lead to further prosecution. For example, in a case where five uniformed police officers stood over the 10-year-old suspect with Uzis while the suspect was in a county jail cell, the court held that the suspect's confession to burglary was not voluntarily given. Here, only one officer was present, Officer Casey was in casual clothes, Officer Casey did not have a gun or other police-issued weapon, Chad was in the middle of a field, and Chad was 45 years old. However, Officer Casey did poke him with a stick, and Chad's crying and asking for his mother seems to indicate he might be closer emotionally to a child than an adult. It's also unclear whether Chad understood he was making a confession, considering the fact Officer Casey did not identify himself and wasn't wearing a uniform. However, since Chad did not seem to be faced with any of the things that can make an officer situation coercive or frightening (like several officers, weapons, uniforms, or a jail cell) and Chad's answer just seemed spontaneous to Officer Casey's

question, a court would likely find his confession was voluntarily given.

D. What Does a Terrible Outline Look Like?

As stated above, the worst thing you can do is simply paste in your briefs. You will end up with an 80-page outline that isn't actually going to help. It could also encourage you to write a page on the exam simply telling the professor all you know about a case you read for class. The professor doesn't particularly care, and you won't earn points for it.

I have found that terrible outlines are often the result of fear. The student is afraid that something is being left out, so he or she includes enormous amounts of unhelpful material. Here's an example of a terrible outline of the tort of battery (these cases are made up, so don't go looking for them):

Battery—*Buddy v. Mary, 2010 WL 344567, 234 P.2d 455, 123 Cal. Reporter 3444, 345 LA Law 2 (1989).*[1] *Battery is touching another person or according to the Restatement 2d touching or putting someone in fear of being touched or otherwise apprehensive that such a touching could or might occur without the actual touching within the zone of danger of the participant. In this case, doctor didn't get permission to operate on shoulder that wasn't injured, so there was no consent to the touching.*[2]

Plaintiffs usually lose.[3]

Intent—knowing or substantially knowing that some sort of result could or will occur if the person goes through the actually planned act that can or cannot happen but is in fact intended.[4]

Rosemary v. Walter—a woman was getting on a crowded bus when a man brushed against her while trying to fit inside. This was not dangerous per se, but made the bus really

[1] You won't need the case citations on the exam—imagine how cruel it would be if you did. Consequently, don't include them in your outline.

[2] This rule is written in a way that is incredibly confusing—imagine trying to say this out loud to a client. It's certainly not something you'd ever want to write on an exam.

[3] Who said this? The professor? In regards to what?

[4] Again, a rule that seems translated from a foreign language.

crowded and tight. When the man brushed against the woman the woman screamed and tried to beat him up until the bus doors opened again and he was able to flee.[5]

Can't just go throwing people off bus—would be no implied consent to that

Jim v. Mercado—blowing tuna fish breath on someone can count.[6]

Egan v. Palmer, 2010 WL 3456677, 456 N.W.2d 123, 5566 Mont. Laws 344 (1983).

Judge Pollard, presiding.[7]

FACTS: Egan, a 43-year-old structural engineer with a bald spot, and Palmer, a young woman who hated all team sports but especially baseball and ultimate Frisbee went to the July 4th party at the Bigmore Beach Club, a club in Long Island, NY. The club had a pool, two handball courts, a basketball court, a small beach, playground, and a concession stand. The club was very crowded on July 4th. Egan was very touchy about his bald spot. To cover it up, he went to the beach club wearing his favorite baseball cap, which depicted the logo of the New York Throwers, a professional ultimate Frisbee team. He had gotten the baseball cap from his friend Gibby. Egan and Palmer did not get along, going back to their time in preschool together when Egan stole Palmer's blocks. Over the ensuing years they had grown up together, and Palmer knew how embarrassed Egan was about his bald spot. During the sand castle contest, Palmer saw the baseball hat, which seemingly combined the two sports she hated most in the world. She took it as a personal insult from Egan, who knew she didn't like baseball or ultimate Frisbee. Palmer went over to Egan and knocked his hat off in front of everyone, screaming "Ultimate Frisbee is ultimate lameness!" Egan was

5 Too much info—probably not much about bus safety on torts exam.

6 Count as what?

7 Who cares about what judge said this? Judges are only important when their name is actually the title of a rule or concept or you are comparing differing opinions on the U.S. Supreme Court.

embarrassed and ran away in tears. Soon thereafter, he sued Palmer for battery in New York superior court.[8]

ISSUE: Is it battery when someone knocks off someone else's baseball hat during a July 4th sand castle competition?

HOLDING: Yes.[9]

RATIONALE: Judge Pollard stated in his decision that Egan's use of the hat to cover up his bald spot made the hat a closely associated part of Egan. Ultimately, knocking the hat off, although Palmer did not touch Egan's actual skin, was just as harmful (and possibly more so) than if she had actually just touched his skin. Palmer did not like Egan and knew he was sensitive about his bald spot. Palmer clearly intended to hurt and humiliate Egan, and in fact did so because he went home in tears.[10]

As should be apparent, this example has far too much information, written in a way that the student will never, ever use on the exam.

E. What Does a Good Outline Look Like?

A good outline is the product of logical thinking and should be something you could basically paste into an exam to answer a question. You should build around the legal concept, not the individual cases, **because the legal concept is the important point.** It doesn't matter that a specific case said a rule. What matters is that you understand and can apply and explain that rule. For example, here is a good outline of the information presented above. Again, although the legal rules are real, these are made-up cases, so don't cite them in an exam or add them to your outline:

---

[8] There is no way you would have the time to use all these facts on an exam. Most of them are completely irrelevant.

[9] On the exam, you wouldn't write "issue" and "holding" like this.

[10] Way too much information in the rationale section—can easily condense this.

Battery

A. Battery—Intentional Touching of Another that is Unpermitted and Harmful or Offensive[11] **I**ggy **T**ouched **A**cid **U**ntil **H**e **O**ozed[12]

1. **Intentional Touching**
   a. Person must actually intend to touch other person (can't be accident/forced touching)
2. **Unpermitted**—consent is a complete defense to battery
   a. Express Consent—Actual consent by plaintiff—consent to one kind of touching does not mean all touching

      Example: Doctor who operated on left shoulder when right shoulder was injured liable for battery because patient did not consent to surgery on left shoulder—Buddy v. Mary.
   b. Implied Consent—can be implied by individual actions or generally accepted societal norms.

      Example: Brush someone to get on crowded bus. Rosemary v. Walter.

      Non-example: Push someone out of the way because the person is blocking the bus door, and defendant knocks plaintiff to floor. Decking someone not generally accepted societal norm.
3. **Harmful/Offensive**
   a. Must actually injure person in some way.
   b. Can be done with smoke or perfume if actually intended to be offensive

      Example: blowing tuna fish breath after losing card game—Jim v. Mercado.[13]
   c. Doesn't have to be physical person—just something closely associated with that person if intent is to harm or offend.

Example: knocking off baseball cap and revealing bald spot—Egan v. Palmer.

B. Checklist—

1. Was there a touching?
2. Did person intend the touching?
3. Was it unpermitted, harmful, or offensive?
4. Did plaintiff consent?

F. Commercial Materials/Other Student Outlines

As stated above, you should use commercial outlines and outlines provided by other students as examples and ways to check your work, but you must make your own outline. Year after year, weak students simply get an outline and try to memorize it. They almost always end up in the bottom of the class. Even the best outlines have mistakes. At the school where I teach, the "best" student outlines that are passed down from one year to another have names like "The Jones Outline." A few years ago, a ton of students made the same mistake on an exam, and I traced it back to a mistake in the "genius, number-one-student" outline. This mistake really hurt the grades of several students. Feel free to use other student's outlines in making your own, but be wary.

G. How Your Good Outline Will Help on the Exam

A really good outline should be set up and written in such a way that you could cut and paste it into your exam. In fact, if you have written a good outline, you've already got the rules and the structure of your analysis figured out. The only things you don't know when you sit down for the exam are the exact

---

[11] Although the cases are made up, the rule isn't. However, you should formulate rules in the manner stated by your professor. A legal rule is the same everywhere, but a professor could change the emphasis, wording, or order to make a point or clarify the rule for you, or use a statement of the rule from one particular case or another. Your outline and exam should reflect that.

[12] This sentence is goofy enough that I will easily remember it.

[13] On the exam, it's unlikely you will need to know the case names, but I find having the names on your outline makes everything easier to keep straight.

scenario and names in the question. For example, here is an exam hypothetical involving battery:

> Skippy decided to play touch football with his other law school pals. Everyone walked out to the fields, and the game started. People pushed, shoved, and sometimes even grabbed each other during the game, but since touch football specifically excludes tackling, no one tackled each other. Slappy saw Skippy playing. Slappy was angry at Skippy for stealing his girlfriend, Sweetie. Slappy joined the game on the opposite team from Skippy. Slappy yelled, "I'm going to woop you on the next play, Skippy!" As Skippy was running down the field on the next play, Slappy punched Skippy in the neck, crushing his larynx. Discuss.

If you had written a good outline, the only things you didn't know when you sat down for the exam were that the question would involve touch football, guys named Skippy and Slappy, a girlfriend named Sweetie, and a crushed larynx. Since you took the torts class that had the battery rule in it, you should have known a question in this area was coming.

Here is what a sample answer to the above question should look like based on the good outline provided earlier. Notice now much of it is pre-written. Everything in italics comes straight from the outline. Out of 192 words in my model answer, 53 came straight from my outline:

> The issue here is whether Slappy committed a battery against Skippy. *Battery is the intentional touching of another that is unpermitted and harmful or offensive. Consent is a complete defense to battery. Importantly, consent can be implied by an individual's actions or generally accepted societal norms. For example, gently nudging someone while trying to get on a crowded elevator would not be a battery.* Here, the punch was intentional, because Slappy told Skippy he was going to "woop him" on the next play. The punch was harmful because it crushed his larynx. The main issue is whether the punch was consensual. Here, by playing touch football, Skippy impliedly consented to touching, pushing, and grabbing (his friends were doing

it). However, while Skippy consented to some touching, he likely did not consent to being punched in the neck, which seems to go far beyond the bounds of a 'touch' football game, since "touch" football expressly excludes tackling. Consequently, a court would likely find Slappy liable for battery because neither Skippy's actions nor societal norms in the touch football game would imply consent to being punched in the larynx hard enough to crush it.

4. REVIEW YOUR NOTES ❐

Take the time you have set aside to go through your notes. Now that you know the point of outlining, you should have a pretty good idea of which things you should highlight.

5. LEGAL WRITING ASSIGNMENT TO TUTOR/PROFESSOR ❐

Week Four

1. MAKE SCHEDULE ❐

A. Suggestions to Speed up Your Reading

If you don't have enough time to get everything done because your reading is still going slowly, there are a few things you can do to try to tackle the issue:

1. Make sure you are using the reading strategies presented earlier. Don't read cases like a novel. Figure out who the parties are and what they want, look for the

holding, read the endnotes before the case, use clues from the case's placement in the textbook, and look at where the case is in your syllabus.

2. Look at a commercial or student outline or commercial case brief first to see what the case is supposed to be about before reading. In fact, you can simply Google the case name and a brief will likely pop up. You have to use these materials with a grain of salt, and you still must read the case, but it might give you some direction to speed up your reading. Remember that outlines, commercial case briefs, and online materials sometimes have mistakes, so don't simply substitute reading these materials for reading the cases. Use them as hints and guides, but nothing more.

3. Absolutely force yourself to read within the time you've set aside. Remove all distractions. When your time is up, move on to something else.

4. As stated earlier, when students arrive at law school, they sometimes discover that they have a learning disorder like ADD/ADHD. While the student may have already adopted coping mechanisms to get through undergraduate, these may no longer work with the increased workload of law school. If you suspect you have a learning disorder, ask your Academic Success Office or Dean of Students about the procedure for getting tested. Do this as soon as possible in the semester, so any available accommodations will be in place before exams start. Usually, these accommodations involve extra time on exams and quiet areas to take those exams.

2. CONTINUE TO BRIEF ❒

3. CONTINUE OUTLINES ❒

A. Complete One Syllabus Section in Each Class

If you haven't completed a syllabus section in your outline yet, try to do so. For example, if your class has completed Intentional Torts, see if you can get that section on your outline completed. Completing a section will likely be dependent on your class, but if you have completely covered the section in class, you should be able to outline it now. Pace your outlines by working on them continually. It is important to space out your outlines over the course of the semester because they will help you with class participation, understanding new concepts, and following the class. If you try to jam a ton of outlining in at the end of the semester, you won't get as much out of it and you will give yourself ulcers.

4. ASK RELEVANT QUESTION IN CLASS OR GO TO OFFICE HOURS ☐

Throughout the book I have included check-off boxes asking you to ask a relevant question in class or go to office hours. Being "required" to speak up sometimes takes a lot of the stress out of the whole endeavor. Eventually, speaking up will become second nature. Make yourself say something meaningful or relevant, then check off the box.

A. Email

Some professors prefer receiving questions over email. However, you need to be careful when emailing your professor. You probably know this already, but email lends itself to a lot of unintentional faux pas. Don't be too familiar ("Hey Dude-arino!"). Don't be passive-aggressive ("I know you're not really teaching this important legal concept, but I'm worried about the Rule Against Perpetuities.") Don't take the opportunity to complain about assignments ("Since we had over 50 pages of reading to do in your class, I couldn't do the worksheet"). Don't make one class seem more important than another ("Since I had civil procedure to do last night, I couldn't get to my legal writing assignment"). Don't ask for the impossible ("Can you look at my rule for proximate cause?"—sent at 3 a.m., when paper is due at 8 a.m.).

Most professors I know have received puzzling or vaguely insulting emails from law students. Like anything else on the Internet, use email, but take a minute or two to read over and think about what you are saying and how it might come across to the reader.

Importantly, **READ YOUR EMAIL from your school.** You might get tons of stuff every day, but this is the main way your professors and your school will pass along information. Every year, I have at least a few students who miss out on something important simply because they felt they were getting too much email and didn't want to read it.

5. REVIEW YOUR NOTES ❒

6. LAW SCHOOL STRESS ❒

By this point in the semester, the workload has probably picked up and the excitement of doing something new has probably worn off. At this point, a lot of students start to feel stressed out.

A. Where's the Stress Coming from?

Stress in law school is inevitable. When I was a law student, it was deeply implied that if a student was not in the top 10 percent of the class he or she wouldn't ever get a job, would end up in a gutter, and no one would ever love him or her. From the first day, everyone was talking about Big Law and how I really should go to Big Law or I was a loser. I didn't think I wanted to do Big Law. I didn't know what Big Law was. But everyone else was talking about it like I should. Suddenly, I was really worried about something I didn't know about that I wasn't sure I wanted to do.

You need to recognize the law school "buzz" for what it is. Law school is inherently stressful because suddenly you are thrown into a situation where everyone is as smart or smarter than you, you are all shooting for the same goal, you are all taking the same classes, and you will be ranked against each other in determining grades (which then determine job opportunities, clerking opportunities, etc.). Also, in the past 10 years, the bashing that law school, lawyers, and the legal profession have taken has been pretty relentless. Even so, this bashing is not a new phenomenon—I just read the 1917 novel *Princess of Mars* by Edgar Rice Burroughs (of *Tarzan* fame). In the novel, John Carter, the main character who has magically travelled to Mars, says, "In one respect at least the Martians are a happy people; they have no lawyers." Considering the

Martians solve all their problems by killing each other, this is a debatable statement.

In my experience, some law students get stressed about not feeling too stressed. This is normal. I get about 10 or so students every year that come into my office with this problem.

Intentionally or not, law students stress each other out. A fellow student might tell you, "My study group and I study every night until 2 a.m." Assuming you do not also study until 2 a.m. every night, such a statement might stress you out. However, realize the statement for what it is. With little to no feedback from professors, your fellow student is simply trying to get some positive feedback regarding his or her study habits compared to yours. If you want to be a nice person, you can respond, "Wow! That's great! You're definitely going to get an 'A' plus-plus!" If you want to be a mean person, you can respond, "Wow! I'm there until 3 a.m. every night and I don't usually see you."

Ultimately, there's probably nothing you can do to avoid stress entirely. However, you can and should try to contain it. Below are some strategies that may help.

B. Stress Test

As with any problem in law school, you need to evaluate the problem before you can tackle it. Ask yourself if you are engaging in any of these behaviors:

- ❑ Drinking more than three caffeinated beverages a day.
- ❑ Habitually drinking alcohol before bed.
- ❑ Failing to get seven to eight hours of sleep a night.
- ❑ Getting drunk regularly.
- ❑ Abusing any kind of drug.
- ❑ Drinking nothing but caffeine or alcohol.
- ❑ Eating a lot of junk food.
- ❑ Gaining or losing a significant amount of weight.
- ❑ Believing yourself too busy to exercise.
- ❑ Believing yourself too busy to eat one decent meal a day.
- ❑ Believing yourself too busy to keep your home neat.

- ❒ Believing yourself too busy to seek help.
- ❒ Believing yourself too busy to have fun with friends.
- ❒ Lashing out at friends or family.
- ❒ Spending more than an hour a day goofing on the Internet.
- ❒ Avoiding work and procrastinating.

These are the kinds of things people start doing when they are stressed out. These things build up in your system to make you feel worse. Getting bombed and eating a bag of potato chips can make you feel less stressed in the short term, but you need to make sure you don't let things get out of hand. If you recognize any of these behaviors in yourself, address them. Realize you are not alone and you can absolutely get through this.

C. Symptoms

If you are too stressed, you'll feel it. You'll get sick more often, avoid class, and avoid doing your work. You'll sleep way too much. You might start thinking your professors or the school are out to get you. If you find yourself running from law school, you need to address the problem immediately. Years ago, I would see a student in the gym no matter what time of the day or night I went in there. He was basically fleeing from law school by working out constantly and ended up failing out.

D. Coping

There are plenty of terrible ways to deal with stress. If you find yourself drinking more, avoiding human contact, taking drugs, or eating to excess, you need to stop now. You don't want to turn into the stereotype of the "drunken lawyer."

You also need to take a close look at your habits. For example, I once had a student who drank energy drinks all day and then knocked himself out at night with a six-pack of beer. He gained a lot of weight and started looking a bit like a zombie. His fellow students were actually so worried about him that they asked me to stage an intervention. If you find yourself staying up all night, you need to adjust your schedule so you can get some sleep. If you eat only microwave burritos and drink only diet soda, you need to make time to eat some healthy meals.

There's a lot of things that are probably adding to your stress. Some of it, like law school buzz, is fairly unavoidable. But other stuff can be contained. I would stay off the Internet, because it wastes time and every time I read an article about politics or someone being hurt I feel miserable. I would also stay off Facebook or Twitter or whatever is the cool thing at the moment you are reading this book. To use Facebook as an example of general Internet and social media behavior, people only post to Facebook those things that make their lives look great and fun. For example, before Facebook, I had never thought I should own a boat or take my kids on an African safari. After looking at Facebook, I feel like everyone else is doing those things and I am letting my family down by not doing them. While you're in law school, it's probably not going to help your mood to see the posts of that one friend who is riding a jetpack through Europe with Brad Pitt and Kermit the Frog.

Also, cut back on caffeine, sugar, fast food, and television shows involving murder or torture. Make sure you exercise. Make sure you have down time so you can hang out with friends and family. Try to keep your weight and basic physical wellbeing under control. Watch something funny on television instead of something dark. Keep up those hobbies that make you "you": keep playing guitar, painting pictures, writing vampire fan fiction, etc. Build all that stuff into your schedule so you will actually do it. As long as you are also doing the things in this book that are necessary for law school success, you shouldn't feel guilty about the time you take away from your studies.

Taking 15 minutes a day to meditate can really help. Almost every form of religion known to man has some version of meditation. Find a quiet place, sit or lie down, and close your eyes. Try to pay close attention to your breathing. Whenever a thought pops into your head, imagine encasing it in a bubble and gently letting it float away and out of your mind. Remind yourself that you can think about it later. It will be really hard at first, but keep at it until you train yourself to let your mind rest. You can also look at the meditation material in Week 10 in the Second Semester.

Finally, realize this time will pass. At the end of it all you will have your law degree and then you can use it as you see fit.

Keep your eye on the prize. It may seem silly, but if you want to use your law degree to represent children, put away criminals, support your family, or buy the most expensive townhouse in New York, tape a picture that represents this goal to your bathroom mirror. It will really help on those days when you are feeling down.

While the suggestions above can help, don't think you need to deal with the stress of law school alone. If you find yourself severely stressed or depressed, you need to ask your Dean of Students or Academic Success person about mental health counseling at your school. Many schools have inhouse mental health counselors that know everything you are going through. Even one meeting with a professional can help. Don't try to tough things out. Your school's mental health office will help you with strategies to deal with any stress you feel.

WEEK FIVE

1. MAKE SCHEDULE ❑
2. CONTINUE TO BRIEF ❑

3. CONTINUE OUTLINES ❐

A. Complete Second Issue for Each Class

4. REVIEW YOUR NOTES ❐

5. BACKUP YOUR COMPUTER ❐

Every year, students lose their notes and outlines because their computer died. Make sure you start regularly backing up your work on a flash drive or some other device. You can also just email all of your material to yourself. While you can always get notes and whatnot from your friends, the stress of losing everything is not something you want to go through.

WEEK SIX

1. MAKE SCHEDULE ☐

A. State of the Union

Now that you have a few weeks of law school under your belt, you should evaluate where you stand in relation to your classes, legal writing assignments, and your exams. Make any necessary adjustments now so you are not overwhelmed at the end of the semester. Are you keeping up with the material? Are you behind in anything? Is one class proving to be more difficult than another? Do you have enough time to both read and outline? Are you satisfied with how law school is going? Ask yourself all of these questions and then change what needs to be changed.

2. CONTINUE TO BRIEF ❑

3. CONTINUE OUTLINES ❑

A. Complete Third Issue for Each Class

4. ASK RELEVANT QUESTION OR GO TO OFFICE HOURS ❑

5. REVIEW YOUR NOTES ❑

Week Seven

1. MAKE SCHEDULE ❑
2. CONTINUE TO BRIEF ❑
3. CONTINUE OUTLINES ❑

A. Complete Outline Necessary for Midterm

Even if you do not have a midterm in your classes, get your outlines up to date as if you did have one. If you do have a midterm, getting caught up with your outlines is essential. Even if it is ungraded, treat any midterm as you would a real exam so you can clearly see where you stand before the end of semester exam. Otherwise, any wrong answers or any poor writing skills can just be attributed to not being prepared and you won't get much from the experience.

B. Check Outline with Academic Success

Meet with your Academic Success Office and see if they will take a look at some of your outlines. The help they can give you with structure can prove to be invaluable.

4. REVIEW YOUR NOTES ❒

5. HOW TO APPROACH A MIDTERM IF YOU HAVE ONE ❒

If you have a midterm, skip ahead and also read the advice on exam-writing in Weeks 10, 11, and 12.

A. Take It Seriously Because It Is the Best Practice Available

If you are lucky enough to have a midterm, take it absolutely seriously. Prepare and study just as you would as if this were a final exam. You'll get invaluable insight and practice for your study skills. Especially when they are ungraded, students often make the mistake of blowing off midterms. Don't do this. Also take advantage of any of your professor's offers to grade or go over your work. It's likely you won't get many of these.

B. Go over It by Yourself by Reading Professor's Comments and Score

After your midterm, you should go over it and carefully read the professor's comments and score to get an idea of where your weaknesses are. If you don't take a hard look at it afterward, you've really wasted your time. Even if you did fantastically well, you'll still find places where you can improve. Your fellow classmates are likely finding places where they can improve, and you don't want to be left behind. If you did well, don't start getting cocky and slack off now.

If you performed poorly, was it something that happened with your studying? Did you fail to study hard enough and thus did not know the Black Letter Law? Did you see all the issues? Did you run out of time?

The most common issue with a poor exam is that there was a problem with the answer structure. Look at your exam. Did you clearly state the rules? Did you state specific facts in the analysis? Did you write to a client, or did you write to your professor? Did you state counterarguments? Did you write every sentence with an eye to getting points, or did you dither around by repeating the question asked or writing a recap to everything you had just written? Did you do a brain dump, or did you answer the question asked? Did you use every one of the relevant specific facts that was provided in the question? Did you see all the relevant issues?

C. Go over It with Your Professor

By and large, students do not take enough advantage of professor's office hours. Especially if you did poorly on the midterm, you should meet with your professor to go over it. But even if you did O.K., or think you know what your issue was, you should meet with your professor. Students are often poor judges of their own work. For example, you might think you were simply off in your rule statements, when the reality is you missed many large issues.

First, ask if the structure of your answers was clear and complete. Did you have an obvious rule? In your analysis, did you use enough of the specific facts? Did you see and explain the relevant counterarguments?

If the basic structure of the answer seemed good, did you misstate the law or fail to see several issues? Both of these problems could be because of problems in studying or problems in your outline.

Was there enough meat to your answers? Were you too cursory in your analysis?

If your professor is willing, ask him or her to go over a question on the exam and show the difference between your answer and the best answers in the class.

6. BACKUP COMPUTER ❐

There are several good methods for backing up your computer, from saving things to Dropbox, the Cloud, an external drive, or even emailing things to yourself. Make sure you are backing up your work regularly.

7. LEGAL WRITING ASSIGNMENT TO TUTOR/PROFESSOR ❐

WEEK EIGHT

1. MAKE SCHEDULE ❑

A. Add Practice Question Time

At this point in the semester, if you haven't already, you should start doing practice questions. To get used to the skill of recognizing and reciting the Black Letter Law, I suggest you start with some short answer questions. Short questions divided up by subject for each first-year class are provided at the back of this book. I've divided them into sections based on where you are likely to begin your semester. To succeed, you'll need to do more questions than those provided in this book, but use these as a starting-off point. Pick questions relevant to the topics you have covered. Suggested answers are also provided. As stated above, you should do more than just the questions here. You can also get questions from commercial outlines, other study aids, your Academic Success Office, and your professor. You'll need to add some time into your schedule for these practice questions. Hopefully, your reading has gotten more efficient in the last few weeks, so you should be able to put in practice time without expanding the amount of hours you are spending each week on law school. If your reading is still slow, look at the strategies to speed up your reading in Week Four.

Doing practice questions is the best way for you to learn the law. Consequently, don't wait to do practice questions until you are completely done with your outlines or "feel ready." Waiting that long is too late, and doing practice questions even when you don't feel solid in the subject helps with studying and retention. You'll do a question and figure out what you don't know. The best way to learn anything is by practice. If I was teaching you to play guitar, it would be ridiculous if I simply told you about the guitar and you waited until you read enough about the guitar to feel "ready" and then you immediately played a concert. You'd bomb. The only way you would get good enough at guitar to play for an audience is to try it out. The same thing applies to studying and doing well on law exams. Start trying out what you know now. Otherwise, you may not get to do any practice until the night before the exam, which isn't going to help very much.

2. CONTINUE TO BRIEF ❒

3. CONTINUE OUTLINES ❒

A. Complete as Much Material as Covered in Class

If you are behind in your outlines, try to pick up the pace and catch up to where you are in all your classes. Exams are coming soon, and you want to make sure you have the time to do practice questions and have studied enough to make doing those practice questions as fruitful as possible. Practice questions should also alert you to problems in your outlines.

4. PRACTICE QUESTIONS❑

The practice questions in the back of this book cover a few different topics that your first year classes are likely to start with. Some questions are short, some are medium, and some are long. As you're studying, take a run at them as you go. Practice questions are the best way to learn the material. Even if you are not done with that area in your outline, take a run at a practice question. Doing outlines will help with practice questions, and doing practice questions will help with outlines.

A. Focus on Black Letter Law

Any time you are answering a practice question, imagine speaking with a client who has come into your office. He or she will tell you the problem, and you will respond with the relevant law and an explanation of how the person's specific facts fit into that law. There will be more on question answering later in the book, but for now, when you start answering questions, write out a clear statement of the Black Letter Law and then a clear statement regarding how the facts connect to that Black Letter Law. Write out your answers, and do not read the suggested answer before writing your own.

Use the questions to begin practicing issue-spotting, which you will need to do to do well on your exam. "Issue-spotting" means recognizing what Black Letter Law is brought into play by certain situations. On the exam, issues are created by specific facts. For example, if your professor says someone was drunk, or they didn't speak English, or they didn't intend to shoot anyone during a robbery, your professor is trying to alert you to the existence of a specific legal issue and point of Black Letter Law. On the exam, your professor wants you to be able to state the Black Letter Law regarding that issue and show how the facts link to it. Remember, as stated earlier in this book, your Black Letter Law statements need to be precise.

5. ASK RELEVANT QUESTION ❑

6. REVIEW YOUR NOTES ❑

WEEK NINE

1. MAKE SCHEDULE ❑
2. CONTINUE TO BRIEF ❑
3. CONTINUE OUTLINES ❑

4. PRACTICE QUESTIONS❐

A. How Professors Write Questions

To maximize your studying and reduce your stress level on the exam, you should try to make some predictions about the questions you will see on the exam. Take a look at your class so far. Do any current or famous events in the news touch on the subject area of the exam? What questions would you ask if you were in the position of a professor who wanted to make sure his or her students understood the class? What are the major issues in the subject? What areas were most interesting? What is covered in the notes and problems in the casebook or in professor or tutor handouts?

B. Getting a Read on Your Professor's Exam

You can also predict what is coming on the exam by watching your professor. What topics seemed most interesting to him or her? What topics did the class spend the most time on? What cases kept coming up during class discussion? What legal theories kept coming up during class discussion? What hypothetical questions did the professor ask? How did he or she change the scenarios of the cases you read when you were discussing them in class?

If your professor makes his or her past exams available, make sure you do them as practice. Many professors don't change questions much from year to year, simply because it's difficult to write a good question and there's value in having road-tested the question to see if it works. For example, one of my former colleagues gave almost the same exam question for 10 years.

Even predicting the small things can help make you feel more comfortable on the exam. For example, your professor might have favorite names or locations that seem to be included in all of his or her hypotheticals. My students could correctly guess that the characters in my exam are likely to be named Skippy and Slappy or after some indie rock musician. Even that small amount of familiarity can make you feel more comfortable on the exam.

5. REVIEW YOUR NOTES ❒

6. BACKUP COMPUTER ❒

WEEK TEN

1. MAKE SCHEDULE ❐

A. State of the Union

You're approaching crunch time. Look around and make sure you are caught up on your work and have a plan for getting everything done in the next few weeks.

B. Finding Time

If time continues to be an issue, you should go through the exercise in Week 2 of tracking your time like an attorney. You can gain time by adding more study hours to your goof-off time (don't cut into sleep) or you can see if your loved ones can help out with some stuff around the house that could buy you a little more time. Also, if you've been helping out your family by driving them to appointments or cooking dinner or getting groceries, see if you can pass this off to someone else in your family for a few weeks. Let them know that you need to do it and that it's only temporary. Getting prepared for exams must be the top priority, so make sure you keep to a good schedule that provides time for outlining and practice questions.

2. CONTINUE TO BRIEF ☐

3. CONTINUE OUTLINES ☐

4. PRACTICE QUESTIONS (MEDIUM ONES) ☐

The medium practice questions in the back of the book are a bit longer than the questions meant to help you begin your semester. They have more than one issue and deal with more than one discrete subject. One of the key skills you want to develop is making sure you answer the question that is created by the facts. If you haven't already, you also need to be getting questions from any source you can find. Doing questions improves your skills, but it is also the best way to learn your law subjects and it will alert you to what you do not know yet.

A. IRAC, and the Point of It

IRAC is the acronym for the standard form in which you should be writing your exam answers. If you haven't already been told by one of your professors, IRAC stands for Issue, Rule, Analysis, and Conclusion. You may be using a different acronym in your legal writing class: CREAC, CRAC, TRRAC, TREAT, TICra–FLipC, etc., but they all amount to basically the same thing: tweaked versions of IRAC.

On an exam, you should have one IRAC paragraph for every issue or situation you spot. You should not have one giant IRAC covering the entire exam. Even if your professor states that he or she doesn't care about IRAC, you will likely score higher on your exams if you stick to the IRAC form, and IRAC is absolutely necessary for success on bar exam essays, so you may as well start practicing it now. When students hear a professor say he or she doesn't care about IRAC, they often misunderstand that to mean the professor is fine with students writing down gobbledygook. This is not what a professor means. Professors still want answers that are readable and complete. IRAC ensures that you have logical structure in your answers and hit all the parts necessary to score points on the exam. In general, the only time not to use IRAC is if the professor asks you to write answers in a very specific form to that professor (e.g., he or she might only want bullet points in an answer). If the professor has a very specific way of answering his or her exam, he or she will tell you. Otherwise, go with IRAC.

A good legal answer should be easy to understand. You are not writing to your professor, you are writing to an imaginary client who has come to you for help and advice.

i. Issue

The Issue statement should be the first sentence of your IRAC. You can introduce it with "The issue is . . .", but you don't have to. Imagine a long exam question in your Criminal Law class where a lot of potential crimes are happening. For example:

> Skippy was very angry at Slappy and wanted to hurt him because Slappy had been borrowing Skippy's guitar for months without giving it back. He went over to Slappy's house at midnight to get his guitar back and saw that the door was unlocked. Skippy knew Slappy was out on a date. After he was inside the house, Skippy decided to steal Slappy's expensive computer as well. However, Slappy's gun-wielding father suddenly burst out of the bedroom and chased him back outside. Skippy didn't manage to get his guitar or the computer. Skippy ran across the street into the neighbor's house, grabbed

a wallet in the kitchen, and then ran out to the garage and stole a bike to escape.

In this situation, you want to break out each legal issue and discuss it. For example, "The first issue is whether Skippy committed a burglary when he went inside Slappy's house to get his guitar." There will be a second issue and IRAC for stealing the wallet, another IRAC for stealing the bike, and perhaps another IRAC for Slappy's dad.

ii. Rule

The second sentence of your IRAC is the Rule, or the Black Letter Law you are discussing. Poor performing students often skip this part or bury it somewhere later in the discussion. However, the Rule sentence (or sentences) is the scaffolding on which your analysis rests. Your Analysis section won't make sense if you don't clearly write out the rule with all of its elements. A good rule statement for the burglary issue might be, "Under the common law, burglary is the breaking and entering of a dwelling house at night with the intent to commit a felony therein."

iii. Analysis

The third part of your paragraph is the Analysis section. This is where you get the majority of your points on the exam. In the same order as the elements of the Rule you have just written, you should show how the specific facts of the hypothetical fit into that Rule. For example, "Here, there was a breaking and entering because even though the door was open, Skippy broke the plane of the doorway when he entered it. It was the dwelling house of another because Slappy and his father lived there. It was at night because it was midnight. However, when Skippy entered the door, he only intended to get his guitar back. He did not form any intent to steal the computer until he was already inside. Consequently, Skippy did not have the necessary intent for burglary."

Next, introduce the counterarguments. These statements, often beginning with "on the other hand," are an important part of your analysis. A counterargument is an argument that goes against the main argument you are making. You don't want your answer to be too conclusory, and your professor likely put in several facts that could make the Analysis go both ways. In finding counterarguments, you want to use the facts as they were given in the question and not use facts you make up on your own. For example, "If Skippy had been suffering from a brain injury . . ." is not going to get you points because those specific facts weren't provided in the question.

Here, you want to include, "On the other hand, Skippy did enter the house with the intent to 'hurt Slappy.' If Skippy had intended to physically hurt Slappy in such a way as to constitute a felony or to do significant damage to Slappy's property (such as arson), this likely would be enough to fulfill the intent requirement of burglary."

Once you state your "on the other hand" argument, you then need to explain why you think this won't ultimately change the outcome. Here, you might write, "However, Skippy knew Slappy was not home when he entered the house, so he could not have intended to physically harm Slappy, and he did nothing to indicate he wanted to do significant damage to the property."

iv. Conclusion

Finally, you want to end the paragraph with a Conclusion. Use language such as "Consequently, a court is likely to . . ." or "Ultimately, . . ." You need to make sure you have a Conclusion. Really weak answers will often end with something like, "Ultimately, this will be a question for a jury," but you need to come out on one side or another. Imagine listening to a client's story, stating your Analysis, and then ending with "I don't know—this is a question for a jury." Then sliding over your check. Imagine how that would go over. You need to tell your client how you think things will work out, even if you are ultimately wrong. Thus, a good Conclusion might be something like, "Consequently, because Skippy did not have the intent to commit a felony when he entered the house, he likely could not be found guilty of burglary."

The point of IRAC is that it makes your answer very clear. It is also the most logical way to explain something. While it may be slow going at first, IRAC will get easier, and you will find yourself using it in all kinds of situations. For example, when I talk to my kids about their videogames, it often goes something like this: "The issue is you want to stay inside and play video games. The rule is you are only allowed to play video games on weekends for an hour a day because I don't want you to become little tubs of goo. However, it is raining today and you want to play that video game where you are dancing around. While you are still playing a video game, at least you are getting some exercise, and you can't go outside anyway. Consequently, I will let you play that videogame." The model answers to the medium questions are written in clear IRAC form so you can compare your own answers. With enough practice, IRAC will become second nature to you.

B. Issues Are Created by Facts

On the exam, the issues are created by the specific facts. Consequently, a professor will change a date, make someone a child, make someone a drunk, or make someone fail to sign something. The important thing is that you repeat these specific facts back in your answer. In the real world, specific facts matter and create specific issues. For example, in a real legal case, it matters exactly how fast the car was going or exactly how much money was lost in the deal.

In writing exam questions, professors scatter in specific facts designed to make you think of a specific legal issue. This is why it is so important to read questions carefully. When you see these specific facts, make sure you can relate them back to the law that you have learned in your class.

C. Imagine Explaining This Situation to a Client, Not Another Lawyer or Your Professor

The best way to write out your answer is to imagine you are speaking to a client on the other side of the desk from you. You should not imagine you are writing to your professor, or you'll fail to get all the points available on the exam because you'll leave things out. As much as an exam is an exam meant to rank you among your peers, it is also a test of what you might be able to do in the real world. In the real world, you wouldn't listen to a widow's story about a will, say "Yep! Sounds like you win," and slide your bill over to her. You want to be explicit and clear in explaining her options, and you can't assume she has any prior knowledge regarding her situation. Do the same thing on your exam.

For a criminal law exam, you might imagine that you are in your office with a new client. A 15-year-old boy is sitting in the chair in front of you. He recently threw a frozen turkey off the roof of his school. He was unaware that frozen turkeys bounced on concrete. When he threw the turkey, it bounced into the freeway and killed a young woman. The boy's dad is in one corner of your office methodically ripping pages out of one of your law books, and the boy's mom is in the other corner of your office crying through several boxes of tissues. Imagine explaining the situation to them. You have to be clear and complete. For example, you might say to them, "The worst crime your son can possibly be convicted of is second degree depraved heart murder. Depraved heart murder is when you kill someone with a callous disregard for human life. Here, your son threw a frozen turkey off the roof of the school. The turkey weighed at least 10 pounds. The school was five stories tall. Your son's actions in throwing the turkey could show callous disregard to human life. But there was no one below him and there was no indication he knew the turkey would bounce into the street, so he probably didn't have callous disregard for human life. Thus, it is unlikely he'll be convicted of depraved heart murder." This is the way you would need to talk to your clients so they understand you. It is the same way you should write on your exams.

D. Seek out and Use Questions Provided by Your Professors (and Questions from Academic Success or Commercial Materials)

Going over practice questions is the best thing you can do while you are studying. This is a great time to get a study group together to go over your answers. Seek out questions provided by your professors. Sometimes the professors might hand them out, and sometimes they might be in a bank in the law review office, SBA office, or library. If your professor doesn't have any questions of his or her own you can use, use questions provided by either your Academic Success office or commercial materials like this book or other outlines. All of these materials are dealing with the same world of law, so doing any of the questions can be of great help. However, keep in mind, they may not cover subjects you covered in class, or they might cover subjects your professor told you to ignore. Use these materials with some caveats, but they can be an invaluable tool.

5. ASK RELEVANT QUESTION OR GO TO OFFICE HOURS ❒

6. REVIEW YOUR NOTES ❒

7. LEGAL WRITING ASSIGNMENT TO TUTOR/PROFESSOR ❒

Week Eleven

1. MAKE SCHEDULE ❐

2. CONTINUE TO BRIEF (CONSIDER MOVING TO BOOK-BRIEFING) ❐

A. What Book-Briefing Looks Like

As exams approach, some students move from classic briefing to book-briefing. If you have done 10 solid weeks of traditional briefing, you should be able to move to book-briefing without much difficulty.

Book-briefing simply means that you are marking up the case in your book instead of writing out an actual brief. As you read the case, clearly mark the relevant facts, issues, holding, and legal arguments and label "facts," "issues," etc. clearly in the margins for when you get called on. Sometimes students like using different colored highlighters for this purpose, but underlining with a pen works just as well. Just make sure you don't mark up the book so much that it's basically meaningless. A page of a book-briefed case might look something like this:

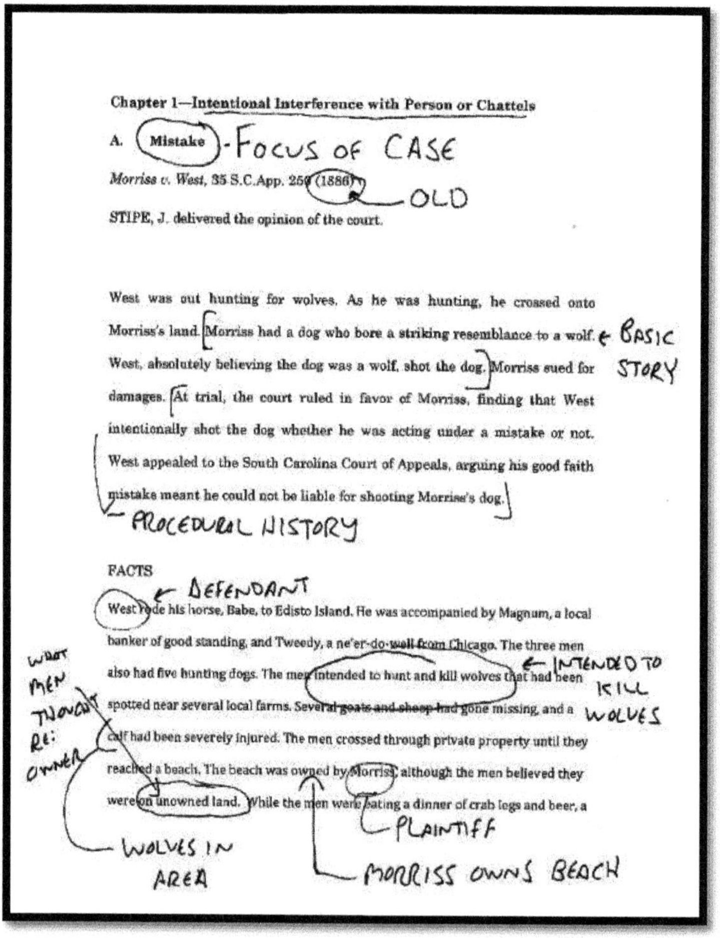
Chapter 1—Intentional Interference with Person or Chattels

A. Mistake

Morriss v. West, 35 S.C.App. 259 (1886)

STIPE, J. delivered the opinion of the court.

West was out hunting for wolves. As he was hunting, he crossed onto Morriss's land. Morriss had a dog who bore a striking resemblance to a wolf. West, absolutely believing the dog was a wolf, shot the dog. Morriss sued for damages. At trial, the court ruled in favor of Morriss, finding that West intentionally shot the dog whether he was acting under a mistake or not. West appealed to the South Carolina Court of Appeals, arguing his good faith mistake meant he could not be liable for shooting Morriss's dog.

FACTS

West rode his horse, Babe, to Edisto Island. He was accompanied by Magnum, a local banker of good standing, and Tweedy, a ne'er-do-well from Chicago. The three men also had five hunting dogs. The men intended to hunt and kill wolves that had been spotted near several local farms. Several goats and sheep had gone missing, and a calf had been severely injured. The men crossed through private property until they reached a beach. The beach was owned by Morriss, although the men believed they were on unowned land. While the men were eating a dinner of crab legs and beer, a

B. Drawbacks of Book-Briefing

The major downside of book-briefing is that you won't have everything on a single sheet in front of you if you get called on in class. Also, you won't be able to edit your briefs as you should have done in the past, so you won't be able to give yourself the kind of in-class feedback you did before and you still need to synthesize your briefs into your outline. However, it is extremely important that you make time to do as many practice questions as possible (both from this book, your professor, and other sources), so if you have to sacrifice traditional briefing to do questions, do so.

3. CONTINUE OUTLINES ❑

4. PRACTICE QUESTIONS (MEDIUM ONES) ❑

A. How to Use Policy

i. Policy in a Traditional Exam Question

You will sometimes want to use policy when you answer a traditional exam question. By traditional exam question, I mean something similar to the hypothetical questions that have already appeared in this book.

"Policy" refers to the principles, guidelines, and wisdom regarding following one rule or another or interpreting a Black Letter Law in a particular way. You probably spent a lot of your time in your legal classes talking about policy considerations. Often, you may find it is a way to decide which conclusion to the legal issue is correct. Importantly, if the legal rule itself has an element that mentions public policy, you need to make sure you include a public policy analysis in your argument. But, a big mistake weak students make is to write answers that are all about policy and what *should* be done. You need to base your answers in the Black Letter Law, with policy thrown in simply to show that you understand how those Black Letter Laws work and how a particular policy might lean the court one way or another.

ii. Pure Policy Questions

There are no pure policy sample questions in this book, just as there are no multiple choice questions. However, if you get a pure policy question, you need to write in such a way as to get as many points as possible. A "pure policy" question is one where a professor asks you to make an argument regarding what should be done. For example, if you get a question like "Was *Katz* correctly decided?" you need to mention all the relevant arguments and counterarguments from your class. In that particular case (*Katz* dealt with the legality of police eavesdropping on a telephone conversation), you would want to argue several points. First, the fact the Fourth Amendment says it protects "persons, houses, papers, and effects," and an oral conversation is none of these things. Second, that earlier cases required a physical intrusion for there to be a search, and here the police had a listening device on the outside of the phone booth. Third, that the Fourth Amendment is dependent upon people's reasonable expectations of privacy. And so on and so forth, until you ultimately choose and defend the position you think is best. There is no right answer in a question like this. The question is calling on you to show your professor you can take all the things you've learned regarding the *Katz* decision and make some cogent argument as to why it was or was not correctly decided. Importantly, you are not being asked to win the argument—you are being asked to show all the possible arguments and how they play off each other. While a pure policy question can sometimes be answered in a manner more similar to the way you likely wrote English composition papers in undergraduate, IRAC likely works better in making sure you score maximum points. I would stick to IRAC. Using the above question, each of my suggested arguments would get its own IRAC.

If you know your class has a policy question on the exam, pay special attention to class discussion. If your professor has a pet peeve or keeps returning to a certain area or question in the law, you can bet the policy question is coming from there, and he or she is likely to bring it up a lot in class. When I was in law school, I had a professor who kept mentioning the Federalist

Papers during almost every discussion we had—you can guess what his policy question was about.

B. The Difference Between an "A" Answer and a "B" Answer

The difference between an answer that earns an "A" and an answer that earns a "B" is the answer's thoroughness. "Thoroughness" does not mean flip-flopping back and forth without a clear indication of how you think the law will treat a hypothetical situation, but it does mean noting all the arguments and issues created by the hypothetical. Consequently, it is important to note dissenting decisions in your casebooks and pay attention in class when another student brings up a decent argument you might not have thought of. Study groups are another great place to collect arguments, counterarguments, and different ways of looking at a situation. It's also important that you pay attention to the court's reasoning in cases, because oftentimes the court will be weighing the relative merits of two strong arguments before deciding which one ultimately wins.

As an example of the difference between an "A" and "B" answer, imagine this hypothetical:

> Tracy was a lifeguard at a private pool surrounded by a large security fence. To swim in the pool, a person had to be a member. One day, Chad, a teenage boy who was not a member of the pool, climbed the fence. He hopped in the pool and Tracy failed to see him slip under the surface and die. At the time, she was playing on her phone.

A "B" answer would go through all the necessary elements of negligence—duty, breach, causation, and damages, and likely find that Tracy was negligent in Chad's death. However, an "A" answer would bring up the counterargument that Chad had hopped the fence and was not actually a member of the pool. If you contractually agree to protect one group of people, are you responsible for other groups of people? Did Tracy's duty to rescue extend to non-members? Even if it did not, did her presence there as a lifeguard keep away other potential rescuers? Would there be any way to tell if a drowning person was a member or not? Does public policy want public safety to rest on membership and payment? What kind of trespasser would Chad be classified as? In answering questions, you need to look at all the specific facts and see if there are some valid counterarguments you can use to make your answer as strong and complete as possible.

C. How to Write Counterarguments

When you include differing arguments in your answer, avoid writing like a ping-pong match. Specifically, don't write something like "The plaintiff will say that the defendant intended to hit him. The defendant will say that the plaintiff consented. But the plaintiff will answer that the consent was not expressed. The defendant will answer consent can be implied." Answers like this take up way too much space and time and are extremely difficult to follow. It is much clearer to state one party's entire position and then the other party's entire rebuttal.

5. REVIEW YOUR NOTES ❒

WEEK TWELVE

1. MAKE SCHEDULE ❑

A. Thinking About Exams

Start planning out a structure and schedule for getting all of your studying and practice questions done. If a class has been particularly difficult, see about scheduling an appointment with the Academic Success Office to see how they can help you. This is often the time illnesses start going around. Stay healthy and get plenty of rest. You don't want to miss a couple of days in the last few weeks because of a stomach bug or a cold.

B. Getting Ready for Thanksgiving

If you are travelling during Thanksgiving, you might want to try and lessen the amount of stuff you are going to need to haul around, especially if you are going to be on a plane. For your case reading, consider making photocopies of the necessary pages in your casebooks so you don't have to carry the entire thing.

In an effort to clear more study time right before exams, it might be a good strategy to try to do all the reading for your classes before you get back. This way, you can quickly review the reading before class starts, but use the majority of your study time to work on outlines and practice questions.

2. CONTINUE TO BRIEF ❏

3. CONTINUE OUTLINES ❏

4. PRACTICE QUESTIONS (LONG ONES) ❏

Grab an appropriate question for each of your classes from the back of the book. If you need more questions, you should seek out your professors' old questions as a first choice, or questions provided in other commercial material if your professor does not have any available questions. Although there are an infinite number of names and situations a professor can come up with, at the end of the day, there are only so many ways for a professor to write a decent exam question and feel like he or she has actually tested the important concepts in a particular subject. In contracts, there has to be some sort of offer, acceptance, and consideration. In torts, someone needs to intentionally or accidentally do something to injure someone else. In property, people need to be fighting over the ownership of some tangible thing or slice of real estate. It would be ridiculous to have an entire criminal law question on the crime of mayhem instead of asking a question covering the different categories of murder and manslaughter. Thus, the more practice questions you do, the more likely you'll get a chance to work through something similar to the hypothetical the professor will give you on the exam. Think of it this way—every lawyer in America has to go through Duty, Breach, Causation, and Damages on their Torts exam. How they did so might have been different (perhaps a puddle left in a supermarket, or a mattress strapped to the roof of a car with twine, or a kid jumping a fence and drowning in a public pool), but the essential rules and analyzing skills are the same.

Also, doing well on the exam is a test of your ability to recall the information. Do the practice questions without looking at any notes or outlines until after you have tried to answer them. You do not want to test your recall for the first time on the exam itself.

A. How to Write an Exam Answer

First, remember to write your answer in IRAC form (discussed above). Second, when you are writing an exam answer, you need to think of it in terms of grabbing as many points as possible. Consequently, anything you do that keeps you from getting the maximum amount of points on an exam question is a mistake.

i. The Classic Time Mistake

It is a classic mistake in law school exam writing to spend too much time on one part of the exam to the detriment of the other parts. For example, imagine you have a three-hour exam with three questions. If you spend an hour and a half on the first question, and an hour and fifteen minutes on the second question, that leaves you only fifteen minutes for the third question. You were supposed to spend an hour on each, and now you are left with a quarter of the suggested time to answer the third question. Don't fall into this very common trap. In fact, when you get the exam, the first thing you should do is write out when you need to be done with each section at the top of that section to remind you when time is up and you need to move on. Otherwise, it is far too easy to steal time from one question to give more to another.

ii. Incomplete and Inaccurate Rules

It's very common on a poor exam to find that the student wrote something like "burglary is breaking into a home and stealing something" instead of the complete Black Letter Law. Make sure you always write the complete rule with all of the elements.

iii. Failing to Use Exact and Specific Facts

The analysis section of a bad exam will say something like, "Here, Jimmy negligently allowed his property to be dangerous." Instead, it should have used the specific facts from the question, like "Here, Jimmy was negligent when he allowed a 100-foot pit to remain open on his unfenced property when he knew children used the property as a shortcut to school."

In the real world and on the exam, exact facts make a difference. For example, imagine you are representing a pizza parlor owner and someone who is carrying a stack of pizza boxes trips over a frost heave in the walkway to the parking lot. The exact size of the frost heave is going to be very important, and perhaps even bring up other potential issues. If the frost heave was three millimeters high, how could anyone have expected the owner to see it? If it was three inches high, that's probably right in the wheelhouse of something the landlord should have fixed. If it was three feet high, how did the guy carrying the boxes manage to fall over it? Is there some contributory negligence there? If it was a three-story frost heave and the guy basically walked smack into a wall, there is definitely a contributory negligence issue.

As another example, imagine you are representing the police department in a case where a person is suing the department and claiming that he was unlawfully stopped. Out of the three choices below, how would you likely explain the facts to a judge or jury to get a judgment in favor of the police?

1. A police officer can stop someone if he or she has reasonable suspicion that criminal activity is afoot. Here, there was reasonable suspicion.

Would the judge or jury have any idea what created the reasonable suspicion? Would they have any idea what the reasonable suspicion was? Would any judge or jury feel particularly compelled to rule for your client? Do you think the judge or jury will simply trust your assertion that there was reasonable suspicion?

2. A police officer can stop someone if he or she has reasonable suspicion that criminal activity is afoot. Here, the suspect's shirt implied he had engaged in criminal activity.

Better, but again, what does that mean? What kind of shirt was it? A punk rock T-shirt that said "Anarchy"? A shirt with horizontal black-and-white stripes? A shirt with a gangster on it? Was it a shirt that had been reported stolen? Again, would this really explain things to a judge or jury?

3. A police officer can stop someone if he or she has reasonable suspicion that criminal activity is afoot. Here, the suspect was wearing a blue silk shirt with a giant gold lion on the back. Fifteen minutes before, the president of First Bank had called the police and said the bank was robbed by a man in a blue silk shirt with a giant gold lion on it. The fact the suspect was wearing a shirt matching the Bank's description seems to imply he had been involved in the bank heist, and it could be considered as part of the totality of circumstances leading to reasonable suspicion.

In the real world, if you were defending the police, you'd argue, "He was wearing a blue silk shirt with a giant gold lion on it! The Bank had just said they were robbed by a guy in a blue silk shirt with a giant gold lion on it! What do you expect the officer to do?" You wouldn't dance around it because you want to show the court exactly why the officer felt justified in stopping the guy and why that stop fit the rule. You should think the same way on exams. Leaving out the specific facts will rob you of the opportunity to explain the nuances of the situation, and it will cause you to lose points on the exam. You want to get as many points as possible!

iv. You Need to Clearly Connect the Facts

When they were small, my kids loved these panels at the zoo where they had to draw a line from a picture of an animal to a phrase describing that animal. They looked something like this:

If you had a question on common law burglary, you would want to answer it using the same kind of thought process. You want to basically draw a line from the Black Letter Law to the specific fact (without the questionable artwork). Notice the clear statement of the Black Letter Law, and then how the facts in the analysis are presented in the same order:

> Common law burglary is the (1) breaking and entering into the (2) dwelling house of another (3) at night with (4) the intent to commit a felony therein. Here, although the door was open, Skippy had to push the door open further to get inside, and this minimal force would likely be sufficient for a breaking. It was the dwelling house of another because, although Skippy was in the home's garage, it was physically attached to the main house by a wide hallway with no real split between the garage and sleeping area. It was at night because it was 12 a.m. and dark. Finally, Skippy did not have the necessary intent, because when he entered the garage he just wanted to get his bicycle, and he only later decided to grab Slappy's chainsaw.

A common mistake is for students to jump right to the apparent issue of Skippy's intent and fail to pick up the points for linking the facts to the other three elements, which might seem too obvious to mention. But they aren't too obvious to mention! They might seem obvious to you, a person who has studied the law, but they're not going to be obvious to a client who has come to you looking for help. Of course, in this question, you might want to spend more time discussing the intent issue since there seems to be some doubt as to what is going on there, but you still want to get the points available by discussing the other less arguable elements.

v. Terrible Ideas in Writing an Exam Answer

a. The Prologue

Anything along the lines of "You have asked me to answer a question regarding . . ." There is no reason for a professor to give you points for repeating the question. While you want your writing to be clear, there is nothing to be gained by trying to make it "intellectual sounding." Prologues were fine for college papers, but they are only going to hurt you now.

b. The Wrap-Up

Clearly, you need a conclusion for all of your IRACs, and perhaps a conclusion for the question as a whole, but you won't get any points repeating what you have just said. Anything along the line of, "As stated above, Skippy will be liable because . . ." is unnecessary. You already said it once, your professor has already awarded you points, and you're not going to get any more points by saying it again. A good conclusion is simply, "Consequently, a court will likely find Skippy liable for battery."

B. First Steps to Writing an Exam Answer

1. First, carefully read the exam instructions. Even if a professor doesn't take off points because you failed to follow instructions, he or she is going to wonder why you ignored them. This will make your exam look bad and cost you points.

2. Ignore all the typing around you during the exam. Law students often begin typing or writing immediately when they are handed the exam question. If it is a closed book exam, some

students find it helpful to quickly write out their attack outline so they can look at it as they write their answer. You might consider doing that. For open book exams, in which students should have already prepared and have on-hand their attack outlines, I'm not exactly sure what people are doing (for a discussion of "attack outlines," see Week 13). Two seconds into the exam, what could anyone possibly be typing? Don't let it get to you. Consider investing in some earplugs. An exam room full of typing people can be as loud as the Invasion of Normandy.

3. Make sure you read and answer each question that is asked. Avoid the brain dump at all costs. For example, let's say you are taking a class on Music & the Law and I ask on an exam "On a scale of 1 to 10, how funky is this song?" I don't want you to give me all the music history and law we have learned from Gregorian chants to Chuck Berry to James Brown to Parliament Funkadelic to Prince. As a professor, I'm not going to go through and pick out the information that actually matters to the question I asked. I just want to see something like, "10. This song is a particularly funky piece of music. The rule for funky is. . . ."

4. Make sure you stick to the suggested time allocation. For the questions themselves, more debatable issues should be given more time, less debatable issues should be dealt with as quickly as possible.

5. Quickly scan the whole exam. Each question probably represents a discrete area of the course. For example, if your Torts class was divided up into sections on intentional torts, negligence, and products liability, and your exam has three large questions, it's unlikely two of them are dealing with products liability.

6. **Remember, it is one IRAC for each issue, not one giant IRAC for the entire exam.**

7. As long as you have the Issue, Rule, Analysis, and Conclusion, you don't need to label them. If it helps you, do so. But labels can slow you down, and are especially problematic if you have a word limit. Below I suggest a slightly different IRAC model that will keep your answer easy to write and clearly structured.

C. When You Are Ready to Answer the Question

1. Write your end time at the top so you know when you need to move to the next question.

2. Read the call. The call is the sentence after the main part of the question that says "Discuss" or "Explain the issues" or "Can Lumpy succeed on her 12(b)(6) motion?" You should always read the call first because it can help you with the reading of the body of the question. A call like "Discuss" won't really do anything for you. But you might get a call that says "Discuss Frank's liability." In that case, you don't need to write anything about Frank's ability to sue the other parties involved. You only need to focus on what the other parties may be able to do to him.

3. Read the question all the way through without circling anything or making any notations. You want to get the lay of the land and see where the professor is trying to lead you.

4. Read the question more slowly, circling specific facts and making notes in the margins. You want to make sure to circle all of the specific facts, because you are likely going to need to use them. Circle every character, object, time, dollar amount, date, transaction, or action. However, try to circle only the smallest word or phrase that makes sense. That way, you can make sure you are breaking down the question into absolutely every possible issue, and you won't end up with a question that's basically covered in big circles that will not help you.

5. Issues are created by the specific facts. A character might be drunk, or a kid, or a kid who is driving a car, or a drunk kid who is driving a car. Someone might not hear someone else over a loud noise, or someone might fail to sign something. Maybe a bank robber only had a rubber gun and a guard killed his accomplice. These specific facts are what create the issues. Look at the specifics closely.

6. If at this point you still don't know what is going on, you could jump to the next question. But if you do jump, make sure you leave time to come back. Sometimes, if the first question is one you were not prepared for, it is better to get your engine running answering an easier question and then come back. It's

pretty common to feel your brain fall out in that first minute or two of looking at an exam. But it snaps back pretty quickly once you get going.

D. When You Are Ready to Write

1. Outline your answer before you write it down. Most professors agree that this is an essential step. Assuming two students saw the same number of issues, a well-plotted and thought-out answer will beat an answer that bounces all over the place. You want to spend several minutes sketching out your answer, but you also want to do it as quickly as possible because you will be under a lot of time pressure. This is where a good, memorized outline with checklists can really help. In your exam answer outline, you don't need to write out your entire rule (you'll do that in the answer), but quickly put the relevant facts in the appropriate categories. Remember, you won't be graded on what's in your outline. Importantly, your thought process needs to be written out on the exam paper, because if it is not on the exam paper, the professor can't give you any points for it. At most schools, exams are anonymous, and many, many times colleagues have expressed shock to me that a particular student did poorly on his or her exam. Usually they say, "But they were always on point and correct when I called on them." Clearly, in that case, the student knew and understood the law but simply didn't show his or her thinking on the exam. Make sure you use the advice here and do enough practice questions that you do not fall into this trap.

2. Make sure you are set to argue both sides and include any counterarguments (you can use the outline you created for your class to check). You should be thinking of your exam answer as a memo explaining the entire situation to a client or senior partner, not a brief where you are trying to win your case (unless the question specifically says argue for one side—but even in that case, you want to address counterarguments or you won't win the argument). Do not be too conclusory in your answer or willfully ignore the good arguments on the other side. This omission would be like losing a case and then telling your client, "Actually, they did have a great argument, I just didn't tell you about it."

3. Start writing your answer. As you write, cross out every specific fact in your question outline and on the question itself. You should end up with almost all of it crossed out. If you end up with a lot of facts that are not crossed out, you likely missed some issues. One year, a colleague of mine wrote a torts question with a large paragraph in the middle devoted to a doctor. Almost 20 percent of the class failed to write anything about that doctor. If they had been crossing out the words as they used them, they would have seen that they didn't use anything from almost a third of the question, which should have alerted them to a very big problem.

4. Don't make up your own issues instead of the ones that are there. Only use the facts provided in the question. If the professor wanted you to write about another set of facts, he or she would have written them into the question.

5. Make sure you have a Conclusion. Don't leave it hanging or say "It's up to the jury." Say something along the lines of, "Consequently, a court will likely find . . ." If you were explaining the situation to a client or law partner, you would give them some indication of how you think the court will decide.

6. Finally, review your answer. Read your entire answer quickly. Did you actually respond to the precise call of the question? Did you include a Black Letter Law Rule statement for every issue? Did you use the specific facts? Did you state a conclusion? Did you drop any words or make a typo you need to fix for clarity?

7. After that, move on to the next question!

E. This Is an Example of What the Whole Thing Might Look Like

Question:

Alvin was walking down a narrow sidewalk when Bailey brushed past him. Alvin yelled, "How dare you touch me, sir!" and punched Bailey in the ear. Bailey fell onto Chris's yard. Chris saw Bailey fall and yelled, "You don't move! Don't move from that spot! You crushed my petunias! I've got something for you inside!" Chris then went inside the house. Up the street came Dan, a world-renowned ear surgeon. He saw Bailey lying on the ground bleeding from his ear. Dan was pretty sure it was a life-threatening brain bleed that he could easily stop with some of the medical tools he had in his pocket, but he really didn't feel like stopping his walk. Consequently, he went on his way. Bailey later died from his injuries.

What torts have been committed?

Question with end time, circles, and answer outline

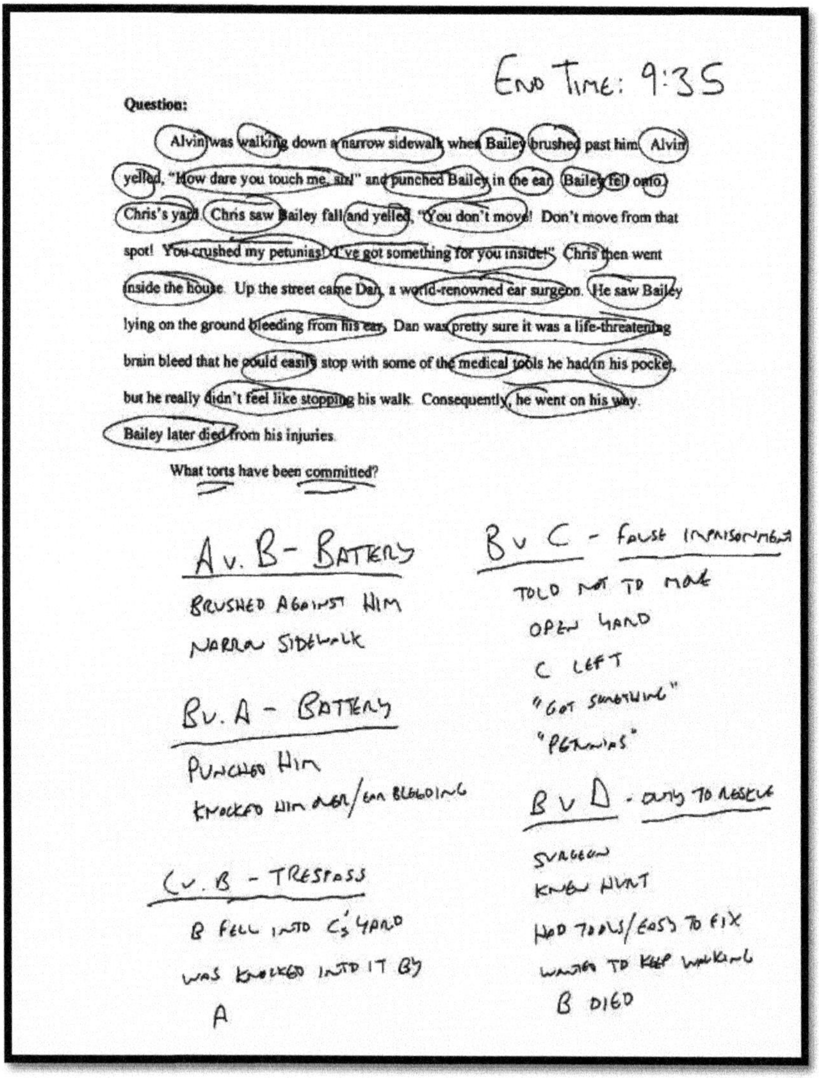

END TIME: 9:35

Question:

Alvin was walking down a narrow sidewalk when Bailey brushed past him. Alvin yelled, "How dare you touch me, sir!" and punched Bailey in the ear. Bailey fell onto Chris's yard. Chris saw Bailey fall and yelled, "You don't move! Don't move from that spot! You crushed my petunias! I've got something for you inside!" Chris then went inside the house. Up the street came Dan, a world-renowned ear surgeon. He saw Bailey lying on the ground bleeding from his ear. Dan was pretty sure it was a life-threatening brain bleed that he could easily stop with some of the medical tools he had in his pocket, but he really didn't feel like stopping his walk. Consequently, he went on his way. Bailey later died from his injuries.

What torts have been committed?

A v. B - BATTERY
BRUSHED AGAINST HIM
NARROW SIDEWALK

B v. A - BATTERY
PUNCHED HIM
KNOCKED HIM OVER/EAR BLEEDING

C v. B - TRESPASS
B FELL INTO C's YARD
WAS KNOCKED INTO IT BY A

B v C - FALSE IMPRISONMENT
TOLD NOT TO MOVE
OPEN HAND
C LEFT
"GOT SOMETHING"
"PETUNIAS"

B v D - DUTY TO RESCUE
SURGEON
KNEW HURT
HAD TOOLS/EASY TO FIX
WANTED TO KEEP WALKING
B DIED

Sample answer:

Alvin v. Bailey—Battery

A battery is the intentional infliction of a harmful or offensive bodily contact. An offensive bodily contact is a contact that damages a person's reasonable sense of dignity. Additionally, consent is a complete defense to battery, and consent can be implied if the person touched engages in some type of action that will likely result in touching (like getting on a crowded elevator). Here, Alvin was walking down a narrow sidewalk when Bailey brushed past him. First, it is debatable whether the touching was intentional, because Bailey simply brushed past him on the sidewalk and seemed to have no particular intent to touch Alvin. Second, it was merely a "brush," which would be unlikely to damage a person's reasonable sense of dignity. However, Alvin was clearly offended when he yelled, "How dare you touch me sir!" and punched Bailey. But, his level of offense seems unreasonable, and the fact he did not seem to make way on the narrow sidewalk to avoid being brushed by Bailey seemed to be an implied consent to being touched. Consequently, a court will likely find Bailey not liable for battery.

Bailey v. Alvin—Battery

The rule for battery is stated above. Here, Alvin yelled "How dare you touch me, sir!" and punched Bailey in the ear, showing his act was intentional. It was harmful because it caused Bailey to fall, bleed from his brain, and ultimately die. Consequently, Alvin is likely liable to Bailey for battery.

Chris v. Bailey—Trespass

A trespass occurs when a person intentionally enters another's land without permission. Even if the person is mistaken, as long as the person intended to commit physical contact with the other person's land, he or she committed a trespass. Here, Bailey did not intend to enter Chris's yard. Instead, he fell into it when he was punched by Alvin. Consequently, he cannot be held liable for trespass.

Bailey v. Chris—False Imprisonment

False imprisonment is the intentional infliction of a confinement, and it can be accomplished by threats. A confinement means the person must be held within certain limits. Here, Chris intentionally meant to keep Bailey in the yard by ordering him not to move and saying, "I've got something for you inside." The difficulty here is what Chris meant by those words. If he meant that Bailey should not move because he had something inside with which he could render aid, this would not be a confinement. However, if he meant that Bailey shouldn't move and that he had something inside to keep him there, like a gun, his threats could have created a confinement. The statement about the petunias seems to indicate some anger, and it would not be unreasonable to believe Chris might be threatening Bailey. However, the problem is that Bailey was in an open yard. There did not seem to be any particular limits he was being kept within, although Chris told him not to move from that spot. Ultimately, considering Chris's unclear statements and the fact Bailey was in an open yard, it is unlikely that Chris could be liable for false imprisonment.

Bailey v. Dan

There is no general duty to act or rescue. Unless there is some special relationship between Bailey and Dan, Dan is not liable for his refusal to assist. There does not seem to be any special relationship between the two men. Even though Dan is a doctor, recognized the problem, and could have easily prevented Bailey's death, he was under no general duty to do so. Consequently, he would not be liable for failing to render aid.

*Note: In a question like this you can save time by simply writing a rule has been stated above.

You may be surprised to see just how different a proper law exam answer is from the type of exam answer you would write on an anthropology, history, or literature exam. Notice that here is no thesis statement, and no transitions between sections.

F. How These Things Are Graded

To make grading as fair as possible, professors usually grade off of a checklist. You want to get as many points as you can. Whoever gets the most points gets the highest grade. A checklist for the above question might look something like this:

Torts question checklist

55 total points

Alvin v. Bailey

_____ Rule for battery (3 points)

_____ Rule for offensive bodily contact (2 points)

_____ Rule for implied consent (2 points)

_____ Narrow sidewalk (1 point)

_____ Brushed past him (1 point)

_____ Maybe not intentional (1 point)

_____ Unlikely to damage reasonable sense (1 point)

_____ Alvin offended/yelled/punched (3 points)

_____ Unreasonable/didn't move over (2 points)

_____ Bailey not liable (1 point)

Bailey v. Alvin

_____ Rule for battery (3 points)

_____ Alvin yelled/punched intentional (3 points)

_____ Harmful/fall/bleed/die (4 points)

_____ Alvin liable (1 point)

Chris v. Bailey

_____ Rule for trespass (3 points)

_____ Bailey did not intend/fell (2 points)

_____ Bailey not liable (1 point)

Bailey v. Chris

_____ Rule for false imprisonment (3 points)

_____ Intent/Chris ordered not to move (2 points)

_____ Did he mean to render aid (2 points)

_____ Was it a threat (2 points)

_____ Open yard (2 points)

_____ Unlikely false imprisonment (1 point)

Bailey v. Dan

_____ Rule for rescue (2 points)

_____ Special relationship (2 points)

_____ Doctor/saw problem/easy/died (4 points)

_____ Not liable (1 point)

The point values are completely arbitrary, but this checklist should give you a pretty good idea of how a professor might look at your essay. As you can see, you want to have clear and complete statements of the rules, use all the specific facts, and note any counterarguments. Otherwise, you'll leave points on the table.

5. ASK RELEVANT QUESTION ❒

6. REVIEW YOUR NOTES ❒

7. BACKUP COMPUTER ❒

If you are travelling, make sure to back-up everything. Your computer could be lost, stolen, or dropped, and now would be the absolutely worst time to lose everything.

THANKSGIVING BREAK

1. EVALUATE WHERE YOU STAND ❑

You may be so together that you can completely goof off during Thanksgiving break. However, must students need to use at least some of the break to work on outlines or do practice questions.

2. DO NOT THINK THAT THIS WILL BE A WORK-A-THON ❒

Many people overestimate the amount of work that can be done during Thanksgiving. At most, you are getting a couple days of relative free time to do work. Unfortunately, sometimes students have the idea they can do all of their outlines in this one week simply because they don't have class for a few days.

At this point of the semester, you will need some down time. More importantly, your friends and family will demand it. Make sure you set up a schedule where you get enough work done that you can sit down and have dinner or watch football without worrying about the studying you are not doing.

A. Being Realistic About What Can Be Accomplished

Consider not staying up late or sleeping in during Thanksgiving break. If you keep going to bed and getting up at the same time you did for school, you'll have a lot more time to get things done before the day really starts. Remember that winter break is not too far off.

Give yourself some doable goals for the break. For example, you might already have enough of your outlines completed that you can realistically finish all your outlines. If not, tell yourself you'll finish one or two. Put together a packet of practice questions and tell yourself that you need to do 10 of them over the week. Having a goal you can meet during the break will make the break feel much more productive, and you won't be beating yourself up with the vague feeling that you didn't do enough work. There is much more work you need to do than can be completed during the holiday. Don't set yourself up for failure by thinking you can do it all.

B. Dealing with Significant Others

If you are going home and all of your undergraduate breaks were basically rage-a-thons, you'll need to make sure your friends and family understand that the first year of law school is extremely important and you're going to have to do some work. Explain to them that you will make time for them, but you have to get some work done to do your best in school.

To make life easier on yourself, find a place (other than where you are staying) to study. If you are at your parents' house, go to the public library or a coffee shop. That way, your friends and family won't be tempted to distract you.

Also, use the carrot approach to keep yourself working and focused. For example, tell yourself that if you study for x amount of hours you can go out and have a few drinks with your friends or play a game with the family. Make sure you set a clear time for when you will stop studying. Otherwise, you might find yourself wasting valuable study time by procrastinating.

You might use the time to make and study flashcards covering the Black Letter Law from your outline. A lot of people really like flashcards, especially if they are into playing board games and whatnot. If you do decide to make flashcards, don't just chop your outline into little pieces. Otherwise, you're going to end up with way too much information for the flashcards to be effective. For example, you might have sat through a PowerPoint presentation with tons of information on the slide. Your eyes probably glazed over.

The best way to make flashcards is to make a card with the basic elements of the Black Letter Law, and then make other cards breaking down those elements. For example, your first card might say, "CONTRACT"—"Offer," "Acceptance," "Consideration." Your next card might say, "OFFER"—"Promise to enter a contract," "Essential Terms," "Communicated to Offeree." Basically, flashcards are likely good for the overall structure of the law, but probably not the place to try to memorize all the little nuances.

Finally, see if there are some things your loved ones can do to help you. If you traditionally cook something for the holidays, can someone else do the shopping for you? Do you have a young nephew or niece that would think it was fun to go over your flashcards with you (in my experience, small children pretty much go along with anything as long as you are paying attention to them)? Can your friends come over to your house or neighborhood so you don't need to travel too far and waste time?

C. Using Your Travel Time

Because of all of the inherent distractions in Thanksgiving break, force yourself to work during your travel time, even if it is not something you usually like to do. If you are travelling by car, see if someone else is willing to drive. If you are on a plane or train, don't bring a fun book or take a nap. The time you spend travelling will likely be the most uninterrupted time you get the entire holiday. Use it wisely.

3. WORK THROUGH ANY PRACTICE QUESTIONS THAT HAVEN'T BEEN COMPLETED ❒

If you haven't kept up with getting all the practice questions completed, the Thanksgiving holiday might be a perfect time for you to finish them up.

WEEK THIRTEEN

1. MAKE SCHEDULE ❑

2. FINISH OUTLINES ❑

A. Making "Attack Outlines"

An attack outline is basically a one- or two-page version of your main outline. You can make one by taking out all the meat of the outline and leaving behind only the Black Letter Law titles you will need for the exam. If you have been studying, you should be able to recall everything you need from looking only at the law.

Even if you have an open book exam, you should make an attack outline for the exam because you don't want to be flipping through your outline or other materials during the exam. You simply don't have time for it. If you have a closed book exam, make an attack outline and memorize it. Many students memorize the attack outline and then quickly write it out on scratch paper when the exam starts. This can be a valuable aid in remembering the material from your larger outline. This is what an attack outline built from the good outline noted earlier might look like:

Battery

1. **Intentional Touching**
2. **Unpermitted**
    a. Express Consent
    b. Implied Consent
3. **Harmful/Offensive**

B. Using Your Outline as Answer Outline

If you have an open book exam, one thing you can do to speed up your test-taking is to write out form answers to statements of Black Letter Law in your outline. This would merely be for the basics of a question, as you will absolutely need to adjust on the actual exam. But, as a basics checklist, it could be pretty helpful. For example:

> The issue is whether __________ gained title to the property through adverse possession. A person gains title to land through adverse possession if he or she engages in use that is hostile, exclusive, open and notorious, continuous, and actual for the statutory period. Here, __________ use was hostile because ____________; it was exclusive because ____________; it was open and notorious because ____________; it was continuous because of ____________; and it was actual

> because of ____________. However, continuous use for the statutory period may be an issue because __________ only used the property during the ____________ months. However, seasonal use can be good enough for adverse possession because courts look at the nature and condition of the land and how a true owner would use it. Here, the land is _______________. . . .

Setting up portions of your outline this way is a great way to make sure you don't forget any issues. The one caveat to this is you don't want to lock yourself into being too robotic in your analysis. Think of it as a checklist you can and will expand upon in your actual answer.

C. How to Memorize Your Outline

There is a difference between reading your outline and memorizing it. You must memorize it.

Poor performing students often tell me that they made an outline and simply read it a bunch of times. As stated above, whether you have an open-book or a closed-book exam, you need to memorize your outline because you will be writing under time pressure, and because you want to test your ability to recall the information before you actually sit down for the exam.

Look at the Memory Strategies in Week 3 of this book and see what works for you. You might even try different strategies for different subjects. The important point is that you memorize.

3. PRACTICE QUESTIONS (LONG ONES) ❑

4. GO TO OFFICE HOURS/REVIEW SESSIONS/PRACTICE TESTS ❑

If you have any unanswered questions, this is your last chance to get them sorted out. Don't go into the exam without getting those questions answered. It might be a foundational question that is likely to show up on the exam.

A. Importance of Going to Practice Exams and Review Sessions Even if You Are Not Totally Ready

Sometimes students fail to go to practice exam and review sessions because they don't feel like they are far enough in their studying to gain anything. This is a huge mistake. Make sure you go to any practice exams or review sessions. They can give you an invaluable window into the exam, and they can help you focus your final days of studying. Even if you are unprepared when you do the practice exam, this can alert you to the areas of the law where you are weakest, so you can focus your efforts there.

5. REVIEW YOUR NOTES ❒

6. BACKUP COMPUTER ❒

Exam Week

1. HOW YOU SHOULD BE STUDYING ❑

Whether it is open or closed book, you should study for all your exams the same way. Break up the exam week to give each class the same amount of study time. All of your classes are likely worth the same number of credits, so don't skimp on one because you think another is more difficult. In my experience, when students tell me they focused on one class that they thought was harder, or less on a class that they thought was easier (or open book), they're in my office telling me this because their semester grades weren't great.

A. Memorizing

During exam week, continue memorizing. Don't make yourself sick by not sleeping, but study to the point that you are basically angry at the fact you have to take an exam. That way, by the time the exam comes, you aren't nervous. Plus, if anything weird happens during the exam, it won't throw you or stress you out. For example, I somehow caught pinkeye the night before my very first law school exam (contracts). The exam went fine because I had studied so much that pinkeye just seemed like a gnarly and vaguely funny example of Murphy's Law.

B. Practice Questions

If you can find some other practice questions you haven't done, exam week is a good time to do one or two more. At this point, your focus should be on memorizing the law, but the practice questions will continue to help.

C. Attack Outlines

Since you've already made the attack outlines, spend time getting them memorized backwards and forwards. Use the same techniques you used with the larger outline and see if you can reproduce it without looking at it. More importantly, can you remember all of the other information the outline contained by only looking at a few words?

D. Flowcharts and Flashcards

If you are a visual learner, you might find flowcharts helpful (especially in something like civil procedure, where the course focuses on a rule book, the Federal Rules of Civil Procedure). You can make the flow charts on your computer, but the quickest and most expedient way is probably to simply write them out by hand. Just like flashcards, don't try to cram every bit of information you have into them, or they're not going to be of much use. Here is a simple example regarding jurisdiction:

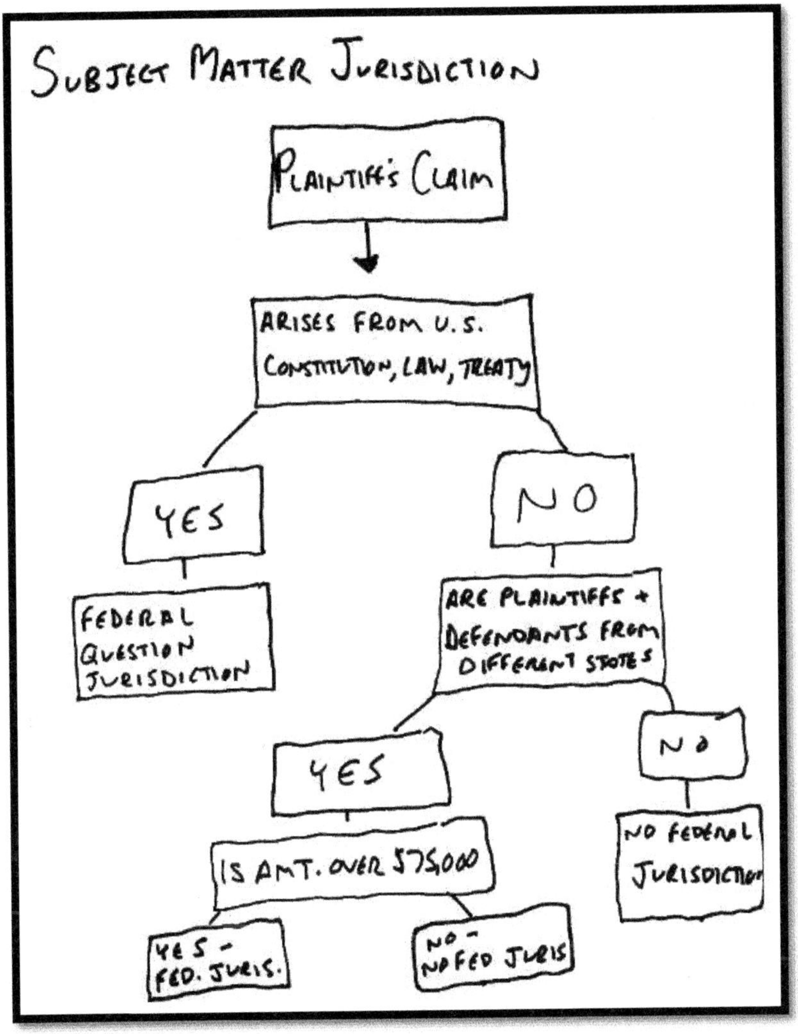

If it helps, you can even post these things on your wall like they do in criminal procedural television shows where the police officers make big boards covered in suspects and information as they try to figure out the case. You can look at your wall of stuff as you brush your teeth in the morning. As I mentioned in the earlier chapter on memory, memory is simply making novel connections between new and old information. Sticking things on your wall is like making a billboard for yourself. There's a reason billboards line every highway in America.

E. Scheduling Your Study Time

i. Priorities

At this point, you need to make your study time your top priority. Tell friends, families, and loved ones that anything not related to exam studying will not be dealt with until after exams. Don't worry about getting your oil changed. Buy a lot of dinners you can easily heat up. If you live with someone, see if they can be responsible for keeping the dog, cat, or plants alive.

ii. Find a Place to Study

The law library and your home are likely the two least effective places to study because those are the two places with the most distractions. Find someplace where your friends and families won't bother you. The undergrad stacks can be good. For me, a coffee house can be pretty good, but the best place I ever found to study was a small public library branch. It was made of gray cinderblock, dark, and completely empty. I could crank out several hours of work without a break, and when I finally was done, I felt good knowing I had done as much as I reasonably could during these hours. Also, there was a Chinese restaurant and bar next door, so after I had done all of my studying for the day, I could treat myself to something as a reward.

iii. Splitting Your Time

In general, it is a good idea to give each class the same amount of coverage, depending upon how those exams are split during exam week. For example, if there are two days between the exams, I would give two entire days right before each exam to that exam and that exam only. If you have a longer period, you can add time. If you have a completely free reading week, I would suggest giving equal time to each class by spending two days on your first exam, then two days on your second, and two days on your third (set in such a way that you will still get two days studying for your first exam right before your exam).

F. What You Shouldn't Be Doing

A lot of common undergraduate study habits don't translate well to law school. If a particular strategy worked very well for you in the past, of course you want to take advantage of it now. However, there are some things you should definitely avoid.

i. All-Nighters

All-nighters might have worked in undergrad where you likely spit out answers to questions that were designed to have a single answer. On a law exam, you need to show how you think, and to be able to think clearly, you need to be rested. The night before the exam, stop studying at dinner. Relax, watch a dumb movie, and go to bed early. You are going to be worked up as it is, and you might not sleep great. Any last minute studying is going to mean little to your grade. On the morning of the exam, wake up early, eat breakfast, give yourself enough time to calmly get to school, and maybe glance over your attack outline one more time. At this point, you are as ready as you are ever going to be.

If you pull an all-nighter, you might be able to spit out some basic legal information, but you will be unlikely to make the necessary connections to make a good grade.

Also, to pull an all-nighter, you're probably going to need to drink a lot of caffeine. Caffeine takes a long time to get out of your system and increases nerves and the necessity to go to the bathroom, two things that won't be particularly useful on the exam.

ii. Typing up Your Notes Is a Common Mistake to Avoid

Some people study by typing up their notes. This is an utter waste of time. Do practice questions instead.

2. MULTIPLE CHOICE QUESTIONS ❐

If your exam has multiple choice questions, try to do as many practice questions as you can from either commercial outlines or commercial multistate bar exam (MBE) books. These should be available at your law library or Academic Success Office. Many professors mine these books for potential questions, and they are the best source of practice for law school multiple choice.

A. "The Yellow Pad of Things I Do Not Know"

As you study and do practice multiple choice questions, set aside a yellow legal pad. Every time you get a question wrong, or get a question right for the wrong legal reason, write that legal point on your pad. Make this list of "Things I Do Not Know" and study it. Go through that set of questions again and see if you can get the questions right the second time. Eventually, you will get to the point where you will never miss those legal issues again.

B. Wrong Answer Choices on Multiple Choice Questions

Your professors are likely to structure their questions around MBE-style or commercial outline questions. Consequently, it is important to understand how the questions are made. Basically, multiple choice questions are designed to make you spit out one undeniably right answer (this is why the Yellow Legal Pad of Things I Do Not Know is so helpful). For example, a question might look like this:

The sun is a . . .

(A) Banana

(B) Monkey

(C) Star

(D) Ball of interstellar gas.

The correct answer is (C). Most multiple choice questions try to have two answer choices that you can dispose of pretty quickly. You are then left with two potentially correct answers. Here, (C) would clearly be the correct answer. While a sun is technically a ball of interstellar gas, many other things are also balls of interstellar gas (gas planets, nebulas, etc.). The most precise answer, and the answer that was likely taught in class, is that the sun is a star. On multiple choice exams, you have to choose the more precise of the two potentially correct answers—namely the answer that was accentuated in class.

A multiple choice question writer will put in the correct answer choice and try to hide it with foils and distractors. Foils are answer choices that make the right answer choice look wrong. For example, they may be longer or have "if" or "unless" wording that flips the facts of the question, like "Yes, if the plaintiff knew this was a unilateral contract." A distractor is an answer choice that sits there like a shiny bauble. It might have a Latin phrase you do not recognize or some other legal idea you don't quite remember. Students who are unsure tend to go for these, thinking that they must have missed something in their studying. If you don't know what the answer choice is talking about, it's unlikely to be correct. This is another reason to study until you're simply angry, not nervous.

Another thing a wrong answer choice might do is provide the basic statement of the law, but fail to note the relevant exception. For example, from civil procedure you might know that a complaint needs to be a "short and concise statement of the claim." However, in claims involving special damages, the plaintiff needs to plead the amount with specificity. On multiple choice questions, as with essay questions, always keep the relevant exceptions and clarifications in mind. This is often where the right answer lies.

Much like essay questions, it's important to remember that there are only so many testable concepts in the law, and if you do enough practice multiple choice questions, you'll probably work through examples of the majority of them.

If you struggle with multiple choice questions, it is likely one of two things. Either you read too fast and jump on the wrong answer, or you pick the right answer initially and talk yourself out of it. Do enough practice questions to figure out which category you fall into and then start actively reminding yourself not to do it as you do more practice multiple choice questions. Try slowing down your reading, or see specifically what kinds of multiple choice questions cause you to doubt your original answer. See if you can figure out a pattern and adjust your thought process. Keep the Yellow Legal Pad going to collect those legal points you did not know. Ultimately, you will never miss them again.

3. TAKING CARE OF YOURSELF ❒

During exam week, it's fairly common to let things like sleep and healthy eating go, but you should continue to take care of yourself.

A. Stress

The exam is going to be a stressful experience. Don't engage in post-mortems of the exam right after taking it. Talking with other students about what they wrote is only going to freak you out. Avoid the scrum right after the exam and tell your friends you don't really want to talk about it. Put the exam out of your head and get ready for the next one.

B. Diet

Try to eat decently over the exam period. This is a great opportunity for significant others or extended family to help out if they want to. When I was in law school, my parents would drive up to Austin during exam week, clean my apartment, and leave me a cooler full of food. They were basically awesome elves.

If you don't have a significant other or other family close by, stock up on some easy to prepare meals or already prepared meals from the grocery store. Don't skip breakfast, lunch, or dinner. Also, treat yourself to a few snacks or special meals. A good mood will put you in a good place for studying.

C. Sleep

Watch your caffeine intake over exam period so you can get decent sleep. Make sure you get some exercise every day to get your muscles tired. If you are having trouble turning your mind off, try meditation as you are lying in bed. Focus completely on your breathing and gently watch any thoughts about the exam or life float out of your head. The classic "counting sheep" trick also works.

One thing you might consider is getting rid of your alarm clock and just using your phone's alarm to wake you up. Don't look at your phone until the alarm goes off. This way, if you're having trouble sleeping, you won't have the time staring you in the face, and you won't be thinking "Oh my God! It's 4 in the morning and I am still up!"

D. Exercise

Keep exercising to keep your mood up and make it easier to sleep. Just be careful that you aren't using your exercise time as a way to avoid studying. I would also make your exercise time a real break. Don't try to study on the treadmill. Your brain needs a rest.

WINTER BREAK

1. LET IT GO AND RELAX ❐

Congratulations on finishing your first semester of law school! You need to recharge your batteries, so don't immediately start worrying about getting prepared for the next semester. Sleep a lot. Read some stupid books. Binge-watch your favorite television shows.

If you are worried about your exam performance, push it out of your mind. You have no idea how you did, and worrying about it now is not going to help anything. Let everything go and relax.

SECOND SEMESTER

Welcome back! In this second semester section, you'll see the same checklist format, although there will be fewer new concepts that will need to be explained. If you didn't read this book in the first semester, you should go back and read the first semester sections. This section assumes you have been using this book all year, so the second semester has much less material because the major components of your law school study have already been explained.

WEEK ONE

1. YOUR FIRST SEMESTER GRADES DO NOT DEFINE YOU ❑

I hope you earned the grades you wanted on your law school exams. If you didn't, it's absolutely fixable. Many, many law students fail to do well in their first semester and recover in their second.

In all honesty, the best thing that ever happened to me during my schooling was after I turned in my first English paper in college. I had never gotten less than an A in anything in my life. I was the "English" guy for the Academic Decathlon Team. I'd won several creative writing contests. I really thought I wanted to major in English.

On my first paper, I got a C. When I went to talk to the professor, a man who wore seersucker suits and looked like a cross between Mark Twain and Colonel Sanders, he said in his genteel Virginia-Tidewater accent, "Is English your first language? Your name is Russian. Are you translating as you write?"

The unfortunate thing was that he was genuinely curious, and English is my first, and only, language. I bet several of your professors have a similar story somewhere back in their academic careers, so realize 1) you're not alone, 2) you can bounce back, and 3) this kind of experience is an integral part of the learning experience that is often overlooked. In fact, this experience made me buckle down, make up a plan, and work harder than I probably would have had if I had not gone through it. Once I figured out where I was making mistakes, I corrected them and ended up getting 'A's on my next two papers.

Keep in mind that everyone at your law school wants to do everything he or she can to help you succeed. Take advantage of everything the law school has to offer. Stay positive, and focus on working on a plan to be the best lawyer you can be.

2. GO OVER YOUR EXAMS ❑

No matter how you did, the first thing you should do is make appointments with your professors and/or Academic Success to go over your exams. Most students are terrible judges of their own work. Oftentimes, what they think are the problems on their exams are off base. Your professors have seen all the other exams in the class and they can tell you how your exam compares to the others. Even though you may never take these professors or subjects again, the advice and guidance they give you can be invaluable. If you did extremely poorly, don't be embarrassed to meet with your professors. The grade is not evaluating you as a person; the grade is evaluating what you put down on an exam paper on a certain day in a certain class and in a certain amount of time. Your professors understand that this is simply part of the learning process.

If you can look at your exams before meeting with your professor, do so. It will be much more productive if you can go in to the meeting with some specific questions. If one area of the exam was especially problematic, you can ask your professor if he or she can sketch out a good explanation of this area for you to go over.

A. Diagnose What You Need to Work on

A lot of times, students make mistakes during the exam that have nothing to do with understanding the law. Sometimes, students think about something during the exam but fail to get it down on the paper. If it's not on the paper, the professor can't give you points for it. The most common mistakes in exams are:

1. Failing to spot all the issues—in that case, you want to make sure you do as many practice questions as possible this semester. Practice questions will teach you where the issues are.

2. Failing to write a complete and accurate rule—this might be a problem from your outlines or memorizing.

3. Incomplete analysis—did you go deep enough in your analysis? Did you assume your professor would understand some of your analysis without thoroughly explaining it? Did you clearly connect the facts to the law? Did you use specifics? Did you fail to write as plainly as possible?

4. Counterarguments—did you mention all the relevant counterarguments? Did you simply argue the point one way without noting that the facts could be argued another way? Did you include the relevant exceptions on your outlines? Did you memorize possible exceptions so you could use them on your exam?

5. Was the multiple choice section a bloodbath? Did you change answers? Overthink answers? Fail to read the questions carefully?

3. MEET WITH PROFESSOR REGARDING YOUR WORST EXAM ☐

Your meetings with your individual professors over the next few weeks will be dependent on the professors' schedules, but try to go over your worst exam first. Your worst exam will probably show your mistakes the clearest. In the following weeks, there will be check-offs for your other exams. Just make sure you are on track to go over all of them. The check-offs are simply here to remind you. Meet with your professors and get as much as you can from looking at your triumphs and mistakes from last semester.

4. MEET WITH ACADEMIC SUCCESS ❐

At the same time you are meeting with your professors, schedule an appointment to meet with your Academic Success Office. They have the expertise to help you diagnose your problems, and they also have materials that can really help.

5. MAKE YOUR SCHEDULE (SEE WEEK ONE, FIRST SEMESTER) ❐

6. CHECK-IN WITH CAREER SERVICES ❐

Introduce yourself to the folks in career services and begin thinking about the summer. You might have already had a mandatory meeting with your Career Services Office. If not, this is a good time to drop in. You should start planning for your summer now. Be proactive and see what the Office can do for you, especially in regards to your resume.

7. EVALUATING LAST SEMESTER ❐

Especially if you didn't do as well as you would have liked, you should take some time to evaluate what you did last semester by filling out the following questions. Figure out the things you want to change. Think of it like a diet. If you decide to just "eat healthier," what does that mean exactly? Thinking "I'll study more . . . or better . . . or harder" doesn't mean anything. As far as diets go, saying "I'll switch to light beer" or "I'll eat a small salad with dinner every night" works better than "I'll eat healthier." Decide on some specifics:

1. Did you make a schedule and stick to it? ______________

____

____

2. If you had a set schedule, how often were you able to follow it? Were there particular things about your schedule that didn't work? ____________________

3. Did you miss a significant amount of class? If so, why?

4. Did you go to Academic Success Workshops and/or Tutoring? How often? Which ones did you go to? __________

5. How much time did you spend each week reading cases for class? ____________________

6. When did you usually do your reading? Did you have enough time to get it done? ____________________

7. Did you take breaks when you were reading? How long did they last? ____________________

8. Where did you study? Were you able to concentrate in this location? ____________________

____

____

____

9. Did you use commercial or other students' outlines? Did you rely on them instead of your own? Did you find a commercial or student outline particularly helpful? ________

____

____

10. Did you make your own outlines? Were they finished before the exam period? Were you able to memorize them?

____

____

11. Did you make flashcards or flowcharts? Were they particularly helpful? ____________________

____

____

12. How many practice questions were you able to do?

____

____

13. Did you go to any official practice exam/review sessions? How many? ____________________

____

____

14. What was your strategy on the exams? Did you use the strategy outlined in this book? Did you do something else?

____

____

____

15. Were your grades consistent? Was there a class you performed particularly poorly in? ____________________

____

____

16. Was your grade in your legal writing course consistent with your other grades? __________________________

____

____

____

17. After going over your exams, did you discover a common mistake (for example, failure to use specifics or completely state the rule)? ______________________________

____

____

____

18. Did your grades get better or worse as the exam period progressed? ___________________________________

____

____

____

19. If you had both essays and multiple choice exams, did you perform better or worse depending on the format?

____

____

____

20. List your classes and grades. For each class, was the grade better or worse than you expected? Did your grades correspond with classes you liked or disliked?

____

____

____

____

____

____

____

21. Were there particular study areas that were difficult? For example, reading and briefing, outlining, time management, or exam writing? ________________________

____

____

____

____

____

____

____

Once you've answered the questions, take a look at your answers and see where adjustments need to be made. Also make an appointment with Academic Success or one of your professors to see what help is available for your particular issues.

WEEK TWO

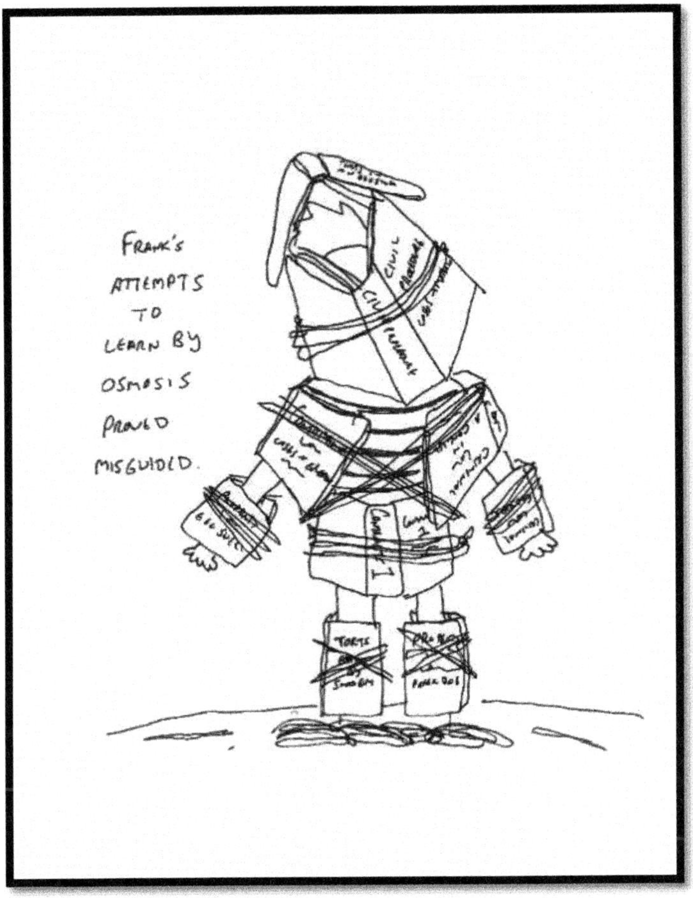

1. MAKE SCHEDULE ❑

2. CONTINUE TO BRIEF ❑

You should treat this semester just like the first when briefing. Even if you moved to book-briefing at the end of last semester, it would be worthwhile to go back to classic briefing for the beginning of the semester. You're likely dealing with completely new subjects. In many schools, these subjects may be "harder" or at least less intuitive than first semester courses. For example, most schools have torts, contracts, and criminal law in the first semester. Even without going to law school, you probably know that you can sue someone if they injure you, you've probably signed a lease on an apartment, and you know you can't go around killing people. The second semester is likely to have courses like civil procedure and property, and there's nothing intuitive about the number of interrogatories you are allowed or the various systems in place for filing a deed.

3. ASK RELEVANT QUESTION ❒

4. REVIEW YOUR NOTES ❒

WEEK THREE

1. MAKE SCHEDULE ❒

A. Meet with Professor from Second Worst Exam

Again, scheduling will be dependent on your professor's schedules, but this check-off is here to keep you on track. Whenever you do manage to meet with a professor to go over your exam, make sure you check off a box here in this book so you know the work was done.

B. Add Outline Time to Schedule

2. CONTINUE TO BRIEF ❑

3. START YOUR OUTLINES ❑

You should learn from last semester's outlines. Ask yourself: Did your course grades correlate with the quality of your outlines? Did you finish them on time? Did you give the outlines sufficient time in your study schedule, or did you spend too much time reading and preparing for class? Did you rely too much on commercial or other student outlines? Would it have helped to look at commercial or other student outlines if you didn't? Did you run parts of your outlines by Academic Success to get some tips?

4. REVIEW YOUR NOTES ❑

Week Four

1. MAKE SCHEDULE ❑

A. Meet with Professor from Best Exam (Unless More than Three Exams)

2. CONTINUE TO BRIEF ❑

3. CONTINUE OUTLINES ❑

4. ASK RELEVANT QUESTION (GO TO OFFICE HOURS) ❐

5. REVIEW YOUR NOTES ❐

6. LEGAL WRITING ASSIGNMENT TO TUTOR/PROFESSOR ❐

WEEK FIVE

1. MAKE SCHEDULE ❑
2. CONTINUE TO BRIEF ❑
3. CONTINUE OUTLINES ❑
4. REVIEW YOUR NOTES ❑

5. CHOOSING CLASSES FOR NEXT YEAR ☐

A. Thinking About the Bar Exam

In choosing classes for next year, you want to keep a few things in mind. First, if you have decided where you are going to sit for the bar exam, take a look at what subjects are covered. If your GPA is not that strong or you are already anticipating having a difficult time studying for the bar, consider taking those classes that cover bar topics. You don't need to take every subject on the bar exam, but you'll likely feel more comfortable in those areas where you took the class in law school. Most law schools have a list of faculty-suggested classes that may be helpful on the bar exam even if they do not directly address bar exam topics. Ask your Dean of Students or Academic Success Office about the bar exam you are planning to take to get an idea of what law school classes would be most applicable.

B. Thinking About What You Want to Practice

When picking classes, also keep in mind what you think you might like to do in law practice. If you are not sure yet, you might consider taking a few different kinds of courses to see what interests you. Also, some classes at your law school might be very difficult to get into, require prerequisites, or might only be offered on alternating years. Finally, if you're thinking you might like to do particular types of summer clerkships or part-time jobs during the school year, you should take some courses that could be helpful in getting that position. Ultimately, it's probably a good idea to roughly sketch out what you want to do over the next two years to make sure you have everything set.

C. Thinking About Your Grades

You also want to pick classes in such a way that you do not create a monster of a semester for yourself. Ask around about professors, work expectations, and general difficulty of the classes. If your GPA is not that strong, it's probably not a great idea to take a bunch of very difficult courses during the same semester, especially if those courses are courses you are not particularly interested in but are only taking because of the bar exam. You also want to think about breaking up your exam period by taking some classes with papers or projects. Finally, consider taking some summer courses to lessen your load during the school year. Many students knock out a required course or two during the summer after their first year because 1L summer clerkships are usually difficult to come by.

6. BACKUP YOUR COMPUTER ❒

WEEK SIX

1. MAKE SCHEDULE ❑
2. CONTINUE TO BRIEF ❑
3. CONTINUE OUTLINES ❑
4. ASK RELEVANT QUESTION (GO TO OFFICE HOURS) ❑
5. REVIEW YOUR NOTES ❑

WEEK SEVEN

1. MAKE SCHEDULE ☐
2. CONTINUE TO BRIEF ☐
3. CONTINUE OUTLINES ☐
4. REVIEW YOUR NOTES ☐
5. BACKUP YOUR COMPUTER ☐

6. IMPROVING YOUR EXAM ANSWERS ❐

A. Keeping Ahead of the Curve

Even if you did well in your first semester, you can't sit back and relax. Everyone else will improve in the second semester. Those people who did poorly are likely to be meeting with Academic Success and taking steps to fix whatever issues they had. Be especially careful if you are right above the line for being on Academic Probation. While schools usually do not dismiss students after the first semester, they do after the second. Keep in mind that everyone should be more comfortable and working smarter this semester. You want to make sure you are doing everything possible to keep up or improve your grades.

7. LEGAL WRITING ASSIGNMENT TO TUTOR/PROFESSOR ❐

WEEK EIGHT

1. MAKE SCHEDULE ❑

A. Prepare for Spring Break

As much as you may really want to, and as much as you may deserve it for all the hard work you've been doing this year, you shouldn't plan a Spring Break like the ones you may have had in college. While you do need to blow off some steam, you will ultimately feel a lot better if you get some work done so you are prepared for exams. Just like you did for Thanksgiving, plan for travel, consider photocopying your cases, and back-up your computer. Set some sensible goals and do the hardest things first so you don't sit around procrastinating about them. Your first year of law school is not the best time to spend an entire hedonistic week partying, especially if you're going to need another week (while back at law school) to recover.

2. CONTINUE TO BRIEF ❐

3. CONTINUE OUTLINES ❐

4. PRACTICE QUESTIONS (SHORT ONES) ❐

5. ASK RELEVANT QUESTION ❐

6. REVIEW YOUR NOTES ❐

7. WRITING YOUR OWN QUESTIONS ❐

A very effective method of preparing for your exams is to try to write your own questions. You've already been through one semester of exams, so you have a better handle on what questions will probably look like. As you are outlining, set some time aside to make your own questions. In deeply thinking about how to put the questions together, you should get an idea of what areas produce the most testable questions and where the natural testing points in those areas are. It is likely your professors will spend a lot of time on these areas in class. For example, in property, adverse possession is a very testable area because the rule has very clear elements and the facts that are necessary for an adverse possession hypo are easy to manipulate. For adverse possession, the main place to manipulate the facts are the facts connecting to the continuous element because there are a lot of things that can be done concerning seasonal use. In torts, you might realize the "reasonable person" is a great place to create issues. You can make the main character a child, a child engaged in an adult activity, a drunk, a doctor, or incredibly stupid. Write up questions and then trade them off with your friends to get even more practice.

Spring Break

1. EVALUATE WHERE YOU STAND ❑

2. DO NOT THINK THAT THIS WILL BE A WORK-A-THON ❑

Like Thanksgiving, you want to get some work done, but you can't assume you'll be working the entire time. Don't plan to get more done this week than you actually can. You'll just end up disappointed in yourself. But don't pretend you've never seen a case book before either. Find a balance.

3. WORK THROUGH PRACTICE QUESTIONS YOU DIDN'T GET TO ☐

While you should get whatever work is necessary done on your outlines, remember that doing practice questions can be a great way to study and pass the time if you are travelling. Practice questions are like crossword puzzles—much easier to focus on than simply reading the newspaper.

WEEK NINE

1. MAKE SCHEDULE ☐
2. CONTINUE TO BRIEF ☐
3. CONTINUE OUTLINES ☐
4. PRACTICE QUESTIONS (SHORT ONES) ☐

5. REVIEW YOUR NOTES ❐

6. BACKUP YOUR COMPUTER ❐

7. LEGAL WRITING ASSIGNMENT TO TUTOR/PROFESSOR ❐

WEEK TEN

1. MAKE SCHEDULE ❑
2. CONTINUE TO BRIEF ❑
3. CONTINUE OUTLINES ❑
4. PRACTICE QUESTIONS (MEDIUM ONES) ❑

5. ASK RELEVANT QUESTION (GO TO OFFICE HOURS) ❏

6. REVIEW YOUR NOTES ❏

7. MEDITATION ❏

Choose a quiet place. Sit in a comfortable chair with your feet firmly planted on the floor. You can rest your hands in your lap, or on the arms of the chair. Set a timer for five minutes. (Your phone's timer is probably the easiest one to find and use.) Close your eyes, and take a few breaths. Choose a word that makes you feel peaceful. It could be the word "peace" itself. But some other good choices could be love, hope, trust, calm, yes, joy, strong, or happy. Perpetuities or jurisdiction are probably not good choices. You can also choose a word from your faith tradition, if that is a source of strength and comfort for you. Hold your word in mind. Say it as you exhale with each breath. You'll notice that even as you say your word, other random thoughts will enter your mind. When you notice that you've been thinking about something else, take note of what it was. It's helpful to realize what's been lurking in the back of your mind. Tell yourself you can think about it later. Imagine encapsulating the thought in a bubble, and it floating away. Go back to holding your word in your mind. That's it. The five minutes will probably feel like a long time at first, but after a few sessions, you'll be shocked when the timer goes off. When that happens, set the timer for 10 minutes. Work your way up to 20 minutes at a time. Doing this will help refresh your mind much more quickly and effectively than fooling around on the Internet or watching TV.

WEEK ELEVEN

1. **MAKE SCHEDULE** ❑
2. **CONTINUE TO BRIEF** ❑
3. **CONTINUE OUTLINES** ❑
4. **PRACTICE QUESTIONS (MEDIUM ONES)** ❑

5. REVIEW YOUR NOTES ❑

6. BACKUP YOUR COMPUTER ❑

7. LEGAL WRITING ORAL ARGUMENTS ❑

Near the end of the year, many legal writing programs have oral arguments. Many people would rather be eaten by a shark than speak in front of someone else. But keep in mind there is at least one other student who is as nervous as you are. Your professor did this as a 1L and was probably nervous as well. Usually, the oral argument is not a huge impact on grades as long as your performance demonstrates that you are prepared. If the argument is making you nervous, practice your argument several times in front of a mirror or a willing loved one. Imagine yourself as an attorney on your favorite legal show, and do it enough times that you basically have everything memorized. If you know your nerves are really going to bother you, skip your morning coffee or other caffeine and just drink a little water. The argument will be over quicker than you think, and you might even discover it's actually kind of fun. If not, keep in mind there are other things in the law than being a litigator.

WEEK TWELVE

1. MAKE SCHEDULE ❒
2. CONTINUE TO BRIEF ❒
3. CONTINUE OUTLINES ❒
4. PRACTICE QUESTIONS (LONG ONES) ❒

5. ASK RELEVANT QUESTION ❑

6. REVIEW YOUR NOTES ❑

7. FINDING THE HOLES IN YOUR PRIOR EXAMS ❑

As you gear up for your second semester exams, make sure you focus on those places where you struggled or were weak on your prior exams. If you had problems stating the rules, using specific facts, or spotting issues, make sure you keep these things in mind as you work through practice questions. Try to run some of your sample answers by Academic Success, tutoring, or your doctrinal professor to see if you are on target.

WEEK THIRTEEN

1. MAKE SCHEDULE ❑
2. FINISH OUTLINES ❑
3. PRACTICE QUESTIONS (LONG ONES) ❑
4. GO TO OFFICE HOURS ❑

5. REVIEW YOUR NOTES ❐

6. BACKUP YOUR COMPUTER ❐

EXAM WEEK

1. HOW YOU SHOULD BE STUDYING ❑

A. Evaluate Last Term's Reading Week

How did last semester's reading week go? Was the place you chose to study an effective one? Were you able to concentrate? Did you find yourself getting distracted by the Internet or other things? Importantly, when you went into exams, how comfortable did you feel? Were you able to study enough that you just felt angry? Could you tell yourself that you did everything you reasonably could do? Is there something you can change in your studying to make yourself feel more comfortable? Did you get everything memorized as solidly as you wanted? Did you feel like you had enough practice? If something did not work, don't think that doing it the same way this time will lead to a different outcome. Take a long look at last semester, and see if there are things you can improve to make this exam session even better.

B. Scheduling Exam Time

Did you give all of your exams enough coverage? Generally, since all of your classes are likely worth the same amount of credits, you want to make sure you don't skimp on one to focus on the other.

2. REMEMBER WHAT YOU SHOULDN'T BE DOING ❒

Things like copying over notes or simply rereading your outlines again and again are not going to help. The best things you can do are memorizing your outline and doing as many practice questions as you can.

3. PRACTICE QUESTIONS AND MEMORIZING OUTLINES ❒

Even if you have an open book exam, you want to memorize the material. That way, the time pressure will not be as much of a factor in your exam performance. Memorizing outlines and doing practice questions are the best ways to internalize the material. Year after year, students underestimate the difficulty of open book exams. As a professor, if I give you an open book exam, it means I'm going to give you less time and judge your answers a lot harsher since you have your materials sitting right in front of you.

Summer

Congratulations! You have completed your first year of law school! Although at the moment almost everyone you know seems to have a law degree or is in law school, keep in mind what a rare feat this is. I hope you enjoyed your first year and that your hard work and dedication resulted in the grades you wanted. Buy yourself a present! Treat yourself!

PRACTICE QUESTIONS

SHORT QUESTIONS

These questions are meant to be very direct. Many times, students jump straight to more convoluted and difficult issues without making sure they can explain the basics, so make sure you start here to build your foundation before moving on. You don't need to worry about timing yourself now, but each question should take about three minutes to answer. The questions are labeled by general topic, and are divided by areas that professors tend to begin the semester with.

CIVIL PROCEDURE

Jurisdiction

1. Bob, a motivational speaker, got in a fistfight with Toby while Bob was giving a speech in New York City. Bob was a citizen of California, and Toby was a citizen of Illinois. Toby decided to sue Bob for his injuries, and learned that Bob was flying through Chicago on his way home to California. During a one-hour layover, Toby had Bob served with a summons to appear in Illinois state court. After receiving the summons, Bob claimed he was just passing through and had no connections to Illinois. Does the Illinois state court have jurisdiction over Toby's action?

2. *Squirrels!*, a national magazine devoted to squirrels and the people who love them, printed an article claiming that Doctor Zidwick, a world-renowned squirrel expert who ran a large non-profit devoted to squirrel research, was using donations to take exotic vacations and build several large houses for himself. The article also claimed his research center abused squirrels and kept them in dirty conditions. *Squirrels!* was based in Maine. Doctor Zidwick filed a suit for libel in his home state of Kansas. *Squirrels!* sold at least 10,000 copies of its magazine each month in Kansas, although this was the only contact the magazine had with the state. Does the Kansas court have jurisdiction over Doctor Zidwick's action?

3. Frank, a resident of the Western District of Iowa, sued David, a resident of the Southern District of California, and Andrew, a resident of the Northern District of California in

federal court for injuries that occurred during an auto accident in the Western District of Nebraska. Assuming there are no personal jurisdiction issues, in which judicial districts can Frank bring his lawsuit?

4. Steve, Scott, Bob, and Mark are all in a band. Steve is a citizen of Oregon. Scott is a citizen of California. Bob is a citizen of California. Mark is a citizen of Illinois. Steve and Scott have brought a federal suit in the Western District Oregon against Bob and Mark claiming missing royalties on a lost recording contract. There is no federal question present. The claim arose in the Western District of Oregon and the amount in controversy is $500,000. Can the Western District of Oregon hear the case?

5. A cable television operator sued an antenna company claiming violations of the federal Telecommunications Act. The operator was a South Carolina corporation with its principal place of business in North Carolina. The antenna company was a South Carolina corporation with its principal place of business in Georgia. The operator brought suit in South Carolina state court. The antenna company would like to remove the case to federal court. May it do so?

Beginning the Lawsuit

1. Rob brought a federal court action against Theresa. The complaint stated in full, "Theresa used fraud to induce Rob into entering this contract." In his action, Rob asked the court to rescind the contact. Assuming the jurisdictional allegations and demand for judgment are adequate, does the complaint fulfill the requirements of the federal rules?

2. Tracy wants to sue Kristine in Texas federal court for injuries sustained during a dance party. Tracy would like to use first class mail for service of process, but Texas law does not allow it. Federal Rule 4 permits substituted service of process. Will Tracy be allowed to use substituted service of process?

3. Biz sued the city after she was struck by a speeding bus. In her complaint, she claimed that she suffered a cracked skull and other physical injuries, physical and mental pain that will last into the foreseeable future, loss of her past and future earnings, and medical expenses of $50,000. Which of these damages need to be alleged specifically?

4. Hakeem was waterskiing when he was run over by a speedboat. Both people in the speedboat fell out when Hakeem was hit, and it's unclear which one was actually driving. Hakeem wants to sue both of them and allege that both of them were the driver. Can he do so?

5. Kelly wanted to sue Melanie for "flirting with married men." What does Kelly need to state in her complaint?

CONSTITUTIONAL LAW

Congressional Power

1. Congress enacted the Education and Training Act, which required all residents of United States military bases to attend school through the 12th grade. Hank, an aspiring musician who lived in Fort Jackson, a United State military base, wanted to drop out of 10th grade to move to Nashville. He challenged the Act in federal court, claiming it was unconstitutional. He pointed out that the vast majority of states only required school attendance until 10th grade. How should the court rule?

2. Congress passed a law that required states to outlaw marijuana if they wanted to continue to receive federal highway funds. Nathalie, who owned a legal medical marijuana dispensary, challenged the law in federal court, claiming it was unconstitutional. How should the court rule?

3. Frances was a bee farmer in Iowa. Due to concerns regarding bee colonies and the market price of honey, the U.S. government placed a limit on how much honey could be produced by any individual bee farmer. Frances was fined after she admitted she was producing honey in excess of the permitted amount. However, she argued that the excess honey was simply for her own private consumption and was never sold to any buyer, so it could not be subject to regulation under the Commerce Clause. Is Frances correct?

4. A federal law gave state courts jurisdiction to hear claims for violations of federal rights committed by corrections officers. After numerous frivolous lawsuits, New Jersey divested its trial

courts of the jurisdiction to hear these cases. May New Jersey do so?

5. Congress enacted a law requiring that pilots of commercial domestic flights carry handguns in case terrorists try to take over the plane. Is it likely such a law would be lawful under Congress's Commerce Clause power?

Individual Rights

1. A state passed a law requiring that a garden in front of the State House have special displays for Roman Catholic, Jewish, Protestant, and Muslim organizations. The intention of the law was to further understanding between the state's citizens. A local Buddhist organization asked to put up a display along with the others, and the state responded that it would not allow the Buddhist organization to do so. The Buddhist organization sued in federal court, claiming the state statute was unconstitutional. How should the court rule?

2. A member of a religious sect sued the state department of motor vehicles, claiming the requirement of a driver's license photo violated his religious rights. According to the sect, all members had to wear a head-covering at all times when in the presence of non-members. The head-covering covered everything but a person's eyes, and driver's licenses required a clear picture of the licensee's face. When the man applied for a license, he was refused because he wouldn't take off his head-covering for the picture. The man sued in federal court, claiming the photo requirement could not be applied against members of his sect.

3. A state passed a law that required anyone traveling by plane to register with the state police at least seven days before his or her intended travel date. The registration could be done online or by phone app, and took less than one minute. If a person failed to register, he or she would not be allowed on the plane. In enacting the law, the state said its intention was to protect the public from possible terrorist attacks and to have an easily accessible database of names in case of a plane crash. Harvey, a computer programmer who travelled each week for business, filed a lawsuit challenging the law as unconstitutional. How should the court rule?

4. David was an attorney representing a black woman who had been charged with reckless endangerment for allowing her son to stay alone in a neighborhood park while she was at work. He believed black women would be more sympathetic to his client, so he wanted to have as many black women on the jury as possible. Accordingly, he used his peremptory strikes to remove a white man and two white women from the jury. The state challenged the strikes, and David responded by pointing out the law allowed him to use his peremptory strikes to remove jurors with or without cause. Was David's action lawful?

5. A city passed an ordinance that limited "topless clubs and other adult entertainment establishments" to the "Barrens," a small corner of the city. The Barrens held a few warehouses, but was otherwise vacant land between a large swamp and the city airport. The city justified the ordinance by stating that its intention was to protect property values and reduce crime in the residential areas of the city. Corbin, who wanted to open a topless bar in the city, challenged the ordinance. He argued that the ordinance made topless clubs legal in less than 5 percent of the city's area and that the area allotted to topless clubs was in the least desirable part of the city. Is the city ordinance lawful?

CONTRACTS

Contract Formation

1. Thurston lost his cat, Mr. Bitey. He posted several signs around his neighborhood that read: "LOST CAT: MR. BITEY. REWARD: $50." Kim saw Thurston hanging up the sign and said, "I accept your $50 and promise to return Mr. Bitey to you." Is there a contract between Thurston and Kim?

2. Paul really liked Chris's guitar. One day when they were at Chris's house, Paul asked, "Would you consider selling me your guitar?" Chris responded, "I need money. Maybe I would accept $50 for it." The next day, Paul showed up at Chris's house with $50 and demanded Chris give him the guitar. Chris told Paul he was just kidding around. Is there a contract for the sale of the guitar between Paul and Chris?

3. Yehudi owned a comic book store. He placed an advertisement in the paper that read, "Stack of 100 Comics: Normally $300, Only $5—'First Come, First Served.' " Cameron went to the store the next day, handed Yehudi $5, and demanded the 100 comics. Yehudi refused to accept the money. Did the advertisement create an offer?

4. Eddie offered to sell his car to Sammy for $10,000. Sammy said he would probably buy it. The next day, Sammy decided to accept the offer and went to the bank to apply for a loan. The bank officer told Sammy that he had just bought the car for $8,000 as a gift for his son. He pointed over Sammy's shoulder to a window looking out on the parking lot. The bank officer's son was outside waxing the car. Sammy drove directly over to Eddie's house and told him that he had to get the car back because Eddie had already offered the car to him. Sammy also said that Eddie had to sell him the car for $8,000, since that was the amount the bank owner had bought the car for. Is Eddie required to sell the car to Sammy for $8,000.

5. Jimmy attended Mary's art show in New York. At the show, he told Mary, "I will give you $5,000 if you paint my portrait. I don't want a promise or anything, I just want the portrait for my boardroom." The next day, Mary drove to the art store and spent $500 buying canvases, paints, and brushes. Mary called Jimmy to arrange a time for her to come to his office for some sketches. Jimmy responded, "What? I was drunk! I don't need a painting." Mary argued that she already accepted his offer by buying the art supplies. Is Mary correct?

6. Becky went to Brandon's garage sale and saw a table she liked. Brandon said, "I want to get rid of it, so I will sell it to you for $50." Becky responded, "I'll buy it for $50, but only if you also throw in this lamp." Is there a contract between Becky and Brandon?

7. Scott and Timothy spent a few days at Scott's beach house. During their stay, Timothy told Scott several times that he would love to buy the beach house if Scott wanted to sell it. Scott said he would probably sell for $250,000, since that was double the price he paid for it and reasonable compared to other properties in the area. A week later, Scott sent Timothy a letter offering to sell his beach house for $250,000. The same day,

without any knowledge of Scott's letter, Timothy sent Scott a letter offering to buy his beach house for $250,000. Is there a contract between Scott and Timothy?

8. Alan ordered 1,000 black t-shirts from Gary's t-shirt shop. Gary shipped 1,000 dark blue t-shirts in response without notifying Alan beforehand. Is there a contract between Alan and Gary?

9. James was worried about his niece, Angela, who he believed was dithering away her life. One day, James promised Angela that if she gave up reading trashy novels and disco dancing until she turned 18, he would give her $10,000 for college. Angela did so, and on her 18th birthday she asked James for the $10,000. He responded, "Everything I asked you to do helped you out! Now you have a scholarship to the best college in the land! My promise has already paid you dividends, so you haven't given me any consideration for my promise!" Is James correct?

10. Skip's daughter, Skippette, was kidnapped and held for ransom. Skip placed a large advertisement in the local newspaper offering $25,000 to anyone who could save her. Officer Darger, who was assigned to the case, discovered Skippette was being held on a boat in the harbor. He rescued Skippette and sent Skip a note demanding the $25,000 reward. Is Officer Darger entitled to the $25,000?

CRIMINAL LAW

Physical Act and Mens Rea

1. Derek, Hans, and Meek were walking back from a bar. Derek, in an effort to be funny, tripped Hans. Hans fell and accidentally pushed Meek out into the middle of the street where he was run over by a truck. The police charged Hans with murder. Can Hans be held criminally liable for Meek's death?

2. Al and Fredo went to an alligator park to look at the alligators. While at the park, Fredo tripped on his shoelace and fell into a large pond where an alligator feeding show was about to start. The alligators reached the pond through a short tunnel that was usually blocked by a metal grate. However, the grate

was open in anticipation of the show. At the moment, no alligators were in the pond, but Al could tell from a large countdown clock on the wall that they were coming to be fed. Al noticed a large red button on a pole next to him that said, "In case someone falls in water before the show, push button and gate will close!" Al could have easily pushed the button and stopped the alligators from entering the pond, but he decided he really hated Fredo and wanted to see him get eaten. Al got out his cellphone and waited to take a selfie in front of the alligators eating Fredo. Fredo screamed for help, but was ultimately eaten. After Al posted his selfie on the Internet, the police charged him with murder in the death of Fredo. Can Al be held criminally liable for Fredo's death?

3. A statute imposed criminal liability on anyone who "knowingly makes a sale of a tobacco product to a person under the age of 18." Ian was a cashier at MartMart, a small grocery store. Sally, who was 17 years old, went to MartMart to buy Tobacha, a chewing gum made with tobacco. She presented Ian with a fake driver's license that listed her age as 20. Ian sold her the gum. A police officer in line behind Sally immediately arrested Ian for violation of the statute. Ian claimed he thought Sally's driver's license was real and had no idea that Tobacha was actually a tobacco product. If Ian's statements were true, could he be found criminally liable under the statute?

4. Ron was a park ranger. One day, he came across a camper who was dying of thirst. Although Ron had a water bottle, his shift was about to end, so he ignored the camper. The camper later died of dehydration. Is it likely Ron can be held criminally liable for the camper's death?

5. Iggy had a brain disorder that caused him to lose consciousness on occasion. One night after a party where all his friends had been drinking, Iggy decided to act as the sober driver. While driving his friends home, Iggy lost consciousness and drove off a bridge, killing three of his friends. Can Iggy be held criminally liable for the death of his friends?

Homicide

1. Tom bought a live hand grenade from an online seller. He brought the hand grenade to school and showed it to his friends

in the school cafeteria. His friends didn't believe the hand grenade was real, so Tom pulled the pin and tossed it towards the food line where dozens of people were standing. The hand grenade exploded and killed several people. Tom was charged with murder. At trial, Tom argued he didn't intend to kill anyone when he tossed the grenade. Can Tom be convicted of murder?

2. Melissa's husband was killed while serving in the military. At his funeral, a religious group widely known for protesting soldiers' funerals showed up and said Melissa's husband deserved to die. One of the protestors had a sign he had made showing Melissa's husband burning in Hell. The protestor approached Melissa and her six-year-old daughter, Buffy. The protestor stood a foot away from Buffy and yelled "Your daddy's burning in Hell!" Buffy, who was already crying, fell onto the ground sobbing and the protestor spit on her. Melissa, enraged, grabbed the sign out of the protestor's hand and clubbed him with it. The blow killed him instantly. What is the most likely crime Melissa will be charged with?

3. Anthony was a huge fan of his local high school football team. One night after this team's latest victory, Anthony went to the house of the losing team's coach and set it on fire. He didn't want to hurt anyone, and knew the coach and his family were not at home because he had seen them eating dinner at a local diner. However, shortly after the fire started, the coach came home and tried to put out the fire with a garden hose. He had a heart attack and died on his front lawn. The local fire department responded to the scene, and a volunteer firefighter died when the fire truck accidently backed over him while trying to get the hose connected to a fire hydrant. Finally, the coach's elderly neighbor woke up, saw the fire and two bodies, and had a stroke. She died later in the hospital. Is Anthony guilty of murder, and of whom?

4. Ezra decided he wanted to kill his neighbor, Henry. He decided the best way to do so would be to shoot him with an arrow. Ezra set up a target in his backyard to practice his archery. As he was practicing, he missed the target. The arrow went over the fence and struck Henry in the neck, killing him. Ezra had no idea Henry was out there, but he was pretty happy with how everything turned out. Is Ezra guilty of murder?

5. Mike was angry at his ex-wife and decided to kill her. Mike knew she had a dangerous heart condition, so he called her and told her that the school called and told him that both of their children were killed in a horrible bus accident. This was a lie. His ex-wife had a heart attack and died from the shock. Can Mike be found guilty of murder?

PROPERTY

Personal Property

1. Job was an avid trout fisherman. One day, he went fishing in an unowned river and hooked a wild trout with his fishing rod. He fought the trout for over an hour until the fishing line broke. The trout, noticeably tired, started to swim away when Matt arrived on the scene and scooped up the trout with his baseball hat. Job yelled, "Hey! That's my trout! I tired it out!" Matt responded, "Nope! It's mine! I caught it!" Who is correct?

2. A man was staying at a hotel when he found a small bag under the mattress of the bed. When he opened the bag, he found that it was full of old baseball cards. Several months later, he took the cards to "The Old Stuff Show," a television program where people had antiques appraised on camera. The appraiser told the man the cards were incredibly rare and likely worth at least $1 million. When the man told the appraiser where he had found the cards, the hotel owner, who was standing nearby waiting to have a lamp appraised, said, "I had no idea they were there, but you found them in my hotel and they belong to me!" The man responded, "You didn't even know they were there! They aren't yours—someone lost them! Finders keepers, losers jerks!" Who is right?

3. Tory visited his fraternity brother, Rob, at Rob's office and admired Rob's rare medical device collection. Tory picked up a Hambrick Scraper, an ancient medical device for removing "the vapors", and said, "Brother! This is totally my favorite! If we were truly brothers, you would totally give it to me." Rob said, "Brother! It's yours—I hereby give it as a gift to you to symbolize our brotherhood!" Tory responded, "I will cherish it always!" Tory put the device back in its stand and the two promptly forgot

about it. Three years later, Rob was run over by a rhino while on safari. At Rob's funeral, Tory asked for the scraper, telling Rob's executor that Rob gave it to him as a gift. Did Rob make a valid gift to Tory?

4. Marshall wanted to show Doc how much he cared for him. He said, "Doc—To show you I could never forget about you, I want to give you my gold microphone." Doc responded, "Thanks! I love it." Just as Marshall was about to hand the microphone to Doc, Marshall said, "Wait—I can't give it to you now." Instead, Marshall grabbed a piece of paper and wrote, "I, Marshall, transfer title to my gold microphone to Doc, but I need to keep it for two years as I embark on my world tour." He then gave the piece of paper to Doc. While on tour, Marshall died in a bus accident. Doc called Marshall's executor and asked for the microphone. Did Marshall make a valid gift to Doc?

5. Mac gave his guitar to a music shop to be restrung. After the shop restrung the guitar, it sold the guitar to Dennis by mistake. Mac asked Dennis for the guitar back, but Dennis refused to give it to him. Can Mac force Dennis to return the guitar?

Adverse Possession

1. Pogue bought a small cottage on a beach near Boston as an investment. The cottage was unheated, and since Pogue always summered in Italy, he never visited the property. George started spending his summers in the cottage since no one else was around. He did so every summer for 15 years until 2009. In 2009, George "sold" the property to Bailey for $10,000. Bailey continued to spend his summers in the cottage until 2015. In 2015, Bailey met with his attorney to find out if he had any rights in the cottage. The attorney told him the relevant statutory period for adverse possession was 20 years, so Bailey now owned the cottage. Is Bailey's attorney right?

2. Twenty-five years ago, Lisa sold Mellowacre, a 20-acre farm in rural Iowa, to Rose. Mellowacre was known throughout Iowa as the "20-Acre Heart of the Country." At the time, Lisa did not in fact have legal title to Mellowacre, although Rose was unaware of this fact. Rose immediately moved onto a one-acre parcel of the property, built a small house, and lived there continuously. Last week, Elizabeth, the true owner of

Mellowacre, sued Rose. Elizabeth acknowledged that Rose had title to the one-acre she had been living on through adverse possession since she had lived on it for over 20 years, but she claimed the other 19 acres still belonged to her. Rose argued she had gained title to the entire 20-acre farm. Is Rose correct?

3. Bob and Ray were neighboring farmers. Bob told Ray that he knew his crops were encroaching onto Ray's land and that Bob would remove the crops if Ray asked him. Ray didn't respond. Twenty years later, Bob claimed that he had gained title to the part of Ray's land where his crops had encroached. Is Bob correct? The relevant adverse possession period is 20 years.

4. Charlie and Alex inherit a beach house as co-tenants. Charlie moves into the house as his primary residence, but Alex continues to live on the other side of the country. Charlie pays all of the property's taxes and insurance and makes all repairs. Alex pays nothing. After 20 years, Charlie claims he's gained Alex's interest in the property by adverse possession. Has he done so? The relevant adverse possession period is 20 years.

5. Zanna moves onto Chadwick's property without permission. Zanna lives on the property for 10 years, then leases her interest to Lola for 10 years. Lola remains on the property during those 10 years, then gives the property back to Zanna. Does Zanna own the property through adverse possession? The relevant adverse possession period is 20 years.

Estates in Land

1. Kerry was the owner in fee simple of Brittneyacre. As a gift, Kerry delivered a deed to her son, Jimmy, which read, "to Jimmy for the life of James." If the jurisdiction follows the common law rule, what estate does Jimmy have in Brittneyacre?

2. Tobias conveyed Bananacre "to Bob for life." What estate and interest does this create?

3. Christina conveyed Sodaacre "to Yiyun life, but in no way may it continue past 10 years." What estate does Yiyun have in the property?

4. Lou conveyed Velvetacre "to Steve for life." Steve entered the property and immediately set up a mining operation. May Steve do so?

5. Vincent conveyed his farm "to my nephew Topher and his heirs so long as the property is never used for hunting; but if the farm is ever used for hunting, to the local animal shelter." What interest does the local animal shelter have?

TORTS

Intentional Torts

1. Bill and Hal were at a toga party when they started arguing about a song playing on the stereo. In anger, Hal grabbed Bill's toga and yanked it off to embarrass him. Everyone at the party laughed and pointed and Bill cried. A few days later, Bill sued Hal for battery. Does Bill have a claim?

2. Kirby and Jaclyn were in a bar when they started arguing. Kirby jumped off her bar stool, pulled back her fist, and yelled, "Jaclyn! Prepare to meet my haymaker!" Kirby then threw a punch at Jaclyn's head. Jaclyn ducked, and Kirby missed her entirely but hit Quentin straight in the nose. Quentin fell to the floor in pain, blood spouting from between his fingers. What torts have been committed?

3. Charles was packing up his bag in the gym locker room when Coach Skinner saw him. There had been several recent thefts in the locker room, and Coach Skinner thought Charles looked suspicious. He walked over, grabbed Charles's bag, and said, "I think you're a thief! I'm taking this to my office right now to see what you have inside!" Coach Skinner disappeared with Charles's bag. Because Charles's wallet and gym clothes were in the bag, Charles stayed in the locker room until Coach Skinner returned with the bag an hour later. Coach Skinner gave the bag back and mumbled, "Sorry." Charles wanted to sue, but he was unsure if Coach Skinner had actually done anything to create tort liability. Did he?

4. Jojo was hiking in a state park. He followed a path clearly delineated by blue blazes. Unbeknownst to Jojo, the blue blazes had been placed in error. Jojo followed the blazes onto land owned by Old Man McGee. Old Man McGee saw Jojo and rushed out with his shotgun. He yelled, "You hippy whippersnapper! You're trespassing!" Jojo responded, "I thought I was still in the

state park." Jojo had no reason to doubt the blue blazes or believe that he was on any land other than the state park. Could he be liable for trespassing?

5. Landon has a video channel where he plays pranks on strangers. He decides to act like he is going to shoot Tina, who is standing at a bus stop. Landon walks up to Tina with his finger in his pocket and says, "I have a gun! I'm going to shoot you!" Tina immediately punches Landon in the face and breaks his nose. Landon sues Tina for battery. Does Tina have any defense to the suit?

Negligence

1. Emma was employed as a bus driver. Emma was helping Harry get on the bus when he dropped a package. The package was full of high explosives. The explosion caused a wall a substantial distance away to collapse onto Cameron. Cameron was severely injured. If Emma was negligent in helping Harry onto the bus, could she be liable for Cameron's injuries?

2. Frances and Paulo were crossing a bridge when Frances thought it would be funny to shove Paulo off. The bridge was only six feet off the water and during the summers many people jumped off and swam there. In fact, Frances and Paulo had done so many of times. Paulo splashed into the water and then bobbed up. He was really mad because his phone was in his pocket and was probably ruined. As he was swimming along and yelling at Frances, Captain Amazepants, a local vigilante hero, leaped into the water yelling, "I'll save you!" Unfortunately, Captain Amazepants's cape caught on the bridge and he gave himself whiplash. If Frances was found negligent in shoving Paulo off the bridge, would she be liable for Captain Amazepants's injuries?

3. Murph was an astonishingly stupid man. One day, he and his even less intelligent friends were at a gas station when they started a "gas fight" and sprayed gasoline all over each other. When one of them lit a cigarette, the entire gas station exploded. Murph truly did not understand that gasoline was explosive. Could he still be held liable in tort?

4. Truck drivers in the state are required to carry $1 million in liability insurance. Harmony, an uninsured truck driver, drove

the wrong way down a street and crashed into oncoming traffic. Is his lack of insurance negligence per se?

5. On New Year's Eve, a woman was walking in front of a hotel when she was hit with a falling armchair. No one saw the accident, although it was a safe assumption that the armchair came from one of the hotel's windows. Can the woman use res ipsa loquitur to make her claim against the hotel?

MEDIUM QUESTIONS

These questions are a bit longer, and are designed to take you 20 minutes to answer. Importantly, they have more than one issue. One of the key skills you want to develop is making sure you answer the question that is created by the facts. Again, the question topics are labeled.

CIVIL PROCEDURE

Subject Matter Jurisdiction

1. Piston was a famous rap star based in Detroit, Michigan. The American Pig Wrestling Federation was a business incorporated in Delaware, with a large plant employing 10,000 workers in Arizona and a small base of key executives and decision-makers in New York City who make all the decisions regarding the company. The Federation asked to use one of Piston's songs in their advertisements. Piston refused. Several weeks later, Piston saw a Federation advertisement using a song that sounded exactly like the one the Federation asked to use, although it was being done by a "soundalike" artist. In addition, the cartoon pig singing the song on the advertisement looked very much like Piston. Piston filed suit in federal court in New York, claiming the advertisement presented him in a "false and misleading light." He claimed $50,000 in damages for the advertisement. He also threw in an unrelated breach of contract claim against the Federation for an additional $25,000. Can the New York federal court hear Piston's claims?

Personal Jurisdiction

2. Hugh, who was from South Carolina, was called to be a witness in a case in Georgia. He took a flight from South Carolina that had a 10-minute stopover in North Carolina. During the stopover, the pilot said there would be a delay and passengers might as well get out and stretch their legs. As Hugh was wandering around the terminal, a process server ran up and served process on him. He looked at the claim, which stated a magazine he ran, *Widespread*, was being sued for libel for a story it did on a South Carolina politician who was presently appearing on a reality television show. *Widespread* was

marketed throughout the southeast, including in Georgia, South Carolina, Florida, and North Carolina. Can Hugh and his magazine be sued in North Carolina?

Supplemental Jurisdiction

3. Lenny sued Rick, claiming Rick violated federal copyright laws when he used excerpts from Lenny's book in a performance art piece. Lenny also sued Jay, his agent, on a state contract claim involving an alleged sale of the book for the same performance, which Lenny claimed involved the same factual questions as the copyright claim. Lenny and Jay were residents of Texas, while Rick was a resident of New York. Lenny claimed $40,000 in damages for the copyright violation, and $45,000 in damages for the contract claim. Lenny would like to bring both suits in federal court. May he do so?

Jurisdiction and Venue

4. Paul sued Tommy in the federal district court of South Carolina for a car accident that occurred in Florida. Paul claimed he suffered $100,000 in damages. Tommy rented an apartment in South Carolina and lived and worked there as a professor for 10 months of the year, but he owned a small house in Rhode Island he visited for two months every summer. Paul was a sea captain who was out at sea for 10 months of the year, but he owned a house in Rhode Island where he received his mail and was registered to vote. After filing suit, Paul requested a transfer of the case to Florida since all of the witnesses and evidence were located in that state. The court granted his request. After the case was transferred, Tommy moved to dismiss, stating that under Florida law Paul's claim was barred by the statute of limitations although it was not barred under South Carolina law. Discuss.

Discovery

5. George and Pogue were two former business partners who had a falling out after George had an affair with Pogue's wife. Pogue sued George for breach of contract regarding their business agreement, and Pogue also requested a mental examination of George "because he was so crazy, he married my wife!" George challenged the request. What result?

Federal Jurisdiction

6. Wendy, who resided in Minnesota, sued PurpleCo. for personal injury after a PurpleCo. delivery truck ran her over during a fair wage protest outside PurpleCo.'s corporate headquarters. Wendy claimed $50,000 in damages. PurpleCo. was incorporated in Delaware and had all of its factories in Texas. Its corporate headquarters and board of directors were in Minnesota. PurpleCo. filed a counterclaim for $30,000 in damages caused to its truck. Analyze whether Wendy's cause of action could be heard in federal court.

CONSTITUTIONAL LAW

Case or Controversy

1. Ellen challenged a state affirmative action program, claiming that she was passed over for a law school scholarship because she was not a minority. While her suit was pending, she was admitted to the law school and at this point in the litigation was about to graduate. Ellen's uncle was the president of the American Optometrist Organization, an organization composed entirely of optometrists whose purpose was to promote the professional well-being of optometrists. Ellen told her uncle about her lawsuit, and he thought Organization members would be very interested in the lawsuit's outcome because many children of optometrists and other similar professionals went to law school. Consequently, he also filed suit on behalf of the Organization challenging the affirmative action program and its grant of law school minority scholarships. Discuss.

Federal Power

2. In an effort to promote green energy in the United States, Congress enacted a statute that created Go Green Grants. The grants provided money to state governments who could then distribute the grants to people and organizations in their states who converted homes and businesses from fossil fuels to solar panels. The intent was to help combat global warming. GreenFrance, a French activist group, protested the grants, claiming the grants were a sham and were merely blinding people to the real dangers of American energy consumption. The

protests became violent, and Serge, the GreenFrance leader, was arrested by state police in California after a police officer was shot and injured. Serge was ultimately convicted and sent to state prison. During critical negotiations with France regarding a new pipeline, the U.S. President pardoned Serge and directed the governor of California to release him. The governor refused to do so. Discuss.

Protected Speech

3. The Town of Terrible is widely known as having the rudest, most offensive citizens in America. In an effort to promote tourism, Mayor Brown passed several ordinances in an attempt to improve the image of the town. The first ordinance, called "Winning Our Kids Back," banned the sale or rental of violent videogames to minors. It stated that its intent was to "return kids to a kinder, gentler state where youth violence isn't a factor." The second ordinance, "Respect Our Authority," banned all speech that "in any manner" questions a police officer in the performance of his or her duty. Its intent was to promote "respect for police and other public servants." The third ordinance, "Parades That the Whole Family Can Enjoy," creates a Parade Commission that gives the Mayor complete authority to grant or deny parade permits to different groups. Its intent was to make sure that "any organization involved in a town parade was family-oriented." Are these ordinances lawful?

Equal Protection

4. A civil rights group was studying several state laws. The first law established districts for the election of congressional representatives. The law had no racial language of any kind, but several of the districts had bizarre shapes that allowed minority race voters to control the outcome of the election. The second law allowed attorneys to strike potential jurors from a jury with or without cause. A study of the judicial system showed many attorneys representing private parties used the strikes to remove minority jurors, although the same study showed government attorneys never did so. The third law required that applicants to the police department pass a written exam. A study showed that racial minorities consistently scored lower on the test than white applicants. Are any of these laws likely to be found racially discriminatory?

Legal Standards

5. In preparation for hosting the Olympic Games, a state passes three new laws. The first prohibits all air travel to and from the city during the two weeks of the games. The second states that only male candidates will be considered as security guards for the games because of their greater size and strength. The third imposes a 1% sales tax on all items sold during the two weeks of the games. In determining constitutionality of these laws, what standards will the court use?

State Taxation

6. A state is very unhappy with the location of a federal nuclear power plant in its state. In response, it passes two laws. The first law creates a state tax levied directly against the power plant itself. The second law subjects federal employees to the same state taxes faced by state employees. Discuss the validity of the two laws.

CONTRACTS

Statute of Frauds

1. A baseball retailer placed a telephone order for 40 batting helmets at the manufacturer's list price of $2,000 "for delivery in 30 days." The manufacturer orally accepted the offer and immediately emailed the retailer a signed memo: "Confirming our agreement today for 40 helmets for $2,000, shipment delivered in 30 days." The retailer received and read the email. Two weeks later, the retailer stated "I'm not accepted this crud!" when the manufacturer's conforming shipment arrived. Is the retailer liable for breach of contract?

Conditions

2. Fenix and Oberon agree that "provided that on November 1, Fenix's rental properties are producing $1,000 a month in income, Oberon will loan Fenix $80,000 at 3% interest for one year." They also enter into an agreement that states: "In consideration of Fenix selling his car to Oberon, Oberon will pay Fenix $40,000. Fenix may retain the car until January 1, provided the car is kept in a locked garage during the night." On

November 1, Fenix's properties are only making $500 a month in income. That same night, Oberon drives by Fenix's house and sees his old car parked out on the street. Oberon refuses to loan the money and asks for the car back. Discuss.

Consideration

3. Telly told Becky, "Hey, come by my house today and I'll give you my old guitar." When Becky arrived, Telly was standing on a ladder. He turned to wave hello, and fell backwards. Becky caught him before he hit the pavement. Telly said, "Thank you so much! I'll give you $1,000 in thanks!" Telly couldn't give Becky the money or the guitar right away, but he promised to give them to her soon. When Becky got home, she wrote a letter to her credit card company. The letter said, "I know I owed your company $2,000, and you can no longer collect on me because the statute of limitations has run, but Beckies always repay their debts! I just came into some money, so I will pay you $500 ASAP." Please discuss whether any of the promises are enforceable.

Promises and Promissory Estoppel

4. Bob decides to open a hamburger stand near downtown. He signs an agreement with T-Bone Meat Purveyors that states, "Bob agrees to purchase from T-Bone as much meat as I may need to buy from T-Bone." Tony, the owner of a local ice cream factory, hears about Bob's plans. He tells Bob, "If you also get an industrial cooler and sell ice cream, I'll give you free ice cream for six months." Based on Tony's promise, Bob buys a cooler for $5,000. Tony then tells Bob he doesn't want to give him the ice cream for free. Please discuss whether any of the promises are enforceable.

Mistake

5. Franklin wants to build a new basement for his house. Ben bids $20,000 to do the job, and Franklin accepts. While digging under the home, Ben discovers a system of small underground streams. In order to complete the basement, Ben will have to spend an additional $5,000, which will eliminate his profit on the job. At the same time, Bob discovers a large shiny rock under Franklin's house. He shows Franklin the stone, and both of them decide it's a geode worth about $100. Ben offers to buy the geode

for $50, and Franklin accepts. On the way home, Ben stops at a jewelers and discovers the stone is actually a rare diamond worth $1 million. Franklin is driving to the grocery store when he sees Ben dancing in the streets. When Ben tells him about the stone, Franklin demands it back. Please discuss whether any of the potential agreements are enforceable.

Article 2—Additional Terms

6. BuildCo. offers to sell to WorkCo. 2,000 bricks at $2 each plus transportation costs. WorkCo. replies, "We accept, but the price is $2.20, which includes transportation costs. We also get a 2% discount if we pay within 60 days. Finally, any disputes will be settled by mutually acceptable arbitration." Please discuss whether an agreement has been formed between the parties.

CRIMINAL LAW

Criminal Basics and Property Crimes

1. Elsa hadn't sleepwalked in 20 years. However, one dark and very stormy night, Elsa started sleepwalking. She got up from bed, took a lamp from her nightstand, and went outside. Chip was walking his dog. Elsa, still sleepwalking, thought Chip's umbrella was the head of a very large alien. She clubbed Chip over the head and killed him. Chip's screams woke Elsa and she panicked and ran down the street. As she was running, she saw a hand reaching out from a rapidly flooding storm drain. Her neighbor, Bitsy, had been swept into the drain and was crying for help. Elsa was too scared to stop so she kept running, and the drain soon filled with water and drowned Bitsy. Elsa was getting really cold in the rain, so she ran to a house with a partly open door. She pushed the door and went inside. While inside, she saw a warm winter jacket. She took the jacket and headed back outside where she was soon arrested by the police. Elsa is charged with the murder of Chip, the murder of Bitsy, and common law burglary of the home. Discuss.

Property Crimes

2. Hermione worked as an editor at a large publishing company. One day, she took several copies of a new book she was working on home with her. Don came by her house and complained about having nothing good to read. Hermione said, "This book I've been working on is sure to be a big bestseller. I'll sell you one for $20." Don agreed, but said he didn't have any cash on him. Consequently, he wrote out a note saying he would pay her $20 next Tuesday. Hermione accepted the note and gave Don the book. Don had just lost his job, had no money in his bank account, and had no intention of ever paying Hermione. On the way out, Don saw another book on Hermione's shelf. He offered to buy that book as well. Hermione agreed to sell it for $30 for another note promising to pay. However, as she handed over the book, she said, "That one's special to me—so consider it borrowed until you actually pay me the money." What crimes have been committed?

Property Crimes

3. Eunice was getting out of her new car when Harpy approached her. Harpy said, "Give me that violin you are carrying, or I'll smash the car window in." Eunice immediately handed him the violin. Harpy ran over to Gummy's pawn shop and said, "Hey, want to buy a violin?" Gummy asked, "Where'd you get that?" Harpy said, "It fell off a truck" and winked at him several times. Gummy agreed to buy the violin. When Gummy examined the violin, he found Eunice's name inside. He called Eunice and said, "Eunice—if you don't pay me $500, I'm throwing your violin in the river!" What crimes have been committed?

Analyzing Statutes

4. A town was very concerned about gun control, so it enacted two statutes. The first stated, "Any fully automatic machinegun must be registered with the local police department." The statute did not include a mental state, but violation of the statute resulted in a 20-year prison sentence. The second prohibited "knowingly making a sale of a fully automatic weapon to a minor." After the ordinances went into effect, Jesse sold an unregistered fully automatic weapon to Owen, a 15-year-old boy.

Jesse was charged under both offenses. What possible defenses does he have?

Merger and Crime

5. Tina was arrested on a street corner with a large amount of drugs in her possession. As she was being put into the patrol car, she escaped and ran down the street. At the end of the street, she saw her friend Amy and screamed for help. They ducked into an alley, and Amy said, "We really need to steal a car." Amy picked up a metal pipe. Tina said, "I don't want to hurt anyone." Amy nodded and then the both of them rushed a woman who was getting into her car. Amy hit her with the pipe, and the woman died. Tina and Amy took the car and sped away until they were stopped at a police roadblock and arrested. At trial, Tina is charged with (1) illegal possession of narcotics, (2) illegal possession of narcotics for sale, (3) illegally labeled narcotics, (4) armed robbery, and (5) felony murder. May Tina be convicted of all five offenses?

Murder

6. Dave hated Taylor. One night, he snuck into his apartment and stabbed him to death with a knife. He fled the scene and returned to his apartment. As he ran inside, he found his wife in bed with another man. Dave screamed, and then stabbed the man to death. He fled his apartment and jumped into his car. He drove all night to get away, finally getting tired after 12 hours of driving. He fell asleep at the wheel and swerved, hitting a man walking along the roadside. The man died from his injuries. The police eventually caught Dave and arrested him. Under the common law, what crimes will he likely be charged with in regard to the three deaths he caused?

PROPERTY

Wild Animals

1. Mikael was hunting bears in Big Wood, an unowned forest. He soon found bear tracks and started following them down a ravine. As he followed the tracks, he left the boundaries of the Wood and entered Ivor's farm. He immediately spotted three

bears. He shot the first one dead, and the other two darted into the Wood. Mikael had placed a net in the Wood, and this fell on the second bear, trapping him. Mikael ran past the second bear, shot again, and hit the third bear in the leg. He followed the third bear's trail until he heard gunfire. He eventually came upon Lydia, who had shot the third bear dead. Mikael yelled, "Hey! That's my bear!" At the same time, he heard gunshots back behind him and ran back to the net. There, Brunhilde was shooting the second bear dead. Mikael yelled, "Hey! That's my bear!" He then heard more shots and ran back to Ivor's field. Ivor was standing over the first bear firing shots into the air in celebration of having a new fur coat. Mikael yelled, "Hey! That's my bear!" Is Mikael right about any of this?

Personal Property

2. Jorge was walking on the sidewalk past a beachside bar when he tripped over a watch. At the same time, he noticed a briefcase sitting on the bar although no one was seated at the bar or working behind it. He thought about picking up the briefcase when he was hit in the forehead by something hard. He looked down and saw that a bracelet had hit him. He looked up and saw an angry couple screaming at each other on a balcony 12 stories above him. He heard the man yell, "Fine! I hate you too!" Then the man took off his bracelet and hurled it from the balcony, hitting Jorge in the head again. Jorge picked up the watch, the briefcase, and the bracelets. Do any of them belong to him?

Adverse Possession

3. Tyrone owned a ski chalet on Mount Ski, a popular skiing resort. However, Tyrone hated skiing, so he only used the chalet for two months every summer as he worked on his book, *Family is the Greatest Gift*. Unbeknownst to Tyrone, James used the chalet every winter when he came to Mount Ski. He was very careful not to let any of the neighbors know he was there, because he didn't want anyone to tell Tyrone. This went on for 10 years. In year 11, Tyrone decided to try skiing. When he showed up at the chalet, he discovered James handing over a title to the chalet to Danny and Danny handing him a large sack of gold. James said, "Dude! I owned this place and I just sold it! The statute of limitations in this state is 10 years!" Danny said,

"I just bought this place, and it's totally mine because I had no idea it wasn't James's to sell!" Assuming James is right about the statute of limitations, is either James or Danny right about who owns the chalet? There is no recording act in the jurisdiction.

Future Interests

4. Susan owned several pieces of property that she decided to grant to her friends and neighbors. Susan granted Alphaacre to Alex, stating "to Alex and his heirs, on the express condition it is only used to raise alfalfa, and if it is ever not used to raise alfalfa, then me or my heirs may enter and terminate the estate." Susan granted Betaacre to Beatrice, stating "to Beatrice and her heirs, provided that beets are only grown on the premises. If something other than beets is grown on the land, Susan and her heirs may enter and terminate the estate hereby conveyed." Finally, Susan granted Gammaacre to Greg, stating "to Greg and his heirs, provided however that if the premises ever cease to be used to grow grapes, title shall pass to George and his heirs." Assuming the Rule Against Perpetuities does not apply, what interests are created by Susan's grants?

Concurrent Estates

5. Eddie granted Corin, Janet, and Carrie a house on the beach. The grant simply said, "To Corin, Janet, and Carrie." After moving into the house together, the three of them got into a fight. Corin took black masking tape and marked off "her part of the house" and said that if either of the other two crossed the line, she would club them. Carrie then decided she didn't want to share the house with the other two anymore, so she sold her interest to Chris. Janet got fed up with the whole situation and came to you for advice regarding everyone's ownership rights. How do the parties own the property?

Landlord and Tenant

6. Larry owns several properties he rents out to students. Quentin rented a large house form Larry while he was taking summer courses, and the lease stated that "Quentin leases the premises from Larry for three months." Art saw the house and decided he wanted to rent it for the fall and spring terms. Art signed a lease stating, "Art leases from Larry the premises at a

rent of $1,000 a month." At the end of three months, Quentin decides he wants to stay in the house. When Larry shows up with Art to get the keys from Quentin, Quentin says, "What evs! I'm staying! I want a month's notice before I move out!" Larry comes to you for advice.

TORTS

Intentional Torts

1. Michael, Peter, Mike, and Bill were all in a band together. They were practicing a new song when Michael told Peter he wasn't playing it right. Peter raised his guitar over his head and said to Michael, "Say it again!" Michael backed away as Mike got between the two of them. Mike put his hand on Peter's chest and said, "Dude, calm down." Peter raised his guitar higher and said, "If you weren't such a nice guy, I would bean you too!" Bill yelled, "Guys! Knock it off!" Bill took an unloaded gun from under his drum set and pointed it at Peter. Peter put his guitar down and said, "It's cool. Don't shoot." Discuss.

Intentional Torts

2. Professor Plug was finished teaching his class and all of his students had left the room except for Darcy, who was asleep at her desk. He didn't want to wake her, but he also didn't want to leave the room unlocked because the lab equipment in the room was extremely valuable. Consequently, he tip-toed out of the room and locked the door from the outside, intending to come back before Darcy woke up since she wouldn't be able to get out without someone unlocking the door. As Professor Plug walked down the hallway, his student, Billy, jumped out from behind a plant while wearing a Halloween mask. Billy yelled "Boo!" and Professor Plug stumbled back holding his chest. Professor Plug had a massive heart attack and died. Discuss.

Intentional Torts

3. Francis, who was blind, was playing in the backyard with his friend, Kim. Kim told Francis she was an expert with a bow and arrow. Francis picked up an apple and put it on his head. Kim got her bow and arrow from her backpack and tried to shoot

the arrow off Francis's head. Unfortunately, she was lying about her expertise, and shot Francis square in the forehead. Francis was knocked unconscious and rushed to the hospital. Doctor Oboe did brain surgery to remove the arrow and save his life. While he was working on Francis, he noticed that Francis had a weird growth on the back of his optic nerve. Doctor Oboe removed it, and when Francis woke up, he could see. Discuss.

Negligence

4. Charlie, Lionel, Bubba, and Doctor Biz were playing football in the playground. Charlie was three years old, Lionel was 14, Bubba was 15, and Doctor Biz was 30. As they were playing, the four of them uncovered an old artillery shell buried in the sand. Charlie kicked the shell hard and it exploded, sending the four of them flying in different directions. After the explosion, Lionel got up and decided he needed to go for help. He jumped on his bicycle and took off out of the park without looking where he was going. Patty was riding by on her motorcycle and had to swerve to avoid Lionel, causing her to crash into a tree. Both Lionel and Patty were knocked unconscious. Bubba ran up and grabbed the motorcycle to go for help and started riding down the sidewalk, accidentally running over Sally. Doctor Biz rushed out of the park to where Lionel and Patty were lying. She noticed Patty wasn't breathing, so she pounded on her chest to get her heart started again. Patty gasped awake just as Doctor Biz's pounding broke her collarbone. Discuss the potential negligence claims.

Negligence

5. Christina decided to decorate her yard for Halloween with a fake graveyard. Two weeks before Halloween, she put up fake tombstones and skeletons, but decided it didn't look scary enough. Consequently, she dug a six-foot hole in front of the tombstones to put a coffin in. As she was working, it started to rain, so she went inside. Trilby and Tricia, two children who lived nearby, were riding their bikes home in the rainstorm. They saw the decorations and stopped to look. Tricia got off her bike and went into Christina's yard to look closer and fell into the hole, breaking her arm. At the same time, Trilby, who had stayed on his bike on the sidewalk, was knocked unconscious by a falling tree branch from a tree in Christina's yard. Would Christina be liable to either of the two children for their injuries?

Negligence

6. Willie lived on a ranch far out in the country. Dozens of "No Trespassing" signs were posted around his property. Josh decided to go hunting on Willie's land without telling Willie. Josh walked onto the property and crossed a river on a rope footbridge Willie had built. Willie had no idea how to build a decent footbridge, and Josh lost his footing and fell into the water, where he drowned. When the police were investigating, they told Willie a lot of hunters went onto his land without permission despite the signs. Consequently, Willie put up warning signs around the footbridge, telling people to stay off of it. A few months later, Francesca asked if she could hunt on Willie's land, and Willie gave her permission. Despite the warning signs, Francesca also fell on the footbridge and drowned. After the second death, Willie hired Charlie, a building contractor to build a decent bridge. As Charlie was planning the new bridge, he also slipped off Willie's rope bridge and drowned in the river. Discuss Willie's potential liability.

LONG QUESTIONS

For these longer questions, give yourself 35 minutes to answer. There are no subject tags on these questions because you won't have tags on the exam, and you should be able to handle almost any question at this point in the semester.

CIVIL PROCEDURE

1. Pilgrim filed suit against Acme Funds, Inc. in federal court in the State A, where he lives. Acme Funds is incorporated in State B, with its principal place of business in State C. Acme Funds owns a small independent subsidiary in State A. Acme's primary business is an Internet site where customers can buy and sell stock. Since 1995, along with several other investment opportunities, Acme advertises and provides links for the State A Educational Plan, which helps State A citizens buy stocks to help pay for college. Pilgrim's complaint alleged that Acme Funds negligently sold stocks belonging to Pilgrim that he had obtained through the website. The stocks were valued at $1 million. Pilgrim seeks actual damages in the amount of $1 million and punitive damages in the amount of $200,000. Acme filed a Motion to Dismiss under the Federal Rules of Civil Procedure 12(b) contending that the complaint should be dismissed for lack of personal and subject matter jurisdiction. The court denied the motion. Discuss.

2. Ripper Guitar Company makes effects pedals for electric guitars. In making the pedals, Ripper buys all of its wiring from Copely's Copper Wire Company. Dukes of the Victorian Era, a hard rock band, used Ripper's pedals on stage. During a concert, Josh and Dave, two members of the band, were electrocuted when the wiring on the pedals failed. Josh and Dave come to you for advice. Assuming the potential jurisdiction of the federal court is not at issue, they wonder whether they can file a suit together, and whether that suit can go after both companies or only Ripper. Discuss.

CONSTITUTIONAL LAW

1. Governor Billy was the governor of State A. In an effort to create a new "Technology Passageway" in State A's eastern mountains, the governor wanted to pass legislation to help technology start-ups within the state. His proposed bill would prohibit companies licensed within the state from using out-of-state businesses for their technology needs. However, the bill included a process whereby companies could petition the state for an exception if they had a valid reason for needing to use an out-of-state provider. You work in Governor Billy's office, and he asks you whether you see any constitutional problems with the proposed law. Please advise him.

2. After a huge student riot during State A's annual Apple Festival, the legislature in State A decided it wanted to create a special unit of police officers for its Riot and Anti-Terrorism Unit. The legislation creating the unit limits membership to male U.S. citizens over the age of 30. Governor Billy once again asks you if there are any potential issues with the legislation. Please advise him.

CONTRACTS

1. Nick was kicked out of his band, Dukes of the Victorian Era, after he made fun of the band's guitarists for getting themselves electrocuted. He decided to quit music altogether and sell all of his gear in a yard sale. He placed an ad in the local paper saying, "FOR SALE—AMPLIFIER AND GUITAR USED IN D.V.E.!" Stone came by the sale and told Nick he was interested in buying the amplifier, but did not have any money on him. He said he needed to go run by the bank, and asked if Nick would wait and sell the amplifier to him. Nick said, "Sure—I'll sell it to you for $200. Just get back by 5 p.m., because that's when I am closing up shop." Stone said, "Thanks!" and left. A few minutes later, Darby came by and said, "Hey—I read your ad in the paper and want to buy your guitar for $100! I'll be back soon with some money to buy it!" Darby left before Nick could say anything. Finally, Kim came by and bought both the amplifier and guitar. As she was loading up her car, Stone and Darby showed up and

said, "What gives, Nick? I thought we'd bought that stuff?" Nick needs some advice.

2. Taylor was the drummer for the band, Dukes of the Victorian Era. After two of the members were electrocuted and one was kicked out, he decided to start his own solo tour. On September 1, he entered into a written contract to play the Nielsen Bar and Grill for $500 on October 31. On September 15, Taylor released a new song on the Internet. The song was a viral sensation and Taylor started getting offers to play huge stadiums for large amounts of money. Taylor called the bar on September 17 and said, "I've become a big star. Look, I can't play the Halloween gig for less than $5,000." Leslie, the owner of the bar, said, "No way I'm paying you more than $500." A day later, Taylor got a call from Trent, who owned a large hotel in Vegas. Trent said, "I want to hire you for a year's worth of gigs from October 15 of this year to October 15 of next year." Taylor said, "I accept!" Taylor called the bar to tell them he wouldn't be playing, and Leslie told him Taylor would find himself "snoozing with the sharks" if he didn't play. Taylor got scared and called Trent back, saying he couldn't start the shows with Trent until November 1. Trent said, "We have a deal dude—you better be here by October 15." Taylor is upset and comes to you for advice.

CRIMINAL LAW

1. Steve was a bully at school. Consequently, Bruce, Clarence, and Max decided to break into his house and steal his computer to teach him a lesson. When they got to Steve's house, Max jimmied open a window with a crowbar. At the same time, Bruce saw that Steve had left his keys in his car. Bruce got in Steve's car and started backing down the driveway, shouting "Let's dump this in the ocean!" Steve heard Bruce's shout and ran out with a large pistol. He immediately started shooting. Clarence and Max took off running, and Max was hit in the head by one of Steve's shots. Max died instantly. Bruce panicked and threw the car into drive, running over Clarence and killing him instantly. Unsure of what to do, Bruce jumped out of the car. The car kept rolling down the street, finally smashing into a telephone pole. The pole snapped in half and fell, landing on

Steve and killing him instantly. Bruce then stumbled into a nearby bar, grabbed the tip jar (which had $3 in quarters in it), and stumbled back out to a bus waiting at the bus stop. He used the quarters to pay his fare and fled the scene. Assess what crimes may have been committed by Bruce, Clarence, and Max.

2. Tina and Amy were actors. After they were cast in *Waiting for Godot—The Musical,* they tried to get parts for their boyfriends, Alec and Tracy. Jimmy, the director, refused. The next night, Tina asked Amy if she would kill Jimmy for $5,000. Amy asked if Tina was serious, and Tina assured her that she was. Amy said, "That's a little nutty—I don't think so." Tina responded, "You know I'm insane in the membrane! If you don't do it, I'll kill you instead." In the face of Tina's threat, Amy agreed to kill Jimmy. The next night, Amy waited outside the theater until Jimmy came out to get into his car and go home. Amy grabbed Jimmy and shoved him in her trunk. She drove him out to the woods, intending to kill him there, but along the way she changed her mind and decided to let him go. When she got to the woods and opened the trunk to let him out, Jimmy wasn't moving. She thought Jimmy had died of a heart attack. She took Jimmy out of the trunk, dropped him in a grave she'd already dug, and then drove off without filling it. In fact, Jimmy was not dead and had only passed out from fright. He tried to get out of the hole but couldn't get a handhold. He called for help, but it started to snow, and he was soon buried in a huge blizzard. Ultimately, he died from exposure. Discuss.

PROPERTY

1. Yehudi was a comic book artist. He needed more space, so he rented a floor in Larry's building. The lease was set to begin July 1 and stated "Rent was payable on the First of Every Month." When Yehudi arrived to move in, Cameron was still in the process of moving out. Cameron's lease had expired on June 30, but it took him until July 30 to get all of his stuff out. Consequently, Yehudi did not pay any rent until he moved in August 1. A month later, the air conditioning in the building broke and started emitting sulfur gas, which made the entire place smell like rotten eggs. The stench was so bad, Yehudi could

barely breathe. Yehudi called Larry to fix it, but Larry was vacationing in Tahiti. Consequently, Yehudi moved into his girlfriend's apartment and didn't pay rent for September. When Larry returned in October, Larry fixed the air conditioner, and Yehudi moved back in. However, several books of Yehudi's art had been severely damaged by the gas. In November, Lyda rented the floor above Yehudi and opened a modern dance studio. The incessant drumbeat of feet on his ceiling drove Yehudi nuts, and he moved out on December 1 without giving any notice or paying any of December's rent. Discuss.

2. Lord Crabtree was getting older and wanted to pass along his lands to his children. He asked his three daughters, Jeannine, Biz, and Roey to dinner. He said to Jeannine, "I want you to have Crabtree Beach, because I know how much you love the beach—but I don't want you moving there until I tell you that you can." He handed Jeannine a deed that read, "Lord Crabtree conveys Crabtree Beach to have and to hold." To Biz he said, "I want you to have Crabtree Gardens, but I don't want you to ruin it." He handed Biz a deed that read, "Lord Crabtree conveys Crabtree Gardens to Biz and her heirs, so long as the property is used as a garden; if it is ever not used as a garden, the property goes to The Ladies Garden Society." To Roey he said, "Crabtree Mountain is yours! But, I want you to finish college first." He showed Roey a deed that read, "Lord Crabtree conveys Crabtree Mountain to Roey for life." He then placed the deed in his coat pocket. All of the deeds were signed by Lord Crabtree and notarized. Jeannine immediately moved onto Crabtree Beach and opened a sand and surf shop, Biz moved onto Crabtree Gardens, and Roey went back to college. Ten years later, Lord Crabtree died. The three Crabtree sisters come to you for advice.

TORTS

1. Bob owned a helicopter and a monkey. He started dating Molly and wanted to impress her by introducing her to his monkey and taking her on a helicopter ride. There was a state law that forbid flying helicopters with monkeys aboard, but Bob figured the monkey would be OK. Bob, Molly, and the monkey

got in the helicopter and started flying around the city. The monkey became frightened, grabbed the controls, and sent the helicopter into a steep dive. Bob struggled to regain control, but the helicopter crashed into Steve's van, which was parked in a clearly marked no-parking zone. Steve was sitting in the front seat of the van when the helicopter hit, and he suffered severe cuts on his face when the windshield smashed in. Bob and the monkey got out of the helicopter, but Molly was trapped. Bob sent the monkey for help, but the monkey just ran around the corner, climbed up a tree, and went to sleep. Steve stumbled out of the van and asked Bob where the hospital was. Bob didn't know, but he pointed over his shoulder and said, "That way." Steve went in the direction Bob pointed and ended up walking 25 miles before passing out on the side of the road. A few hours later, a police officer happened to drive by and he was able to free Molly using a crowbar. Molly's blood loss caused her to lose permanently the feeling in her hands. Discuss.

2. Linus decided to spray Kill'Em All bug killer on the peach trees on his farm. As he was spraying, the wind kicked up and blew the spray onto a neighboring baseball field, where the yearly Old Stars of the Baseball Diamond Game was being played. Willie "Wheezy" Walter, a short stop from the 1940s, inhaled the gas. Unknown to Kill'Em All, another poison had been accidentally mixed into the Kill'Em All poison at the factory. This new poison was extremely toxic. Because of medication Wheezy was on, he suffered a very rare allergic reaction and dropped dead. Discuss.

SHORT QUESTION ANSWERS

All of the suggested answers are written in a form similar to CRAC (Conclusion, Rule, Analysis, Conclusion) with the rule bolded so you can see how logical and clear CRAC is for the reader. The second conclusion is cut off because these are short answers and there's no reason to repeat the conclusion in an answer like this. In CRAC, IRAC, whatever, the important part is not following the exact letter of the form, the important part is that you give the reader a clear and complete answer. That's what a professor means when they say they don't care about IRAC—they still want a clear answer, they just don't care if you write "The issue is . . . ," "The rule is . . .".

CIVIL PROCEDURE

Jurisdiction

1. Yes. **Most state courts have in personam jurisdiction over any defendant who is served with process within the state. This is true no matter how long the defendant is in the state.** Here, since Bob was served while he was in the airport in Illinois, the Illinois state court would have jurisdiction even though Bob is only passing through Illinois on his way home to California.

2. Yes. **Under *International Shoe*, to assert jurisdiction, the defendant must have sufficient minimum contacts with the forum to make the exercise of jurisdiction reasonable and fair. In determining this issue, courts look at purposeful availment and foreseeability. "Purposeful availment" means that the defendant had to purposefully make contact with the state. "Foreseeability" means the defendant must have known or reasonably anticipated that his or her activities would render it foreseeable that he or she would be haled into court in the forum state. For example, in *Keeton v. Hustler Magazine*, the Court found that a national magazine should reasonably anticipate being haled into court in each state where the magazine is sold.** Here, since *Squirrel!* is a national magazine that has sold over 10,000 magazines in

Kansas, a court would likely find it purposely availed itself of the forum state and that it was foreseeable that it could be sued in the forum state.

3. Frank can bring this suit in either the Southern District of California, the Northern District of California, or the Western District of Nebraska. **In a federal suit based on diversity, the case may be heard in any judicial district where any defendant resides, if they all reside in the same state, or in the district where a substantial part of the events giving rise to the claim occurred. See 28 U.S.C. Sec. 1391.** Here, David and Andrew are defendants and are both residents of California, making the Southern District of California or the Northern District of California appropriate. The Western District of Nebraska would also be appropriate because the accident that is the subject of the suit occurred there.

4. No. **Because there is no federal question present, federal subject matter jurisdiction must be supported by diversity of citizenship. Importantly, there must be complete diversity, which means that no plaintiff can be a citizen of the same state as any defendant.** Here, both Scott and Bob are citizens of California. Consequently, despite the citizenships of Steve and Mark, there is no diversity of citizenship to support the case.

5. Yes. **A defendant can remove an action to federal court if the action could have originally been brought in the federal court. Section 1441(a).** Here, both parties are citizens of South Carolina, so federal jurisdiction could not be based on diversity of citizenship. However, the operator is suing under a federal act, which meets the requirements for jurisdiction based on a federal question. Consequently, the action can be removed to federal court.

Beginning the Lawsuit

1. No. **Under Rule 9, certain "special matters" must be pleaded with particularity. One of these is fraud. Under Rule 9(b), "in alleging fraud or mistake, a party must state with particularity the circumstances constituting fraud or mistake."** The bare assertion that Theresa committed fraud would not be enough. Importantly, Rob would likely need

to show what the fraudulent misrepresentations were or how Theresa knew they were false. Consequently, the complaint does not seem to fulfill the particularity requirements.

2. Yes. **A federal court sitting in diversity jurisdiction is required to apply the substantive law of the state in which it is sitting. However, the federal courts apply federal procedural law in diversity cases. Here, the Federal Rule is on point, valid, and arguably procedural.** Consequently, the court will allow her to use substituted service of process.

3. **Under Federal Rule of Civil Procedure 9(g), special damages must be specifically stated. General damages, which do not need to be specifically stated, follow naturally and necessarily from the occurrence causing the basis of the action.** Here, the only general damages claimed by Biz is the physical injury caused by the accident. Future pain, earnings, and medical expenses all have to be alleged specifically.

4. Yes. **Under Federal Rule of Civil Procedure 8(d), a complaint can set out two or more alternative statements of the claim and those statements do not need to be consistent.** Consequently, Hakeem may claim that both people were driving the speedboat even if those claims are inconsistent.

5. Kelly cannot sue Melanie for "flirting with a married man." **Under Federal Rule of Civil Procedure 8, a complaint must show that the pleader is entitled to relief.** Because "flirting with a married man" is not a recognizable cause of action, Kelly cannot sue Melanie.

CONSTITUTIONAL LAW

Congressional Power

1. The Act is constitutional. **Congress has the virtually unlimited power to make laws regarding conduct in the District of Columbia and on federal property.** Here, since Fort Jackson is a United States military base, Congress has the power to require Hank to attend school until 12th grade.

2. The law is likely constitutional. **To be constitutional, a condition on the receipt of federal funds has to be rationally related to the purpose for which the federal funds are allocated. For example, the United States Supreme Court has held that there is a rational relationship between a 21-year-old drinking age and the receipt of federal highway funds. *South Dakota v. Dole.*** Here, for the same reasons as *South Dakota v. Dole,* a court would likely find that the ban on marijuana would promote safe highways by cutting down on the amount of drivers who may be driving while on drugs.

3. No. **Congress has the power to regulate any activity that either by itself or in combination with other activities has a "substantial economic effect" upon interstate commerce. For example, the United States Supreme Court has held that Congress can control a farmer's production of wheat for home consumption because the cumulative effect of many farmers growing wheat for their own use would substantially affect the market for wheat. *Wickard v. Filburn.*** Frances's situation is similar in that the cumulative effect of many bee farmers producing honey for their own use could affect the price of honey on the commodities market. Consequently, Congress would have the power to regulate Frances's honey production under the Commerce Clause.

4. No. **Valid congressional acts or federal regulations supersede any state law that conflicts with the federal rule.** Here, New Jersey's refusal to hear these types of claims directly conflicts with the federal rule creating state jurisdiction. Consequently, the New Jersey rule is invalid.

5. Yes. **Under its Commerce Clause Power, Congress can enact laws regulating the instrumentalities or people that travel or work in the channels of interstate commerce.** Because this law deals with the pilots of domestic commercial flights, this law is likely lawful under the Commerce Clause.

Individual Rights

1. The law is unconstitutional. **Under the Establishment Clause, a state statute cannot discriminate among religions unless it is closely fitted to furthering a compelling government interest.** Here, a court is unlikely to find the garden displays for understanding are closely fitted to furthering a compelling governmental interest.

2. The photo requirement is lawful. **Under the Free Exercise Clause, a law will be upheld if it is a neutral law of general applicability and not motivated by an intention to interfere with religion. Importantly, the Clause does not require exemptions for those who choose not to follow a law because of their religious beliefs.** Here, the state can require the sect member to have a picture of his uncovered face taken if he wants a driver's license.

3. The law is unconstitutional. **Under the Equal Protection Clause, a court will apply strict scrutiny when the law infringes on a fundamental right. Fundamental rights include the right to travel, the right to privacy, the right to vote, and all First Amendment rights. In strict scrutiny analysis, a law will be upheld only if it is necessary to promote a compelling or overriding interest.** Here, the registration law affects a fundamental right because it hinders a person's ability to travel. A court will likely find the registration law does not promote a compelling or overriding interest because it does little to protect against terrorist attacks and is unnecessary for the identification of victims in the event of a plane crash. Consequently, a court is unlikely to uphold the law.

4. No. **The Equal Protection Clause prohibits discrimination based on a person's race or sex. Although the peremptory strike law is neutral on its face, its application can be unlawful if a person's use of the law is discriminatory. Importantly, since the state is significantly involved in trials and juries, even private attorneys are prohibited from making discriminatory preemptory strikes.** Here, although the law states that an attorney can make preemptory strikes with or without cause,

David is basing his strikes on racial and sexual classifications. Such a use of the law is unlawful.

5. Yes. **A land use or zoning regulation limiting the location of adult entertainment businesses is lawful if the regulation is intended to reduce the secondary effects of such businesses, such as crime and loss of property values. The only thing the regulation can't do is ban such businesses completely.** Here, the city has not banned such businesses entirely and has specifically stated its intention in enacting the ordinance is to protect property values and reduce crime. With these goals in mind, the Barrens seems to be a logical location despite its relatively small size and desirability. Consequently, a court would likely find the city's ordinance lawful.

CONTRACTS

Contract Formation

1. No. **An offer to the public, such as a reward, is an offer for unilateral contract under Article 2 and Restatement (Second) of Contracts. Importantly, a unilateral contract can only be accepted by performance of the requested act.** Here, Kim cannot accept the contract by telling Thurston she will return Mr. Bitey. A contract will only be formed if Kim actually finds Mr. Bitey and returns him to Thurston.

2. No. **A contract requires offer, acceptance, and consideration. For a valid offer, there must be an intent to enter into a contract rather than a mere invitation to start preliminary negotiations. Although specific language such as "I offer" is not required, certain language is usually considered a mere invitation. Courts will also look at the surrounding circumstances of the transaction. Importantly, courts will look at the actions of the parties objectively and interpret the transaction according to what a reasonable person would believe.** Here, Chris only stated, "Maybe I would accept $50 for it." This seems to be a mere invitation for preliminary negotiations, as he did not state any definite intention to sell the guitar to Paul.

However, whether Chris was joking or not would likely not decide the issue because there is no indication that a reasonable person viewing the conversation would realize that Chris was making a joke.

3. Yes. **Advertisements are usually mere invitations for offers. However, if an advertisement contains a promise, contains certain and definite terms, and clearly identifies the offeree, courts will construe it as an offer.** Here, the advertisement promises to sell the stack of comics for $5 to the first person who accepts it. Since there is nothing left to negotiate, a court will likely find that the advertisement was an offer.

4. No. **An offer may be revoked by indirect communication if the offeree receives correct information from a reliable source that the offeror has acted in such a way as to indicate to a reasonable person that the offeror has revoked the offer.** Here, the bank officer appears to be a reliable source as he proved his ownership of the car by pointing out his son waxing it in the parking lot. The fact he told Sammy he bought it and had the car in his possession would indicate to a reasonable person that Eddie no longer wanted to sell the car to Sammy.

5. No. **An offer for a unilateral contract is irrevocable once performance begins. However, mere preparation to perform does not make the offer irrevocable.** Here, although Mary has spent $500 in supplies, it appears clear that this is merely preparation since she hasn't actually begun to paint the portrait. She may be able to make a claim based on detrimental reliance, but Jimmy effectively revoked his offer since she had not begun performance.

6. No. **If an acceptance is made conditional upon additional terms, it acts as a rejection of the original offer and a counteroffer by the offeree.** Here, since Becky told Brandon she would only buy the table if he threw in a lamp as well, the original offer was terminated by rejection. At this point, Becky has made a new offer that Brandon may accept or not, but there is no contract between the parties.

7. No. **In order to accept an offer, the offeree must know of the offer.** Here, although Scott and Timothy spoke about selling the house and both letters contained identical prices, neither one of them knew about the other's letter. Consequently, no contract was formed.

8. Yes. **A shipment of nonconforming goods acts as an acceptance creating a bilateral contract and also as a breach of that contract unless the seller seasonably notifies the buyer that the nonconforming goods are only being offered as an accommodation.** Here, since Gary did not contact Alan and sent him 1,000 dark blue shirts instead of black ones, a contract was created that Alan immediately breached.

9. No. **A contract requires consideration, which is a bargained for exchange.** Here, Angela has a legal right to read trashy novels and disco dance, but has given it up based on James's promise to pay her $10,000 for college. Consequently, her actions are consideration for James's promise to pay her.

10. No. **A contract must be supported by consideration, which is a bargained-for legal benefit to the promisor or detriment to the promisee. Importantly, the promise or performance of an existing legal duty is not consideration.** Here, as a police officer assigned to the case, he has a preexisting legal duty to try and rescue Skippette.

CRIMINAL LAW

Physical Act and Mens Rea

1. No. **For a defendant to be criminally liable, that person must have either performed a voluntary physical act or refrained to act in a situation where he or she had a legal duty to do so. Voluntary means that the defendant must have actually chosen to perform or not perform the act.** Here, Hans could not be held criminally liable for Meek's death because he did not choose to push Meek, but merely fell into him after being pushed by Derek.

2. No. **For a defendant to be criminally liable, that person must have either performed a voluntary physical act or refrained to act in a situation where he or she had a legal duty to do so. Importantly, there is no general legal duty to act to save someone in peril. Such a legal duty would only arise through a statute, contract, special relationship, creation of the peril, or voluntary assumption of care.** Here, there is no indication of any particular legal duty between Al and Fredo, and Al did nothing to try to save Fredo, so Al had no legal duty to act despite the fact he could have easily saved Fredo by pushing the red button. This is true despite the fact he took pleasure in seeing Fredo get eaten and took a selfie that he posted on the Internet. Consequently, Al could not be held criminally liable for Fredo's death.

3. No. **When a statute establishes a state of mind for culpability, that state of mind is required for all material elements of the crime.** Here, to be criminally liable, Ian would have to know he was making a sale, that the thing he was selling was a tobacco product, and that the person he was selling it to was under the age of 18. If Ian is telling the truth, he did not know that Sally was under 18 and did not know he was selling a tobacco product. Consequently, he could not be held criminally liable under the statute.

4. Yes. **For a defendant to be criminally liable, that person must have either performed a voluntary physical act or refrained to act in a situation where he or she had a legal duty to do so. Such a legal duty can arise through a statute, contract, special relationship, creation of the peril, or voluntary assumption of care.** Here, it is likely that Ron, as a park ranger, had a contractual or statutory duty to come to the camper's aid.

5. Yes. **For a defendant to be criminally liable, that person must have either performed a voluntary physical act or refrained to act in a situation where he or she had a legal duty to do so. Voluntary means that the defendant must have actually chosen to perform or not perform the act.** While Iggy was unconscious when he drove off the bridge,

the criminal act was Iggy getting into the car and driving when he knew he was prone to losing consciousness.

Homicide

1. Yes. **Murder is the unlawful killing of another with malice aforethought. Importantly, malice aforethought exists if the defendant had an intent to kill, intent to inflict great bodily injury, reckless indifference to human life, or intent to commit felony murder. Also, intentional use of a deadly weapon creates an inference of an intent to kill.** Here, although Tom said he didn't intend to kill anyone, he tossed a hand grenade, which is a deadly weapon. He tossed the hand grenade towards dozens of people, which clearly showed a reckless indifference to human life. Consequently, he could be convicted of murder despite not actually intending to kill anyone.

2. The most likely crime would be voluntary manslaughter. **Voluntary manslaughter is a murder that takes place because of adequate provocation. At common law, adequate provocation is made up of four elements: (1) the provocation must arouse sudden and intense passion in an ordinary person, (2) the defendant must have actually been provoked, (3) there must not have been a sufficient time to cool down between the provocation and the killing, and (4) the defendant did not in fact cool down between the provocation and the killing.** Here, an ordinary person would likely be provoked by the protestor telling Melissa her husband was in Hell during his funeral, making her daughter cry, and then spitting on her daughter. Melissa was in fact provoked because the protestor's actions "enraged" her. Finally, she immediately hit the protestor with his sign, so there was no cooling down period between the provocation and the killing. Consequently, the most likely crime Melissa will be charged with would be voluntary manslaughter.

3. Anthony is likely guilty of first degree felony murder in the deaths of the coach and the firefighter, but not the elderly neighbor. **A killing, even if it is accidental, is a murder if it occurs during the commission of a felony. First degree felony murder is a killing that occurs during an enumerated felony, and most states include arson in this**

list. **Arson is intentionally setting fire to a dwelling. Importantly, the majority of courts require the death to be a foreseeable result of the felony.** Here, Anthony committed arson by intentionally setting fire to the coach's house. Even though he didn't want to hurt anyone, coach's death was a foreseeable result of the felony since he was the homeowner and was trying to extinguish the blaze. Similarly, the firefighter's death was a foreseeable result of the felony because he was run over while trying to put out the fire. However, the death of the neighbor from stroke was likely unforeseeable because neighbors having strokes does not seem to be a foreseeable result of setting a fire (even so, foreseeability for felony murder is fairly loose, and Anthony could very well be convicted based on the neighbor's stroke—the situation is not a slam dunk). Consequently, Anthony is most likely only guilty of murder in the deaths of the coach and the firefighter.

4. No. **To commit a crime, a defendant must have the necessary intent to commit the crime at the time he or she committed the criminal act. Murder requires malice aforethought, including intent to kill.** Here, Ezra intended to kill Henry with an arrow at some point in the future, but at the time he killed Henry he had no idea Henry was in the backyard and was only intending to practice his archery skills. Consequently, he could not be found guilty of murder.

5. Yes. **Murder is a malicious illegal killing.** Here, Mike wanted to kill his ex-wife and did so by lying and telling her their children were dead. The fact he killed his ex-wife by lying to cause a heart attack does not change the analysis.

PROPERTY

Personal Property

1. Matt is correct. **To gain ownership rights in a wild animal, a person must exercise dominion, control, and possession over the animal. Mere pursuit of the animal is not enough, although if a person mortally wounds a wild animal, he or she obtains a vested property right in the animal.** Here, although the trout was noticeably tired, it did not

appear to be mortally wounded and was freely swimming when Matt scooped it up in his hat. At that point, he gained dominion, control, and, importantly, possession over the trout. Consequently, the trout is his.

2. The hotel owner is right. **Mislaid property is property that is intentionally placed somewhere and later forgotten. Determining mislaid property is dependent upon where the property is found. If the property is mislaid instead of lost, the owner of the place where the property is found is entitled to possess the property over all but the true owner.** Here, the bag is likely mislaid property because it was found under the mattress of the bed, a spot the bag could only end up in if it was intentionally placed there. Consequently, since the hotel owner owns the hotel where the bag was discovered, he is entitled to possess the property over all but the true owner.

3. No. **A valid gift requires (1) the donor's intent to make a gift, (2) delivery, and (3) acceptance by the donee.** Here, while Rob seemed to intend to make a gift by saying "I hereby give it as a gift to you," and Tory seemed to accept it by saying "I will cherish it always," Rob did not actually give Tory the scraper or any symbolic or written instrument representing the gift. Consequently, no gift was made.

4. Yes. **A valid gift requires (1) the donor's intent to make a gift, (2) delivery, and (3) acceptance by the donee. Importantly, the delivery requirement can be satisfied in most states if the donor gives some type of written instrument to the donee.** Here, Marshall seemed to intend a gift when he said, "I want to give you my gold microphone." Marshall seemed to deliver the gift by creating a written instrument saying the microphone was a gift to Doc and giving the paper to Doc. Finally, Doc seemed to accept the gift by saying, "Thanks! I love it." Consequently, Marshall made a valid gift to Doc.

5. No. **If a possessor has voidable title to a good and sells it to a bona fide purchaser, the bona fide purchaser is entitled to the good. Voidable title is when a person gains possession to a good by a voluntary transfer. A bona fide purchaser is a good faith purchaser without any reason**

to think the seller is not the proper owner. Here, Mac voluntarily gave his guitar to the shop, and Dennis was a good faith purchaser who had no reason to know that the guitar did not belong to the shop.

Adverse Possession

1. Yes. **To gain title to property through adverse possession, a person's use must be (1) open and notorious, (2) actual, (3) hostile, and (4) continuous for the statutory period. Importantly, the use is continuous if the person uses the property as a true owner would, and two successive adverse possessors can combine or "tack" their periods of possession as long as they are in privity with each other.** Here, both George and Bailey appeared to use the property openly and notoriously in that nothing indicates Pogue would not have seen them using the property if he had looked. The use was actual and hostile, because only George and Bailey seemed to use the property and neither asked for Pogue's permission. Finally, the use was continuous for the statutory period. Since it was an unheated cottage on the beach in Boston, summer use only would be the appropriate use of the property because Boston winters are very cold and the cottage would likely be too uncomfortable to stay in during the winter. Bailey can "tack" his use onto George's because they were in privity—specifically, there was a deed passing property rights between them "selling" the property for $10,000. George used the property for 15 years, and then Bailey used the property for another six, so their use was 21 years, or one year over the 20-year-statutory period. Consequently, Bailey owns the property.

2. Yes. **When an adverse possessor enters a property under "color of title," he or she gets title to the entire property described in the defective instrument even if he or she adversely possesses only a small portion of it. However, the property must be recognized in the community as one single property.** Here, although Rose only lived on one acre, she had defective title to the entire 20-acre parcel. Importantly, the entire 20 acres was known throughout the community as a single parcel called the "20-Acre Heart of the Country." Consequently, Rose gained title to the entire 20 acres and Lisa owns nothing.

3. Probably no. **Adverse possession requires that the adverse possessor's use be hostile and without the permission of the owner. The owner's knowledge of the use combined with a lack of response would likely be seen as permission to use the land.** Here, because Ray knew about the encroachment and didn't say anything, a court would likely find that Bob's use was not hostile.

4. No. **A cotenant can only take another cotenant's property interest if there is an ouster of the other cotenant. Ouster means that the other cotenant has been kept from the premises.** Here, there is no indication Charlie kept Alex from the premises.

5. Yes. **If an adverse possessor leases his or her interest to another, the lessee's time on the premises counts toward the adverse possessor's time on the property.** Here, Zanna's possession and Lola's possession would combine to fulfill the necessary 20-year period.

Estates in Land

1. Jimmy has a life estate pur autre vie. **A life estate pur autre vie is a life estate measured by the life of someone other than the life tenant and is created with the words "for the life of. . . ." Just like a life estate, the grantor of a life estate pur autre vie retains a reversion, which means title will automatically revert to him or her when the measuring life ends. The person used as a measuring life does not receive any interest in the estate.** Since Kerry used the language "to Jimmy for the life of James," Jimmy will have an estate in the land for as long as James lives. When James dies, it will automatically pass back to Kerry.

2. Bob has a life estate in the property, and Tobias has a reversion. **A life estate is created by using the language "for life" and lasts for the life of the grantee. The grantor of a life estate retains a reversion, which means title will automatically revert to him or her when the grantee dies.** Since Tobias used the language "to Bob for life," Bob will have an estate in the land as long as he lives. When he dies, it will automatically pass back to Tobias.

3. Yiyun has an estate for years. **The grant that states, "to Yiyun for life, but in no way may it continue past 10 years" is not a life estate. Because the estate will definitely end at a fixed period of 10 years, it is an estate for years.** Consequently, Yiyun holds an estate for years in the property.

4. No. **A life estate is created by using the language "for life" and lasts for the life of the grantee. The grantor of a life estate retains a reversion, which means title will automatically revert to him or her when the grantee dies. The owner of a life estate may use the property, but he or she may not commit waste or act in such a way as to damage the interests of the person who holds the reversion. Typically, this means a life tenant may not consume or exploit natural resources.** Since Lou used the language "to Steve for life," Steve has a life estate and Lou has a reversion. Consequently, Steve may not exploit the natural resources of the property by setting up a mining operation.

5. None. **The shelter's interest is a void executory interest under the Rule Against Perpetuities, which states that no interest in land is good unless it must vest, if at all, no later than 21 years after some life in being at the creation of the interest.** Here, the shelter's interest is void because it will not vest until hunting happens on the land, which might occur outside the perpetuities period.

TORTS

Intentional Torts

1. Yes. **Battery is the intentional touching of another that is unpermitted and harmful or offensive. Importantly, the touching can be of something connected to that person.** Here, Hal intended to touch Bill because he grabbed the toga and yanked it off. It was unpermitted and harmful or offensive because Bill did not give his permission and he cried when everyone pointed and laughed at him. Finally, although Hal did not touch Bill's physical person, Bill was wearing the toga when Hal yanked it off, so the toga was

connected to Bill at the time of the touching. Consequently, Bill has a claim for battery.

2. Kirby committed an assault against Jaclyn and a battery against Quentin. **Assault is an act intended to cause reasonable apprehension of an immediate harmful or offensive contact. Battery is the intentional touching of another that is unpermitted and harmful or offensive. Importantly, under the doctrine of transferred intent, intent can be transferred from the intended victim of the tort to the actual victim.** Here, Kirby assaulted Jaclyn because she pulled back her fist and yelled "Prepare to meet my haymaker!" In doing so, Kirby clearly intended to put Jaclyn in fear of getting immediately punched and her actions would cause a reasonable apprehension of an immediate punch. Kirby committed a battery against Quentin because, although she intended to hit Jaclyn, that intent can be transferred to Quentin. Clearly, her punch was harmful because blood was spouting from between Quentin's fingers. Consequently, Kirby committed an assault and a battery.

3. Yes. **False imprisonment is an intentional act or omission that confines another person to a bounded area. False imprisonment can result if a person uses physical force directed at another person, a member of that person's family, or an item of that person's property.** Here, although Charles could simply have walked out of the locker room, he stayed because Coach Skinner had wrongfully confiscated his gym bag and wallet. Consequently, Coach Skinner could be found liable for false imprisonment.

4. Yes. **Trespassing is an intentional physical invasion of a person's real property. The only intent necessary is intent to enter the physical property. Importantly, mistake is no defense.** Here, Jojo intentionally walked onto Old Man McGee's land although he had every reason to believe he was still in the state park. Since mistake is no excuse, he could be held liable for trespassing.

5. Yes. **A defendant can claim self-defense even if it was based on a mistake if the defendant's belief in the need for self-defense was reasonable.** Here, Tina didn't know who Landon was or that he was joking. When he said he was going to

shoot her with his finger in his pocket, it was likely reasonable that she believed she needed to defend herself.

Negligence

1. It depends. **Generally, a duty of care is owed only to foreseeable plaintiffs. However, a duty to an unforeseeable plaintiff could arise when a defendant breaches a duty to a foreseeable one. Liability depends on whether the court follows the majority Cardozo rule or the minority Andrews rule. Under Cardozo, the unforeseeable plaintiff can only recover if he or she was located in a foreseeable "zone of danger." Under Andrews, the defendant owes a duty to anyone who suffers an injury as a proximate result of his or her breach of duty.** First, Cameron appears to be an unforeseeable plaintiff because the question states the wall was a substantial distance away. If Cameron is unforeseeable, the fact he is a substantial distance away likely means he was not in the zone of danger. Consequently, he would not be able to recover under the majority Cardozo rule. However, if the court follows the minority Andrews rule, his injuries appear to be a proximate result of Emma's negligence. In that case, he could recover.

2. Yes. **A negligent defendant is liable to rescuers as long as the rescue is not wanton. However, under the "firefighter's rule," professional rescuers such as policeman and fireman may be barred from recovery based on assumption of risk or public policy.** Here, Captain Amazepants's rescue attempt seemed reasonable since Paulo had been tossed off the bridge, was yelling at Frances, and there was no indication Captain Amazepants knew anything about people jumping off the bridge and swimming. It's also unlikely the firefighter's rule would apply to Captain Amazepants since he is a costumed vigilante and not exactly a "professional" rescuer. Consequently, if Frances was negligent in shoving Paulo off the bridge, she would likely be liable for Captain Amazepants's injuries.

3. Yes. **When determining the basic standard of care, courts compare the defendant's conduct to that of a reasonable person. The "reasonable person" has the same physical characteristics as the defendant, the same**

knowledge as an average community member, and average mental ability. An average community member of average intelligence would likely understand that gasoline was explosive. Consequently, Murph could still be liable in tort even though he truly did not understand that the gasoline would explode.

4. No. **For negligence per se to apply, the accident must have been caused by violation of the statute in question.** Here, violation of a statute requiring liability insurance would not be the cause of the accident, so negligence per se would not apply.

5. No. **For res ipsa loquitur to apply, the defendant must have exclusive control of the damage-causing instrument and the accident must have been the type of accident that would not have occurred unless the defendant was negligent.** Here, guests and other visitors to the hotel had control over the hotel's furniture, and one of them could have thrown the armchair from a hotel window with no negligence on the hotel's part.

MEDIUM QUESTION ANSWERS

In evaluating your answers to the medium questions, take a close look at the IRAC used here. Also note how the question is broken into underlined headings, which are easier for a grader to follow. Notice I am using my headings as the Issue in my IRACs—it's simply faster, without losing any clarity.

CIVIL PROCEDURE

1. Federal Jurisdiction

Citizenship

Federal courts have jurisdiction over controversies between citizens of different states when the amount in controversy exceeds $75,000. Importantly, there must be complete diversity of citizenship, and no plaintiff can be a citizen of the same state as a defendant. People are citizens of the states where they are domiciled. A domicile is where a person has his or her true, fixed home. Corporations are citizens of their state of incorporation and the state of their principal place of business. The U.S. Supreme Court has held that a corporation's principal place of business is where high-level officers direct and control the company. Importantly, a corporation cannot have two principal places of business. Here, Piston is likely a citizen of Michigan because he is a person based in Detroit. The Federation is a corporation incorporated in Delaware, and although it has a large plant in Arizona, all of its executive decision makers are based in New York. Consequently, for citizenship purposes, Piston is a citizen of Michigan, and the Federation is a citizen of Delaware and New York. Thus, there is complete diversity of citizenship.

Venue

Venue for a civil action is proper in a judicial district where any defendant resides if all defendants reside in the same state. Here, since the Federation is the only defendant and is a citizen of New York, it could be tried in New York federal court.

Amount in Controversy

If the amount in controversy is exactly $75,000, this does not exceed $75,000 and fails to meet the amount in controversy requirement. Under the majority rule, courts determine the amount in controversy by looking at the plaintiff's claim. To meet the jurisdictional amount, the plaintiff may aggregate all claims against a single defendant whether the claims are legally or factually related to each other. Here. Piston has a $50,000 claim for false light and an unrelated claim of $25,000, and both claims are against the Federation. While the amounts can be aggregated together, Piston, the plaintiff, is claiming that his two individual claims are worth exactly $75,000 when added together. Consequently, his claim likely does not meet the jurisdictional requirement and the New York federal court does not have jurisdiction.

2. **State Jurisdiction**

Service in State

Most states grant their courts in personam jurisdiction when the defendant is present in the forum state and personally served with process. This is true even if the defendant is there for only a short time and merely passing through. However, most states grant immunity from personal jurisdiction for parties and witnesses who are in the state because they are taking part in another judicial proceeding. Here, since Hugh is in North Carolina because he is on his way to a judicial proceeding in Georgia, most states would find him immune. Consequently, the in-state service of process would be unlikely to grant jurisdiction over him.

Long Arm Statute

Most states grant their courts in personam jurisdiction over nonresidents who perform certain acts within the state. Courts require that a defendant have such minimum contacts with a state that jurisdiction would be fair and reasonable. To determine this, courts look at purposeful availment and foreseeability. If a company reaches into a state so as to make money there, a court

will usually find the company has personally availed itself of the state. Foreseeability means that the defendant must have known or a reasonable person would have known that his or her activities could get him or her haled into court there. Importantly, a national magazine is probably subject to trial in every state in which the magazine is sold, since it is a foreseeable occurrence that it might cause injury in any of those states. Here, *Widespread* is marketed in North Carolina, so it is clear it has purposely availed itself of the state. Also, as a national magazine targeting the southeast and North Carolina, it was foreseeable it could be sued there. Consequently, Hugh and the magazine could be sued in North Carolina.

3. Federal Jurisdiction

Federal Question Jurisdiction

A claim can be brought in federal court if it is based on a federal question. Here, Lenny's claim against Rick is based on violation of federal copyright law, so the federal court would have federal question jurisdiction over the matter. Importantly, diversity of citizenship and amount in controversy are irrelevant to a federal claim, so the fact both Lenny and Jay were Texas residents or that the amount in controversy may not exceed $75,000 does not change the analysis.

Pendent Jurisdiction

Under supplemental jurisdiction, if a state-law claim against a second defendant arises under the same nucleus of common fact as the claim against the first defendant, and the federal court has jurisdiction over the claim against the first defendant, the federal court will have discretion to exercise jurisdiction over the second defendant's claim as well. Here, since Lenny claims the contract claim involves the same facts as the copyright claim, it appears that both claims arise from the same transaction or occurrence. Consequently, Lenny could bring both claims together in federal court.

4. Federal Jurisdiction

Citizenship

Federal courts have jurisdiction over controversies between citizens of different states when the amount in controversy exceeds $75,000. Importantly, there must be complete diversity of citizenship, and no plaintiff can be a citizen of the same state as a defendant. People are citizens of the states where they are domiciled. A domicile is where a person has his or her true, fixed home. Here, although Tommy owns property in Rhode Island, he spends 10 months of the year in South Carolina. His job is also in South Carolina. Consequently, South Carolina appears to be the location of Tommy's fixed home, since Rhode Island appears to be simply the place he spends his summer break. Thus, a court would likely find he is a citizen of South Carolina. Likewise, although Paul is a sea captain, he owns a house, receives mail, and is registered to vote in Rhode Island. Consequently, a court would likely find that he is a citizen of Rhode Island. Ultimately, since Tommy is likely a citizen of South Carolina and Paul is likely a citizen of Rhode Island, there is complete diversity of citizenship between the parties.

Amount in Controversy

As stated above, the amount in controversy must exceed $75,000 for federal jurisdiction. Here, Paul is claiming $100,000 in damages, so he meets the amount in controversy requirement.

Original Venue

Venue for a civil action is proper in a judicial district where any defendant resides if all defendants reside in the same state. Here, since Tommy is likely a resident of South Carolina, it was appropriate for Paul to bring his original suit in South Carolina federal court.

Transfer of Venue

Venue is also proper in a judicial district in which a substantial part of the events or omissions creating the claim occurred. Section 1404(a) allows transfer to any other district where the suit might have been brought. In

that case, while venue might have been proper in the original court, a court might find that the convenience of witnesses or parties might favor transfer to the new venue. Under *Erie*, federal courts apply the substantive law of the state in which they sit. If a transfer is made solely because of convenience, the law of the original state is carried to the new court. This is true even if the plaintiff initiates the transfer. Here, since the car accident occurred in Florida and all the witnesses and evidence were in that state, a court could find that transfer for the convenience of the witnesses and parties is proper. Because a statute of limitations issue can decide a claim, such issues are usually considered to be substantive, so the federal court will apply the law of the state in which it sits (here, South Carolina). If the transfer is done solely for convenience sake, the court in Florida will apply South Carolina law and Tommy's motion to dismiss will fail. Importantly, the rule regarding this will apply even though Paul initially chose the inconvenient forum.

5. Discovery

Request for Mental Exam

Under Rule 35, when the mental condition of a party is in controversy, a court may order the party to submit to a mental examination done by a licensed examiner. This rule operates only by court order, and the discovering party has to show good cause why the examination is needed. Here, there is no indication George's mental state is at issue. It simply seems that Pogue wants to insult him for marrying his wife.

Sanctions

A court may order sanctions against parties who behave unreasonably during discovery. George may move for sanctions, claiming Pogue's motion is only for the sake of embarrassment and is completely irrelevant to the issues presented by the case.

6. Diversity of Citizenship

Because Wendy's claim is for personal injury, a federal court could only have jurisdiction based on diversity. **Federal courts**

have jurisdiction over controversies between citizens of different states. Importantly, there must be complete diversity of citizenship, and no plaintiff can be a citizen of the same state as a defendant. People are citizens of the states where they are domiciled. A domicile is where a person has his or her true, fixed home. Corporations are citizens of their state of incorporation and the state of their principal place of business. The U.S. Supreme Court has held that a corporation's principal place of business is where high-level officers direct and control the company. Importantly, a corporation cannot have two principal places of business. Wendy resides in Minnesota, so she is a citizen of Minnesota. PurpleCo. is incorporated in Delaware and has its corporate headquarters and board of directors in Minnesota. Consequently, even though all of its factories are in Texas, it is a citizen of Delaware and Minnesota. Consequently, there is not complete diversity of citizenship between the parties.

Amount in Controversy

In addition to diversity of citizenship, the amount in controversy must be over $75,000. The amount of a defendant's counterclaim cannot be combined with the amount of the plaintiff's claim to meet the jurisdictional amount. Here, Wendy is only claiming $50,000, and PurpleCo's claim for $30,000 cannot be added to hers to meet the jurisdictional amount.

CONSTITUTIONAL LAW

1. Ellen's Claim

For a federal court to hear a claim, a "case or controversy" must be involved. Importantly, a federal court will not hear a claim that has become moot. Here, Ellen's claim is likely moot because she was admitted to law school and is about to receive the same law degree she would have received whether or not the state had the minority scholarship program. Consequently, the federal court will likely not hear her claim.

Organization's Claim

A federal court will only hear a claim if the person bringing it has standing to do so. "Standing" means that the person can show a concrete stake in the outcome. An organization has standing to bring claims that cause injuries to the organization itself or to its members if the organization can demonstrate an injury in fact to its members that would give individual members a right to sue on their own behalf, the injury is related to the organization's purpose, and the nature of the claim does not require participation of the individual members. Here, the Organization's purpose is to promote the professional well-being of Optometrists. While members of the Organization could theoretically be hurt if their children are passed over in the minority scholarship program, the "professional well-being" of an optometrist has nothing to do with where his or her child goes to law school. Consequently, the Organization likely does not have jurisdiction over the matter.

2. Congressional Power

Under Article I, Section 8, Congress has the power to spend "to provide for the common defense and general welfare." Congress may spend for any public purpose so long as it doesn't infringe on other constitutional rights. Here, since the statute is intended to combat global warming and promote a changeover to clean energy, it appears to serve a public purpose and does not seem to infringe on any other constitutional right. Thus, Congress can clearly enact the statute.

Presidential Power

The President may pardon people for offenses against the United States. Here, whether or not he is negotiating with France, Serge was convicted of a violent crime in state court. Consequently, the President cannot compel the state to release Serge.

3. First Ordinance

A regulation burdening the content of speech is presumptively unconstitutional. To justify such a

regulation, the government has to show that the regulation is necessary to serve a compelling state interest and is narrowly drawn to serve that purpose. Here, the ordinance bans the sale or rental of all violent videogames to minors in order to curb youth violence. Since it bans violent games specifically, it is content-based. It is unlikely a court would find this ordinance is narrowly tailored to serving a compelling state interest, because although youth violence is likely a compelling interest, banning all violent videogames would seem to have little effect on that interest. There is likely no direct link to violent videogames and youth violence, and banning all such games would affect the speech rights of many more video game companies and gamers than necessary. Consequently, the ordinance is likely unconstitutional.

Second Ordinance

A regulation that burdens substantially more speech than is necessary will not be upheld because it is overbroad. If a regulation of speech or speech-related conduct burdens a substantial amount of protected speech, the regulation is facially invalid and it cannot be enforced against anyone. Here, the second ordinance bans speech that "in any manner" questions a police officer in the performance of his or her duty. Clearly, this ordinance would burden more speech than is necessary. Under the ordinance, a person could be prosecuted for telling an officer he or she is arresting the wrong person or telling an officer he or she is going the wrong way after a suspect. Consequently, the ordinance is likely unconstitutional.

Third Ordinance

A regulation that gives licensing officials unbridled discretion is void on its face. Here, the ordinance gives the Mayor complete authority to grant or deny parade permits to different groups. This is clearly void and unconstitutional.

4. Racial Discrimination

The Equal Protection Clause guarantees that similarly situated persons will be treated the same. If a regulation shows a governmental intent to discriminate based on racial classification, it will be subject to strict scrutiny.

Strict scrutiny is the highest standard, and under it a law will only be upheld if it is necessary to achieve a compelling government purpose. Intent can be shown in three ways: (a) facial discrimination, (b) discriminatory application, or (c) discriminatory motive.

First Law

Facial discrimination usually means that the law includes a classification on its face. However, in a few cases, the Supreme Court has found a law is facially discriminatory even if the language of the law did not include any racial language. In these cases, the Supreme Court found the law could only be explained in racial terms. Here, the law establishing districts has no racial language on its face. However, the law has resulted in several bizarre districts where minority voters control the outcome of the election. If the bizarre-shaped districts can only be explained through racial classification, it is likely a court would find the law facially discriminatory.

Second Law

Discriminatory application can be shown if a law is neutral on its face but government officials apply it in a discriminatory manner. Even private action can be discriminatory if the action significantly involves the state. Here, the law allows attorneys to strike jurors with or without cause, so it appears neutral on its face. Although government attorneys are not using the law to strike minorities based on race, private attorneys are. In this case, since striking potential jurors from a jury significantly involves the state, a court will likely find that the law is being applied discriminatorily even if it is only done so by private attorneys.

Third Law

Even if a law is neutral on its face and in its application, it will be found discriminatory if a person can show the law was maintained or enacted for a discriminatory purpose. Here, the test appears to be neutral on its face and in its application since all police recruits are required to take the test. However, if someone shows the purpose of the law was to disadvantage minorities, a court would likely find that the law resulted in an equal protection violation.

5. In determining whether a law violates the Equal Protection Clause or the Due Process Clause, courts will use one of three tests: (a) strict scrutiny, (b) intermediate scrutiny, or (c) rational basis.

First Law

Strict scrutiny (the maximum scrutiny) is applied when a law effects a suspect classification or fundamental right. Under this standard, a law will only be upheld if is necessary to achieve a compelling government interest. The burden of proof is on the government, and most laws fail under strict scrutiny. The right to travel is a fundamental right. Here, the law bans all air travel to and from the city, affecting the fundamental right to travel. Consequently, it is subject to strict scrutiny analysis. It is unlikely a court will find this law is necessary to achieve a compelling government interest since there is no indication what the interest is or how banning flights will meet it.

Second Law

Intermediate scrutiny is used whenever a law is based on gender or legitimacy. Under this standard, the law will be upheld if it is substantially related to an important government interest. In most cases, the government bears the burden of proof. Here, the law states that only male candidates will be considering for security guard jobs. Thus, this law will be judged under intermediate scrutiny. Here, the necessity of large guards does not seem to be an important government interest, since there is no indication only large guards can do the job.

Third Law

The rational basis test (minimum scrutiny) is used whenever the other two standards do not apply. Under this test, a law will be upheld if it is rationally related to a legitimate interest. Most laws pass this test, and most laws are upheld unless they appear to be arbitrary or capricious. The burden of proof is on the challenger, and

the court will give deference to the legislature. Here, the law imposes a 1% sales tax on all items sold during the games. Taxation laws like this fall under the rational basis test, and are almost invariably sustained.

6. **First Law**

A state is not allowed to directly tax federal instrumentalities. Without Congressional consent, such a tax is invalid. Here, since the state is levying a tax directly against federal property, the law is invalid.

Second Law

If a tax on the federal government or its property is nondiscriminatory and indirect it is permissible if it does not unreasonably burden the federal government. Here, since the federal employees are simply being held to the same taxation standards as state employees there does not seem to be any unreasonable burden.

CONTRACTS

1. **Sale of the Helmets**

Normally, a contract for the sale of goods of over $500 or more is not enforceable unless there is a signed writing by the party against whom enforcement is sought. However, under U.C.C. Sec. 2–201(2), "Between merchants if within a reasonable time a writing in confirmation of the contract and sufficient against the sender is received and the party receiving it has reason to know its contents, it satisfies the requirements" unless that party provides written notice of its objection within 10 days. Here, although the retailer didn't sign anything, the confirmation makes the contract good because both parties were merchants, the confirmation was binding against the manufacturer because she signed it, the retailer knew the contents of the email because she read it, and there was no indication of any objection. Consequently, there was a valid contract between the parties.

Rejection

An express rejection happens when an offeree makes a statement that he or she does not intend to accept the offer. This terminates the offer. Here, the retailer stated she was not accepting "this crud." This seems like a clear rejection.

Breach

Failure to perform in accordance with contractual terms amounts to a breach in contract. The nonbreaching party must show that he or she is willing and able to perform except for the other party's breach. If the obligee did not receive the substantial benefit of his or her bargain, the breach is considered material. In that case, the nonbreaching party may treat the contract as ended and will have the immediate right to all remedies for breach of the contract. Here, the manufacturer delivered her shipment, thus showing she had the ability to perform. Consequently, she can treat the contract as ended and sue for all remedies due to her because of the breach.

2. Conditions

A contract may provide that a party does not have to perform until a condition is fulfilled. In such a case, any failure in performance is justified.

Loan

A condition precedent is a condition that must occur before duty of performance arises in another party. Here, there is a condition precedent to Oberon giving the loan that Fenix's rental property must be producing $1,000 a month in income by November 1. Since they are only producing $500 a month in income, Oberon is excused from making the loan.

Car

A condition subsequent is one where the occurrence of it cuts off an already existing duty of performance. Here, Fenix's retention of the car is conditioned on the fact that he will have it in a locked garage at night. When Oberon drives by the property at night, he sees the car outside and not in a locked garage. Consequently, Fenix's right to retain the car is extinguished and Oberon can take it back.

3. Guitar Promise

In order to enforce a promise, there must be consideration. Consideration is made up of two elements: (1) a bargained-for exchange between the two parties and (2) the thing bargained for must be a benefit to the promisor or a detriment to the promisee. If a party intends to make a gift, there is no consideration. Importantly, if the party is only stating a condition of receiving the gift, there is no consideration. Here, although Telly told Becky she had to come by his house today to get the guitar, her coming to his house was merely a condition of receiving the gift. Consequently, his promise to give her the guitar is unsupported by consideration and is thus unenforceable.

<u>**$1,000 Promise**</u>

The rule for consideration is stated above. Importantly, if something is already given or done before the promise is made, the promise does not satisfy the "bargained-for" requirement. Here, Becky had already caught Telly when he promised to give her $1,000. Consequently, the $1,000 was not bargained-for, and the promise is unenforceable due to the lack of consideration.

<u>**Credit Card Promise**</u>

The rule for consideration is stated above. However, there is an exception stating that if a past obligation would be enforceable except for the fact of a technical defense like the statute of limitations, courts will enforce a new promise if it is in writing. In this case, the court will only enforce the new promise. Here, since Becky's past obligation is only unenforceable because of the statute of limitations and she wrote a letter to her credit card company (making her promise in writing), her new promise to pay $500 is enforceable.

4. Agreement with T-Bone

In order to be enforceable, consideration must exist on both sides of the agreement. If one party agrees to be bound, and the other does not, the agreement is illusory

and unenforceable due to lack of consideration. Here, Bob's promise to purchase "as much meat as I may need to buy from T-Bone" is illusory because he is still free to buy from other sellers or not buy anything from T-Bone at all. Consequently, the promise is unenforceable.

Tony's Offer

Under promissory estoppel, consideration is not necessary if the promisor should be estopped from not performing. Under Section 90 of the First Restatement, a promise is enforceable to prevent injustice if: (1) the promisor should have reasonably expected to induce reliance or forbearance, (2) the reliance or forbearance was of a definite and substantial character, and (3) the promise does in fact induce such action or forbearance. Under the Second Restatement, the action or forbearance does not have to be of a definite or substantial character, but the remedy may be limited as justice requires. Courts following the First Restatement will award expectation damages, while courts following the Second Restatement might award reliance damages. Here, Tony should have reasonably expected his promise of free ice cream to induce Bob to buy an industrial cooler for his new business. Bob's purchase of a $5,000 cooler was an act of definite and substantial character, and he actually bought the cooler based on Tony's promise. If the court follows the First Restatement, Bob should recover the cost of the free ice cream for six months. Under the Second Restatement, Bob should recover the cost of the cooler.

5. Promise for Basement

If both parties are mistaken as to existing facts regarding the agreement, the contract may be voidable by the adversely affected party if: (1) the mistake involves a basic assumption regarding the contract, (2) the mistake has a material effect on the exchange, and (3) the party trying to avoid the contract did not assume the risk of the mistake. Assumption of the risk usually occurs when one party was in a better position to know about the risks. Here, the problem of the streams clearly involves a basic assumption of the contract and has a material effect on the exchange because it will erase Ben's profits. However, a court will likely find he assumed the risk of the mistake because, as a contractor making a bid on excavation work, he was likely in a better position than Franklin to know what possible problems might lie under the surface. Consequently, he cannot avoid the contract due to his mistake.

Sale of Stone

The rule for mistake is stated above. Importantly, if two parties make assumptions as to the value of the bargained-for object, parties are considered to assume the risk of those assumptions and mistakes in them will not defeat the contract. Here, Franklin cannot void the contract on mutual mistake grounds because the parties assumed the risk of their assumptions.

6. U.C.C. Section 2–207 states that a contract can be formed even though the terms of the offer and acceptance do not match.

2 Percent Discount

If both parties to the contract are merchants, additional acceptance terms will be included unless (1) they materially alter the original terms, (2) the offer expressly limits acceptance to the terms of the offer, or (3) the offeror has already objected or objected within a reasonable time after notice is received. Both BuildCo. and WorkCo. appear to be merchants. Assuming the 2 percent discount is not a material alteration, the parties have formed a contract including this discount (since the offer did not expressly limit acceptance and the offeror has not objected).

Arbitration

The rule for additional terms is stated above. Unlike the discount, the rule regarding the arbitration provision will be construed by most courts as a material alteration that will not be included in the terms of the contract.

Transportation Costs

Some courts treat different terms like additional terms, and follow the same test as set out above for additional terms. Other courts follow the knockout rule, which states conflicting terms are knocked out of the contract

and the gaps are filled by U.C.C. gap-fillers. Here, BuildCo. is offering bricks at $2 plus actual transportation costs. WorkCo.'s acceptance states they will pay $2.20, with the additional $.20 apparently covering those costs. If the court treats this situation like additional terms, the buyer's acceptance will control (so $2.20), unless the seller objects. If the seller objects, the contract is on its terms. If the court uses the knockout approach, the transportation clauses will fall out and the price will be $2 plus the reasonable cost of transportation as determined by the U.C.C.

CRIMINAL LAW

1. Murder of Chip

To be guilty of a crime, a defendant must either perform a voluntary physical act or fail to act under circumstances creating a legal duty to act. To be voluntary, the act must be a conscious act of the will. Importantly, acts performed while the defendant was either unconscious or asleep are not voluntary unless the person knew she might fall unconscious or asleep and engage in dangerous behavior. Here, Elsa hadn't slept-walked in 20 years and likely had no reason to believe she would start doing it again. Consequently, since she was sleeping when she clubbed Chip, she was not engaged in a voluntary physical act sufficient for liability.

<u>Death of Bitsy</u>

There is no general duty to act to save someone. For liability, there must be (1) a legal duty to act, (2) knowledge of facts giving rise to duty, and (3) the act must be reasonably possible to perform. A legal duty to act can arise from statute, contract, familial relationship, voluntary assumption of care, or the creation of the peril by the defendant. Here, there is no known connection between Elsa and Bitsy creating a duty to act, so even if Elsa recognized the danger and could have saved Bitsy, she was under no legal obligation to do so.

<u>Burglary</u>

Burglary is the breaking and entering into the dwelling house of another at night with the intent to commit a felony therein. Actual breaking requires the use of minimal force. Here, although the door was open, Elsa used minimal force to push it open farther. She entered the home, which was the dwelling house of another. It was dark, so it was night. However, when she went inside, she did not intend to commit a felony. All she wanted to do was get warm. Once she was inside, she formulated the intent take the jacket. Since she did not have this intent when she entered the house, she could not be convicted of common law burglary.

2. Taking the Books Home

Embezzlement is the fraudulent conversion of property of another by a person in lawful possession of that property. For the conversion to be an embezzlement, the defendant must intend to defraud. Conversion means that the defendant dealt with the property in a manner inconsistent with the trust arrangement between the defendant and the property owner. Here, Hermione took several books home. As an editor, she was likely in lawful possession of the books, which were the property of the publishing company. It is unclear whether she was allowed to bring the books home, and what her intent was in doing so. However, for at least one of the books, she clearly converted the property when she sold it to Don. Consequently, she is guilty of embezzlement for at least one of the books, and possibly all of them.

<u>Selling New Book to Don</u>

False pretenses is obtaining title to the property of another by a knowing false statement of past or existing fact with intent to defraud. Here, Don gained title to the new book by writing the note for $20. However, he knew he had no money and had no intention of ever paying Hermione. Consequently, he is likely guilty of the crime of false pretenses.

<u>Selling Second Book to Don</u>

Larceny by trick has the same elements as false pretenses above. However, if only custody is obtained and not title, the crime is larceny by trick instead of false pretenses. Here, Don wrote a second fraudulent note to gain possession of the second book. However, Hermione said he should only consider that book "borrowed" until he actually paid her. Consequently, she conveyed custody and not title to the book, so Don is likely guilty of larceny by trick.

3. **Harpy Taking Violin**

Robbery is a taking of the personal property of another from the other's presence by force or intimidation with the intent to permanently deprive him or her of that property. A threat to damage someone's property, unless that property is the person's dwelling, is not enough to meet the force or threat requirement. Larceny is the taking and carrying away of the personal property of another by trespass with the intent to permanently deprive the person of his or her interest in the property. Here, while Harpy did take the violin from Eunice's presence with the intent to permanently deprive, he did so by threatening to smash the car window in. This threat against Eunice's property was not enough to meet the requirements of a robbery. Consequently, he is likely only guilty of larceny since he carried away Eunice's violin with the intent to permanently deprive her of it.

<u>Gummy Buying the Violin</u>

Receipt of stolen property consists of receiving possession and control of stolen personal property known to have been obtained in a criminal manner by another person with the intent to permanently deprive the owner of his or her interest in the property. Here, while Harpy never specifically said he stole the violin, he did say it "fell off a truck" and winked several times. Under the circumstances, it was likely Gummy understood the violin was stolen when he bought it from Harpy (additionally, a jury could find a knowing mens rea based on willful blindness).

Consequently, he is likely guilty of the crime of receipt of stolen property.

Gummy Calling Eunice

Under modern statutes, extortion is obtaining property from another by oral or written threats. In many of these statutes, threats against a person's property may be sufficient. Here, Gummy called Eunice and threatened to throw her violin in the river unless Eunice paid him. This likely meets the requirements of many modern extortion laws, so Gummy is likely guilty of extortion.

4. **Registration Statute**

A strict liability offense does not require awareness of all of the factors making up the crime. Strict liability offenses are generally regulatory offenses regulating health or safety and generally involve a relatively low penalty and little moral impropriety. If no mental state is expressly required, the court can still interpret the statute as requiring one if the penalty is severe. Here, while the registration statute appears to be a strict liability offense generally regulating guns, its imposition of a 20-year sentence for failing to register a gun means a court would likely find the statute did not dispense with the mens rea requirement. Consequently, Jesse could argue that he did not know the weapon in his possession was an automatic weapon that required registration.

Selling Statute

The Model Penal Code breaks up mental state required for a crime into purposefully, knowingly, recklessly, or negligently. A person acts "knowingly" if he or she is aware that his or her conduct is of that nature. Under the Model Penal Code, if a statute establishes a state of mind without indicating whether it is required for any particular element of the offense, the state of mind will apply to all material elements of the offense unless the statute notes a contrary purpose. Here, since the statute does not limit the effect of "knowingly," the Model Penal Code analysis applies and "knowingly" applies to all material elements. Consequently, Jesse could defend himself by showing he did not know that a sale took place, that the object was a fully automatic machinegun, or that Owen was a minor.

5. Narcotics Charges

Under the doctrine of merger, lesser included offenses merge into greater offenses. Basically, a person cannot be tried or convicted for both. A lesser included offense is one that consists of entirely some but not all of the elements of the greater crime. Additionally, under the *Blockburger* test, a person cannot be tried in subsequent trials for a lesser offense and a greater offense that uses the same evidence. Here, Tina could not be convicted of both illegal possession of narcotics and illegal possession of narcotics for sale because all of the elements of simple possession are included in the crime of possession for sale. However, she could still be charged with having illegally labeled narcotics, because this crime requires proof of something that the other crime does not (namely, illegally labeled narcotics).

Robbery and Murder

The doctrine of merger is stated above. Here, the armed robbery is the underlying felony for felony murder, and is thus a lesser included offense of the murder. Consequently, she could not be convicted of both.

6. Killing Taylor

Murder is the unlawful killing of another with malice aforethought. Malice aforethought includes an intent to kill. Here, Dave hated Taylor, snuck into his apartment, and stabbed him to death. His actions clearly meet the requirements of common law murder.

Killing Guy in Bed

Voluntary manslaughter is a killing that would otherwise be murder but there is adequate provocation that lessens the charge. Specifically, the killing must occur in the heat of passion. The provocation must meet four tests: (1) the provocation must arouse sudden and intense passion in the mind of an ordinary person, (2) the defendant must actually be provoked, (3) there was no cooling off time for the defendant, and (4) the defendant did not in fact cool

off. Importantly, adequate provocation is most often found in cases where one discovers their spouse in bed with another person. Here, Dave immediately stabbed the man when he found him in bed with his wife. This was likely adequate provocation, he did in fact appeared to be provoked, the quickness of the stabbing did not create a cooling period, and there was no indication Dave in fact cooled off. Consequently, he would likely be guilty of voluntary manslaughter for this killing.

Running over Guy

If a killing is caused by criminal negligence, it is involuntary manslaughter. Here, while Dave was still fleeing both crimes, this death was very attenuated from the other killings. Consequently, it would be unlikely to fall under the rules for felony murder because a death 12 hours of driving away is likely unforeseeable and it's unlikely he would be convicted of involuntary manslaughter simply based on driving for 12 hours. It is more likely he would be guilty of criminal negligence for driving so long without rest, so the most likely crime is probably involuntary manslaughter.

PROPERTY

1. First Bear

Wild animals become private property when a person reduces them to possession. A landowner is not the owner of all wild animals on his or her land, but a trespasser killing game on someone else's land cannot gain title to it over the landowner. Here, Mikael killed the first bear while trespassing on land owned by Ivor. Consequently, Ivor would have superior title over Mikael and the first bear belongs to him.

Second Bear

The rule for wild animals is stated above. If a person sets a trap or a net and catches an animal, that person has constructive possession over the wild animal and the animal belongs to him or her. Here, the second bear was caught in Mikael's net when Brunhilde shot it. Consequently, since the second bear was in Mikael's net, the second bear belongs to him.

Third Bear

The rule for wild animals is stated above. The first person to exercise dominion, control, and possession over the animal becomes the owner. Mere pursuit will not give a person title in a wild animal unless the person mortally wounds the animal and actual possession is basically inevitable. Here, Mikael shot the third bear in the leg, but it continued to flee. Importantly, there was no indication that the shot mortally wounded the bear. Consequently, Lydia was the first person to exercise dominion, control, and possession over the bear when she shot it, and the third bear is hers.

2. Watch

If a person accidentally loses possession of his or her property, that property is classified as lost. The key factor in determining whether property is lost is the place where the property is found. If the place the property is found would lead a reasonable person to believe the owner had accidentally lost possession, the property is lost. In the case of lost property, the finder is entitled to possession against all but the true owner. Here, the watch was lying on a public sidewalk. Consequently, it would be correctly characterized as lost and Jorge would own the property against all but the true owner.

Briefcase

If property is found in a place a reasonable person would believe the owner had intentionally placed it and then forgotten it, the property is mislaid. In the case of mislaid property, the finder does not acquire possession. The owner of the locus in quo gets possession of the property against all but the true owner. Here, the briefcase was sitting on the bar. From its location, it seems that the true owner likely intentionally placed it on the bar and then forgot about it. Consequently, whoever owns the bar would own the briefcase against all but the true owner.

Bracelets

If a person voluntarily relinquishes all ownership over property, it is classified as abandoned. For property to be abandoned, a person must show an intent to give up both title and possession. Title to abandoned property is acquired by an intent to assert ownership, dominion, and control over the property. Here, the angry couple threw their bracelets off a 12-story balcony. By doing so, they appeared to show an intent to give up both title and possession, so Jorge gained ownership of the bracelets when he picked them up.

3. **James's Ownership**

To gain title to property through adverse possession, a person's use must be (1) open and notorious, (2) actual, (3) hostile, and (4) continuous for the statutory period. Importantly, open and notorious requires use that would give reasonable notice to the true owner and continuous possession must not be broken up by periods of use by the true owner. Here, James appeared to actively hide his use of the property, so a court may find that Tyrone could not have had reasonable notice that he was using the property. James's use was actual in that he stayed at the chalet every winter and it was hostile because Tyrone never gave him permission. However, his use was unlikely to be continuous for the statutory period because, although he arguably used the property more like a true owner would since he actually used the chalet for skiing on Mount Ski, Tyrone stayed at the chalet every summer to work on his novel. Consequently, James is unlikely to have gained ownership over the property through adverse possession.

Danny's Ownership

Unless the statute of limitations has run against the true owner, a bona fide purchaser of stolen property does not gain title to the property over the true owner. Although Danny appears to be a bona fide purchaser of the property since she said she had no idea it didn't belong to James, she still would not gain title to the property over Tyrone. Consequently, since there is no indication any sort of statute of limitations has run (and, she literally just "bought" the property, so it's unlikely it could have), the chalet still belongs to Tyrone.

4. Alphaacre

A fee simple subject to a condition subsequent is created when the grantor has the power to terminate the estate upon the happening of a stated event. If the event occurs, the grantee retains the estate until the grantor exercises his or her power of termination. The grantor's interest is known as a right of reentry. Here, Susan's grant has created a fee simple subject to a condition subsequent. If Alex or his heirs ever fail to grow alfalfa on the land, Susan and her heirs may terminate the estate because Susan and her heirs have a right of reentry.

Betaacre

The rule for a fee simple subject to a condition subsequent is stated above.

Here, Susan's grant has created a fee simple subject to a condition subsequent. Just like Alex and his heirs, if she or her heirs ever grow something other than beets on the land, Susan and her heirs may terminate the estate.

Gammaacre

A fee simple subject to an executory interest is created when the grantor states a third party gains title to the estate upon the occurrence of a stated event. The third party gains an executory interest. A shifting executory interest is one that cuts short the prior estate not held by grantor. Here, Susan has created a fee simple subject to an executory interest because George will gain the property if Greg or his heirs ever fail to grow grapes. George has a shifting executory interest because his interest will cut short Greg's estate.

5. Grant to Corin, Janet, and Carrie

A joint tenancy is a tenancy between two or more tenants with a right of survivorship. In the case of a joint tenancy, when one tenant dies, the other tenants retain an undivided right in the property without the dead tenant's interest. To have a joint tenancy, the interests must be vested at the same time, acquired by the same instrument, be of the same type and duration, and create

identical rights to enjoyment. Under modern law, express language regarding the right of survivorship must be used to create the estate. Otherwise, the tenants have a tenancy in common. In a tenancy in common, each owner has a distinct and undivided interest in the property and there is no right of survivorship. Here, because Eddie granted Corin, Janet, and Carrie the property through a deed grant that simply said "To Corin, Janet, and Carrie," it appears the three women's interests vested at the same time, were acquired by the same instrument, were of the same type and duration, and created identical rights to enjoyment. However, since modern law disfavors joint tenancies and requires such tenancies to be created with express language, it is likely the three women only shared a tenancy in common in regard to the property since no other language was included in the grant.

Corin Divides with Tape

Each co-tenant is entitled to possess the entire property subject to the equal right of his or her co-tenant. Ouster occurs if one co-tenant wrongfully excludes another co-tenant from possession of any part of the whole. In that case, the ousted co-tenant may receive his or her share of the fair rental value of the property. By simply marking off her part of the house with tape, Corin has a very weak argument that she ousted Janet and Carrie. If so, they would be entitled to the fair rental value of the part of the house Corin marked off.

Carrie Sells to Chris

A co-tenant's interest is freely alienable. However, if co-tenants have a joint tenancy, a sale by one of them destroys the joint tenancy only as to that co-tenant's interest. Here, Carrie was free to sell her interest to Chris, who now becomes a co-tenant with Corin and Janet. However, if Corin, Janet, and Carrie held the property as joint tenants (which is unlikely), Chris would be a tenant in common with Corin and Janet, and Corin and Janet would remain joint tenants.

6. Lease to Quentin

If a lease is for a fixed period of time, it is referred to as a term of years. The tenancy expires at the end of the stated

period without notice. Here, by leasing the property for "three months," Larry has created a tenancy for years with Quentin. Consequently, the tenancy automatically terminated at the end of the stated period even though Larry did not give Quentin any notice.

Lease to Art

A periodic tenancy continues from time period to time period and the termination date is always uncertain. While it can be created expressly, it can also be created by implication if the lease has no termination date but states that rent will be paid at specific periods. Here, since the lease states the rent is payable every month, the lease creates a month-to-month periodic tenancy for Art.

Quentin Refuses to Leave

When a tenant wrongfully remains in possession after a lawful tenancy, the tenancy is at sufferance and the tenant is liable for rent. The tenancy ends once the landlord either evicts the tenant or binds the tenant to a new periodic tenancy. Here, Quentin is in the wrong since his tenancy of years has expired. As such, he is liable for rent and Larry may choose either to evict him or create a new periodic tenancy (in residential leases, most courts would say the tenancy is now month to month).

TORTS

1. Michael v. Peter

An assault occurs when the defendant creates a reasonable apprehension in the plaintiff of immediate harmful or offensive contact, the defendant intends to bring about the plaintiff's apprehension, and plaintiff's apprehension is actually caused by the defendant's actions. If a defendant's words and acts combine to create a conditional threat, that is sufficient for an assault. Here, Peter raising his guitar and saying "Say it again" likely combined to create a conditional threat. Although Peter did not specifically say he was going to hit Michael, his actions would lead a reasonable person into believing that was what he meant. Peter was likely standing near Michael when he raised the guitar (since they were at band practice), so raising the guitar and saying "Say it again" would create reasonable apprehension of an immediate harmful or offensive contact. Peter was mad at Michael for saying he was playing the song wrong, so it seemed he intended to bring about the apprehension. Finally, Michael backed away when faced with Peter's threat, so Michael's apprehension was actually caused by Peter's actions. Consequently, Peter likely committed an assault against Michael.

Peter v. Mike

Battery is the intentional touching of another that is unpermitted and harmful or offensive. Here, Mike intentionally touched Peter when he put his hand on his chest. Under the circumstances, Peter would likely not have permitted Mike to touch him, but there is no indication Mike's touch was harmful or offensive. If Peter could show the touching was, Mike could be liable for battery.

Mike v. Peter

The rule for assault is stated above. However, words can negate an assault if they make the apprehension of any immediate contact unreasonable. Here, Peter raised his guitar higher but said, "If you weren't such a nice guy, I would bean you too!" Consequently, there would be no reasonable apprehension of immediate contact because Peter specifically stated he wouldn't hit Mike because he was such a nice guy.

Peter v. Bill

The rule for assault is stated above. Importantly, a plaintiff can be put in reasonable apprehension even if the defendant is not actually capable of causing any injury to the plaintiff. The question is whether the defendant had the apparent ability to do so. Here, Bill's pointing a gun at Peter created a reasonable apprehension, Bill clearly intended to create such an apprehension to get his friends to stop fighting, and Bill's actions actually created apprehension in Peter because he said "Don't shoot" and put his guitar down. Although the gun was unloaded, Peter had no reason to know this and clearly thought it was loaded when he told Bill not to shoot. Consequently, Bill likely committed an assault against Peter.

2. Darcy v. Professor Plug

False imprisonment requires an act or omission that confines or restrains the plaintiff in a bounded area, intent on the part of the defendant to confine or restrain the plaintiff, and causation between the defendant's act and the plaintiff's confinement. Importantly, most courts require the plaintiff to be aware of the confinement. Here, while Professor Plug intentionally locked Darcy in the classroom and did in fact do so, Darcy was asleep. Consequently, it appears Darcy was unaware of her confinement and a court would likely find a false imprisonment did not occur. However, if Darcy woke up and discovered she was confined (which seems plausible considering Professor Plug had a heart attack outside in the hall and had the key), Professor Plug would be liable for false imprisonment.

<u>Professor Plug v. Billy</u>

Intentional infliction of emotional distress requires a defendant's extreme and outrageous act, the defendant's intent to cause plaintiff severe emotional distress or at least recklessness regarding the effect of defendant's actions, causation between the distress and defendant's act, and damages. Liability for this tort is often limited to "outrageous conduct" on the part of the defendant, or conduct that transcends all bounds of decency. Here, while Billy was at least reckless in jumping out to scare Professor Plug and Professor Plug was in fact scared and suffered a heart attack, jumping out with a Halloween mask on and yelling "Boo!" is unlikely the kind of outrageous act that would trigger Billy's liability.

3. Francis v. Kim

Battery is the intentional touching of another that is unpermitted and harmful or offensive. Consent is a complete defense to battery, and consent can be implied by a plaintiff's actions. However, consent induced by fraud is generally not a defense if the fraud regards an

essential matter. Here, Kim intentionally shot Francis in the head, but Francis seemed to consent by placing an apple on his head for her to shoot. However, his consent seemed to come about because Kim said she was an expert markswoman, which was a lie. Consequently, Kim cannot claim Francis's implied consent as a defense, and she is likely liable for battery.

Francis v. Doctor Oboe (Arrow Removal)

The rule for battery is stated above. However, consent is implied by law where action is necessary to save the plaintiff's life. Here, although Doctor Oboe could be liable for battery for removing the arrow, Francis's consent is implied because removing the arrow was an emergency situation requiring life-saving measures.

Francis v. Doctor Oboe (Weird Growth)

The rule for battery is stated above. Consent is implied by law where action is necessary to save the plaintiff's life, but the defendant can still be liable if the defendant goes beyond that implied consent. Here, although Doctor Oboe restored Francis's sight, he still did not have implied consent to remove the growth (which had nothing to do with the emergency). Consequently, he could be liable for battery for removing the growth.

4. Negligence of Charlie

Negligence requires proof of duty, breach, causation, and damages. Importantly, a defendant's conduct must conform to that of a reasonable person. In determining this standard, the majority of courts require a child to conform to the standard of care of a child of like age, education, intelligence, and experience. However, most courts find children under four incapable of having the capacity to be negligent. Here, since Charlie is three years old, most courts would find he is incapable of being negligent, although kicking the shell was likely a negligent act.

Negligence of Lionel

The rule for negligence and children is stated above. Here, Lionel is 14 years old and is required to conduct himself in the same manner of a child of like age, education, intelligence, and experience. A child of 14 would likely know that he or she needed to pay attention while riding a bicycle. Consequently, he could be found liable for riding out of the park without looking where he was going and causing Patty's accident.

<u>**Negligence of Bubba**</u>

The rule for negligence and children is stated above. However, if a child is engaged in an adult activity, he or she will be held to the standard of an adult. Here, although Bubba is 15, he is riding a motorcycle, which is likely an adult activity. As such, he would be held to an adult standard of care, and an adult would clearly know that one should not be riding a motorcycle down a sidewalk. Consequently, he could be found liable for Sally's injuries.

<u>**Negligence of Doctor Biz**</u>

The general rule for negligence is stated above. Importantly, a person who is a professional or has special skills is required to conform to the standard of a reasonable member of that profession or occupation. Here, Doctor Biz got Patty's heart started again by pounding on her chest, but also broke her collarbone in the process. "Pounding" does not seem to mean "CPR," so it seems like Doctor Biz's actions were below the standard of a reasonable doctor (evidenced by the fact she broke Patty's collarbone, which is nowhere near the heart or lungs). Consequently, it appears Doctor Biz could be liable for negligence in pounding on Patty's chest.

5. Injury to Tricia

Under the attractive nuisance doctrine, landowners owe a duty of ordinary care to avoid reasonably foreseeable risks to children caused by artificial conditions on their land. Under the general rule, a plaintiff must show that there is a dangerous condition present on the land the owner should be aware of, the owners know or should know children frequent the vicinity of the dangerous condition, the condition is likely to cause injury, and the expense of remedying the situation is slight compared with the risk. Here, the six-foot hole was clearly a dangerous artificial condition where it was reasonably foreseeable someone could have fallen into it. Christina should have known children would frequent the vicinity since children are the primary audience for Halloween decorations. A six-foot hole is likely to cause injury, and the expense of fixing it is simply filling in the hole or not digging it at all. Consequently, she is likely liable for Tricia's injury.

Injury to Trilby

Generally, a landowner owes no duty to protect people outside the premises from natural conditions on the land. However, there is an exception for decaying trees next to sidewalks in urban areas. Here, Trilby was hit by a tree branch while on the sidewalk. There is no information regarding the state of the tree or area. If the exception doesn't apply, Christina would likely not be liable for his injuries.

6. Death of Josh

A landowner owes no duty to an undiscovered trespasser, or a person who comes onto the land without privilege or permission. Here, Josh had no privilege or permission to be on the land, so he was an undiscovered trespasser. As such, Willie owed him no duty.

Warning Signs

An anticipated trespasser is a trespasser the landowner knows or should reasonably know constantly enters his or her land. Generally, a landowner owes this class of trespasser a duty to warn or make safe artificial conditions that involve a risk of death or serious bodily injury that a trespasser is unlikely to discover. However, "no trespassing" signs might convert an anticipated trespasser into an undiscovered one. Here, Willie has posted dozens of "no trespassing" signs. Additionally, he put up warnings on the footbridge, and although it created a risk of death or serious bodily injury, the footbridge was not the kind of thing a trespasser was unlikely to discover. Consequently, if any other trespassers got hurt on the bridge, Willie would likely not be liable.

Death of Francesca

A licensee is a person who enters land with the landowner's permission, but does so for his or her own benefit. A landowner owes a duty to warn the licensee of dangerous conditions known to the landowner that are unlikely to be discovered by the licensee and create an unreasonable risk of harm. Here, Francesca was a licensee because Willie gave her permission and she was hunting, which was only a benefit to herself. Willie had warning signs up around the bridge, and the nature of the bridge made it something a licensee was likely to be aware of. Consequently, he likely would not be liable for Francesca's death.

Death of Charlie

An invitee is a person who enters land in response to an invitation from the landowner. A landowner owes invitees a duty to make reasonable inspections to discover dangerous conditions and make them safe. Generally, the requirement to make something safe can be satisfied with a reasonable warning. Here, Willie had posted warning signs and invited Charlie onto the property for the express purpose of fixing the bridge situation. Consequently, he is likely not liable for Charlie's death.

LONG QUESTION ANSWERS

CIVIL PROCEDURE

1. To bring a claim in State A federal court, there must be (1) personal jurisdiction over the parties and (2) subject matter jurisdiction over the lawsuit.

Personal Jurisdiction

A federal court may exercise personal jurisdiction over any defendant who is subject to personal jurisdiction in the state where the federal court is located.

Long Arm Statute

A party filing a lawsuit subjects himself or herself personally to the jurisdiction of the court. Personal jurisdiction over an out-of-state defendant is a two-step evaluation: (1) the state's long-arm statute and (2) due process. Under the long-arm statutes of most states, the court in that state has jurisdiction over an out-of-state defendant if the cause of action arises out of the transaction of business in the state. Here, Acme Funds's ownership of a subsidiary business likely constitutes the transaction of business in the state. Further, Acme Funds likely transacts business in the state because it advertises for the state educational fund. Finally, Acme Funds committed a tortious act in the state because it wrongfully converted the stocks belonging to Pilgrim. Therefore, the federal court of State A likely has personal jurisdiction over Acme Funds under its long-arm statute.

Federal Due Process

Due process is a two-step inquiry: The out-of-state defendant must have (1) minimum contacts with the forum state such that it is (2) reasonable to hale it into court there.

Minimum Contacts

The defendant must "purposefully avail" itself of the benefits of contacts with the forum state such that it

should foresee the possibility of defending a lawsuit there. Here, Acme Funds should foresee the possibility of defending a lawsuit in State A because it directed Internet activity toward State A by advertising for State A on its website and providing related links. It also allowed State A residents, like Pilgrim, to buy and sell investments. Acme Funds also owns a subsidiary business in State A. Finally, Acme Funds's actions have created a cognizable cause of action since Pilgrim is suing for the negligent selling of his stocks. Therefore, Acme Funds likely has minimum contacts in State A.

Reasonableness

In determining whether exercising jurisdiction over an out-of-state defendant is reasonable (i.e., not offensive to "traditional notions of fair play and substantial justice"), courts employ a five-part test: (a) the burden on the defendant to answer and defend in the forum state; (b) the forum state's interest in adjudicating the matter; (c) the plaintiff's interest in convenient, effective relief; (d) the national judicial system's interest in efficient relief; and (e) the state's interest in furthering fundamental social policies.

(a) Burden

Here, Acme Funds is not a State A entity; it is incorporated in State B, and its principal place of business is in State C. While it does own a small subsidiary in State A, this is still separate from Acme Funds. Thus, travelling to State A to defend the suit could prove to be expensive. Consequently, this factor does not favor exercising jurisdiction over Acme Funds in State A.

(b) State's Interest in Adjudication

Here, Acme Funds wrongfully sold stocks belonging to a State A citizen (Pilgrim). Acme Funds continues to provide services to State A citizens, and advertises the state's educational plan. Therefore, this factor favors exercising jurisdiction over Acme Funds in State A.

(c) Plaintiff's Interest

Here, Pilgrim is a citizen of State A and alleges losing $1 million from Acme Funds's actions. Therefore, this factor weighs in favor of State A exercising jurisdiction.

(d) National Interest

Here, the national judicial system favors the most efficient and effective resolution to disputes. Since Pilgrim is a citizen of State A, and Acme Funds directs business into State A, it would likely be most efficient to resolve the dispute in State A.

(e) State's Interest in Furthering Policies

Here, there are no facts to suggest that State A, State B, or State C have competing social policies, and each state has an equal interest in protecting its citizens from harm. Therefore, this factor is neutral in determining the outcome of reasonable jurisdiction.

Ultimately, an evaluation of the factors indicates that exercising jurisdiction over Acme Funds in State A would be reasonable.

Also, based on the foregoing, Acme Funds has sufficient minimum contacts with State A such that it would be reasonable to exercise jurisdiction over it. Thus, there is personal jurisdiction under due process analysis.

Subject Matter Jurisdiction

Federal district courts are courts of limited jurisdiction. They have original subject matter jurisdiction over (1) cases arising under federal law and (2) cases involving diversity of citizenship above a certain amount in controversy. As negligence is an issue of state law, there are no facts to suggest that the federal court has federal question jurisdiction.

Diversity Jurisdiction

Diversity jurisdiction requires (1) an amount in controversy greater than $75,000 and (2) complete diversity of citizenship.

Amount in Controversy

The amount in controversy must be more than $75,000, exclusive of costs and attorney's fees. Here, Pilgrim is seeking $1 million in actual damages and $200,000 in punitive damages. Therefore, the amount in controversy is satisfied.

Complete Diversity

No plaintiff may be a citizen of the same state as any defendant. Citizenship for individuals, corporations, and partnerships is established separately. A corporation is a citizen of both (a) the state of its incorporation and (b) the state of its principal place of business. An individual is a citizen of where he or she is domiciled, meaning (a) physical presence in the state and (b) an intent to remain there indefinitely. Here, Pilgrim is a citizen of State A because he lives in State A. Acme Funds is incorporated in State B, and its principal place of business is in State C; thus, it is a citizen of both State B and State C. While Acme Funds owns a small subsidiary in State A, this appears to be a separate entity from Acme Funds itself. Therefore, diversity of citizenship likely exists because Pilgrim and Acme are citizens of different states. Accordingly, the federal court has subject matter jurisdiction over the lawsuit.

In conclusion, Pilgrim may maintain the lawsuit in State A federal court because the court has both personal jurisdiction over the parties and subject matter jurisdiction over the lawsuit. Therefore, the court did not err in denying Acme Funds's motion.

2. Josh and Dave Sue Both Companies Together

If the plaintiffs or defendants have any right or claim against them that arises from the same transaction or occurrence, joinder allows the parties to be in the same suit as long as there is at least one question of law or fact in common. Here, it appears the wiring failure caused both Josh's and Dave's electrocution, and it seems to have occurred at the same time from the same equipment. Consequently, joinder applies to both Josh and Dave as plaintiffs and Ripper and Copely as defendants.

As long as joinder of the parties is proper, any claims against those parties can be joined in a single action. Thus, any claims that Josh and Dave have can be brought in a single lawsuit.

Josh and Dave Sue Only Ripper

Federal courts require the joinder of a party who has a material interest in the case and whose absence would result in substantial prejudice to himself or herself or the parties currently in the lawsuit. Here, a judgment against Ripper will not bind Copely, so Copely's presence in the suit is not required.

Under impleader, if a defendant has a right to potential indemnification from a third party, that defendant can bring the third party into the action. Here, since the wiring caused the electrocution, and Copely made the wiring, Ripper would likely have a valid claim for indemnification. Consequently, even if Josh and Dave only sue Ripper, Ripper could likely implead Copely and join Copely to the lawsuit.

CONSTITUTIONAL LAW

1. Potential Commerce Clause Violation

Under the Commerce Clause, Congress may regulate commerce between the states. While states can also regulate interstate commerce, state regulation that discriminates against another state is unconstitutional unless it is necessary to achieve an important state interest. Here, the proposed legislation clearly discriminates against interstate commerce because it prohibits companies licensed within the state from using out-of-state businesses for their technology needs. While the state has an interest in promoting the Technology Passageway, this is likely not an important enough state interest to justify the legislation. Consequently, the legislation likely violates the Commerce Clause.

Potential Contracts Clause Violation

Under the Contracts Clause, states are generally prohibited from retroactively impairing existing contract rights. However, if the legislation serves an important government interest and the law is narrowly tailored to meet that interest, the legislation will be upheld even if it substantially impairs those contract rights. Here, although there is no information whether the legislation will impair existing contract rights, it is likely to do so since at least some instate companies likely use out-of-state providers. This legislation is not narrowly tailored to meet the interest of creating a Technology Passageway since banning out-of-state technology providers would ban a lot of business that has nothing to do with trying to get the planned Passageway started. Consequently, the legislation likely violates the Contracts Clause.

Potential Privileges and Immunities Clause Violation

Under the Privileges and Immunities Clause, states are prohibited against discriminating against nonresidents' fundamental rights. These fundamental rights include commercial activities, although the clause only protects natural persons. However, if the legislation's treatment of nonresidents is substantially justified and there are no less restrictive means to accomplish the legislation's goal, the legislation can be upheld. Here, while many technology providers are corporations, many of them are also likely to be natural persons. In that case, the desire to create a Technology Passageway likely does not justify the legislation and there are many other ways the state can promote and create the Passageway without banning the use of out-of-state technology providers. Consequently, the legislation likely violates the Privileges and Immunities Clause.

Potential Procedural Due Process Violation

Under the Due Process Clause of the Fifth Amendment, made applicable to the states through the Fourteenth Amendment, the government may not take away a person's life, liberty, or property without the due process of law. Due process usually requires at least notice, a

hearing, and a fair decisionmaker. Here, although the legislation has a petition process for exceptions, there is no indication how such a process would work. Consequently, if the process fails to provide these things, the legislation likely violates due process.

2. **Citizenship Requirement**

If a classification is based on race, national origin, or alienage, the classification is subject to the strict scrutiny test. Under that test, the law is invalid unless it is necessary to achieve a compelling state interest. However, there is an exception when the law discriminates against aliens participating in governmental functions. In that case, the rational basis test is applied. Under that test, the law is valid if there is any conceivable basis for it. Here, it is rational to require members of the unit to be U.S. citizens, since they would be acting as police officers with a direct effect on government functions (namely, public protection). Requiring them to be citizens would conceivably allow them to understand and enforce the laws better than non-citizens. Consequently, the citizenship classification is likely lawful.

Male Requirement

If a classification is based on gender, it is subject to the intermediate scrutiny test. Under this test, a law is valid if it shows a substantial relationship to an important government interest. Here, the male requirement is unlikely to pass the test because the state will likely be unable to show that the work done by the unit is incapable of being performed by female members. This work likely involves the same work as the average police officer, and women are just as able to perform these duties (enforcing the laws, patrolling, capturing criminals, etc.) as men are. Consequently, the male requirement is likely unlawful.

Age Requirement

Age is not a suspect classification like alienage or gender, so classifications based on age will be upheld if they pass the rational basis test. The rule for the rational basis test is stated above. Here, limiting the unit to people over the age of 30 conceivably makes sure that the unit is made up of physically strong people who are mature enough to deal with riots and terrorist situations. Consequently, the age requirement is likely lawful.

CONTRACTS

1. Stone v. Nick

An offer is a statement by the offeror showing an intent to enter into a bargain with the offeree. To be a valid offer, the offer must contain definite and certain terms, including quantity, price, parties, and goods. Here, Nick showed an intent to enter into a bargain by telling Stone he would sell the amplifier for $200. The price, quantity, and goods were all clearly identified. Consequently, Nick made a valid offer to sell the amplifier to Stone.

An option contract occurs when there is an offer, a promise to keep the offer open, and consideration securing the promise to keep the offer open. Stone might argue that there was an option contract because Nick implied that as long as he got back by 5 he could buy the amplifier. However, Stone did not give Nick any consideration to secure this promise, so there was no enforceable option contract.

Under the U.C.C., a merchant can make a firm offer to sell goods without any consideration so long as the offer is in a writing signed by the merchant and the offer expressly states that it will be held open. A merchant under the U.C.C. is a person who has knowledge with respect to the goods involved. Here, Nick is unlikely to be classified as a merchant since the facts do not state he has any particular expertise regarding amplifiers. Also, Nick didn't write down any promise to Stone. Consequently, there was no firm offer regarding the amplifier.

An indirect revocation terminates an offeree's power of acceptance. An indirect revocation occurs when the offeree learns from a third party of the offeror's intention not to conclude the bargain. Here, Stone seeing Kim load the amplifier into her car likely acted as an indirect revocation. Consequently, Stone's ability to accept the offer was terminated.

Ultimately, Stone is not entitled to the amplifier.

Darby v. Nick

An offer is defined above. In general, advertisements are not offers but are solicitations for offers. Here, the ad only said that an amplifier and a guitar were for sale. This was not an offer since all of the terms of the deal were not certain. For example, while the goods and quantity were identified, there is no information regarding the parties or price. Consequently, Nick did not make an offer to Darby. However, Darby likely made an offer to Nick when he said he would buy the guitar for $100.

Acceptance is a manifestation of assent to the terms of the offer that is communicated to the offeror. Here, Darby left before Nick could say anything. Consequently, there was no acceptance of the deal and no enforceable contract. Ultimately, Darby is not entitled to the guitar.

2. Refusing to Play the Bar

A contract can be avoided if it is signed due to some mental defect or illness or other incapacity, duress, or undue influence. A contract can also be set aside if it is obtained by fraud or if the offeror negligently misled the offeree concerning any material fact. Finally, a contract can be set aside on the grounds of mistake, gross unfairness, frustration of purpose, impracticability, or impossibility. Here, Taylor simply had a hit song after the signing of the contract, and he is trying to get more money based on the fact he can now command higher prices and play bigger places. There is nothing in the facts to indicate that any of the valid reasons for avoiding a contract exist, so Taylor is obligated to play the October 31 gig at the bar.

Agreement with Trent

Under the statute of frauds, a contract to employ someone for more than one year must be evidenced by a signed writing. Here, Taylor simply agreed to Trent's one-year engagement over the phone, and there was no evidence any signed writing ever passed between the parties. Consequently, Taylor does not a have contract with Trent for the years' worth of dates, and he can go ahead and play the bar under his agreement with Leslie.

CRIMINAL LAW

1. Conspiracy to Steal Computer

Conspiracy is an intentional agreement between two or more persons to commit a crime. The majority of jurisdictions also require an overt act by a conspiracy member in furtherance of the agreement. Here, Bruce, Clarence, and Max intended to commit burglary by breaking into Steve's house and stealing his computer. Max committed an overt act in furtherance of the burglary by jimmying open the window. Consequently, all three would be guilty of conspiracy to commit burglary.

Larceny of Car

Larceny is the taking and carrying away of the personal property of another by trespass with the intent to deprive the person of his or her interest in the property. Here, Bruce took Steve's car by getting into it and backing it down the driveway. He had no permission to do so, and seemed to intend to deprive Steve of his interest in the car since he shouted, "Let's dump this in the ocean!" Consequently, Bruce would likely be guilty of larceny of the car.

Felony Murder of Max

Felony murder is when a killing (even an accidental one) occurs during the commission of a felony. Generally, a defendant is not liable for a co-felon's death if the death is brought about by a victim's resistance. Here, Bruce and Clarence were in the midst of trying to commit a burglary when Max was killed by Steve (there's no indication the burglary wasn't still ongoing even though Bruce was taking the car). While Max's death could have invoked felony murder, since he was killed by Steve while Steve was defending himself, it is unlikely Bruce and Clarence are guilty of felony murder for Max's death.

Felony Murder of Clarence

The rule for felony murder is stated above. A felony is a crime punishable by death or imprisonment exceeding one year. Here, Bruce accidentally ran over Clarence while he was stealing Steve's car, which is likely a felony since it is likely punishable by imprisonment exceeding one year. Consequently, he'd likely be guilty of felony murder of Clarence.

Felony Murder of Steve

The rule for felony murder is stated above. Here, Bruce was in the midst of stealing Steve's car when he jumped out and it crashed into the pole. Consequently, he is likely guilty of the felony murder of Steve.

Petty Larceny of Tip Jar

Petty larceny usually involves the theft of something worth less than $200. The rule for larceny is stated above. Here, since Bruce "stumbled" into the bar, it didn't seem like he entered the bar planning to do anything in particular. While there, he grabbed the tip jar and left. Since the tip jar only had $3 in quarters in it, he would likely be guilty of petty larceny.

Vicarious Liability of Clarence and Max

Conspirators are not liable for a co-conspirator's acts that are not within the foreseeable scope of the conspiracy. Under *Pinkerton*, co-conspirators are responsible for acts by co-conspirators during the course of and in furtherance of the conspiracy. Here, if Clarence and Max were still alive, they would not be liable for Bruce's theft of the car or the tip jar, since neither of these acts were likely a foreseeable part of the plan to steal Steve's computer.

2. Conspiracy for Jimmy's Murder

Conspiracy is an intentional agreement between two or more persons to commit a crime. The majority of jurisdictions also require an overt act by a conspiracy member in furtherance of the agreement. Here, Tina and Amy planned to kill Jimmy, and Amy grabbed him and took him out to the woods to kill him. Consequently, Tina and Amy are guilty of conspiracy to commit murder.

Solicitation for Jimmy's Murder

Solicitation is intentionally procuring the commission of a crime by counseling, inciting, and inducing another person to commit it. Here, Tina offered Amy $5,000 if she would kill Jimmy. Consequently, she is guilty of solicitation of murder.

Tina's Assault of Amy

The majority of jurisdictions classify an assault as either an attempt to commit a battery or the intentional creation of a reasonable apprehension of imminent bodily harm in the mind of the victim by something other than mere words. Here, Tina only threatened to kill Amy, and there was no indication she meant she would kill her right then and there. Consequently, it is unlikely that Tina would be guilty of assault.

Tina's Defense of Insanity

A defendant's insanity can be a defense to criminal liability. There are several different tests for insanity. Under the *M'Naghten* Rule, insanity is a disease of the mind, caused by a defect in reason, that causes the defendant to lack the ability to know the wrongfulness of his or her actions or the nature and quality of his or her actions. Under the irresistible impulse test, a defendant is not guilty if he or she shows that because of mental illness he or she was unable to control his or her actions or conform his or her conduct to the law. Under the *Durham* test, a defendant is not guilty if he or she shows the crime was a product of his or her mental disease or defect. Finally, under the Model Penal Code test, the defendant is not guilty if he or she suffers from a mental disease and as a result lacked substantial capacity to either appreciate the wrongfulness of his or her conduct or conform his or her conduct to the law. Here, although Tina said she was "insane in the membrane," there is no indication of any actual mental defect. Consequently, unless there is some other evidence regarding a potential mental defect, she will be unable to use insanity as a defense.

Amy's Defense of Duress

Duress can be a defense to criminal liability in any offense other than homicide if the defendant does the criminal act under the threat of imminent death or great bodily harm. While Amy could claim that Tina's threat to kill her caused duress which led her to commit the crime, this defense cannot be used to defend against homicide. Consequently, she could not use duress as a defense.

Amy's Kidnapping of Jimmy

Kidnapping involves the confinement of another person where there is either some movement or the concealment of the victim. Here, Amy kidnapped Jimmy when she threw him in the trunk and drove him out to the woods.

Death of Jimmy

Involuntary manslaughter is a murder committed without malice aforethought as a result of criminal negligence or the commission of an unlawful act. Here, Amy had decided she was not going to kill Jimmy by the time she opened the trunk. Consequently, she would likely not be guilty of murder because she no longer had the intent to kill him. However, she dropped him in a grave in an apparent attempt to conceal his body. As such, she was committing an unlawful act when she left him, and her doing so left him trapped in the grave. She could also be found criminally negligent for failing to discover that he wasn't in fact dead and deciding to dump his body instead of going for help. Consequently, she'd likely be guilty of involuntary manslaughter for leaving him in the grave where he died.

PROPERTY

1. Cameron Still in Apartment

Under the majority rule, a landlord has to deliver actual possession of the premises to the tenant. If a landlord

fails to remove a holdover tenant, the landlord may be liable for any damages suffered by the current tenant. Here, Cameron was still in the apartment even though his lease had expired. Consequently, he was a holdover tenant, and Larry had a duty to remove him. Since Larry did not do so, Yehudi is not obligated to pay Larry any rent for this month. Yehudi did not mention any damages, so he may have waived his right to those damages, but he certainly does not owe Larry for rent.

Air Conditioner Breaks

A constructive eviction occurs when the premises become uninhabitable because the landlord fails to provide a service that he or she has a legal duty to provide. Basically, the property has to be clean, safe, and fit. If the premises are unsuitable for living, the landlord breaches the warranty of habitability. If the landlord does so, the tenant may move out and terminate the lease, make repairs and offset the cost of those repairs in the rent, abate rent, or seek damages. Here, there was likely a constructive eviction when Larry failed to fix the heater because the heater for the building was likely his responsibility as a landlord (since it appears the "heating in the building broke," which implies it was a system serving every unit in the building). The sulfur gas cloud likely made the apartment unlivable, and Yehudi left soon after giving Larry notice. Consequently, Yehudi would not be liable for rent during this time period, and could likely receive damages for the damaged books.

Lyda Moves In

The rule for the warranty of habitability is stated above. Here, Lyda's actions are creating the disturbance, so there is no landlord action and likely no constructive eviction (although a minority of courts hold that a landlord permitting a lessor to interfere with the use of another tenant is in fact an action of the landlord). While the feet on his ceiling drove Yehudi "nuts," there was no indication it created a sufficient injury to Yehudi's health to breach the warranty of habitability in that it did little to make Yehudi's apartment less clean, safe, or fit.

Rent Due from Yehudi

Although the lease did not in fact say that the lease was a month-to-month lease, the fact it said rent was payable on the first of every month made it a month-to-month lease. For a month-to-month lease, one full month's notice is required for termination. Here, as a month-to-month tenant, Yehudi had to give Larry one month's notice, unless there had been some type of constructive eviction. Since he did not do so, Yehudi is likely still responsible for December's rent.

2. Deed to Jeannine

To be valid, a deed must include the names of the buyer and seller, a description of the land, an indication of the present intent to convey, and the signature of the grantor. Here, while the deed describes the land because it says "Crabtree Beach," it seems to indicate a present intent to convey by stating "conveys," and has Lord Crabtree's signature, it doesn't list Jeannine as the grantee. Consequently, the deed was invalid and failed to convey any interest to Jeannine.

Jeannine Opens Surf Shop

To gain title to property through adverse possession, a person's use must be (1) open and notorious, (2) actual, (3) hostile, and (4) continuous for the statutory period. Importantly, open and notorious requires use that would give reasonable notice to the true owner and continuous possession must not be broken up by periods of use by the true owner. Here, it appears Jeannine's use was open, notorious, and actual because she opened a surf shop. It appeared to be hostile because Lord Crabtree specifically told her she couldn't use the property until he said it was OK to do so, and he apparently never gave her permission. She used the property as a true owner would (a surf shop on a beach), but there is no information regarding the length of the statutory period in this jurisdiction. If it is 10 years or less, Jeannine likely has title to Crabtree Beach by adverse possession.

Deed to Biz

The rule for a valid deed is stated above. A fee simple is created by the language "to A and his heirs." A shifting

executory interest is an interest in a third party that cuts short the prior estate after the occurrence of some listed event. Under the Rule Against Perpetuities, no interest in property is valid unless it must vest, if at all, no later than 21 years after one or more lives in being at the creation of the interest. The Rule applies to executory interests granted to charities if that interest cuts short the interest of an individual. Here, the deed has both Biz and Lord Crabtree's names, it states the land is "Crabtree Gardens," it says "conveys," and it is signed by Lord Crabtree. Consequently, it is a valid deed. It attempts to give Biz a fee simple subject to a shifting executory interest, but The Ladies Garden Society's interest violates the Rule Against Perpetuities, so Biz has a fee simple absolute in Crabtree Gardens.

Deed to Roey

The rule for a valid deed is stated above. A life estate is created by the language "to A for life." A valid gift requires (1) the donor's intent to make a gift, (2) delivery, and (3) acceptance by the donee. Here, the deed has both Roey and Lord Crabtree's names, it states the land is "Crabtree Mountain," it says "conveys," and it is signed by Lord Crabtree. Consequently, it is a valid deed. It creates a life estate since it says, "to Roey for life," with a reverter to Crabtree and his heirs when she dies. However, Lord Crabtree may not have made a valid gift. While he seemed to intend to make a gift, he never gave the deed to Roey and specifically told her he was holding onto the deed until Roey finished college. Since there is no indication Roey ever did so, the gift was not completed, and Roey likely has no interest in the property.

TORTS

1. Molly v. Bob

Negligence consists of a duty owed to the plaintiff by the defendant to act reasonably, breach of that duty, causation between that breach and the injury, and damages. Violation of an applicable statute can result in negligence per se if the statute required clear conduct, it

was designed to prevent the harm that occurred, and its purpose was to protect people in the same class as the plaintiff. Here, there was a statute that said monkeys weren't allowed on helicopters, and Bob violated this statute by bringing his monkey. The conduct required by the statute was clear in that it simply said a person couldn't bring a monkey on a helicopter. The statute seemed to be designed to prevent the actual harm that occurred, in that it presumably aimed to prevent monkeys from running around a helicopter, grabbing controls or pushing buttons, and causing it to crash. Finally, it was likely intended to protect people riding in helicopters from injury. Although Bob could argue that the statute was designed to protect the health and safety of monkeys, and the monkey is just fine, a court would likely find his violation of the monkey statute resulted in negligence per se. Additionally, when Bob saw Molly was injured, he sent the monkey for help. This seems to breach the standard of care, as a reasonable person would not send a monkey for help, and the monkey's failure directly resulted in Molly losing feeling in her hands. Consequently, Bob is likely liable for all of Molly's injuries. However, Bob might be able to argue Molly was in fact negligent herself for getting into a helicopter with a monkey (see below). If a court finds Molly was in fact negligent for doing so, her recovery may be reduced.

Steve v. Bob

The rule for negligence is stated above. Traditionally, a plaintiff's contributory negligence barred all recovery. Some states use a partial comparative negligence approach, where a plaintiff's negligence will bar recovery if it passes above a certain percentage of fault (up until that point, a plaintiff's recovery is simply reduced by his or her percentage of fault). However, the majority of states use a pure comparative negligence approach that allows a plaintiff's recovery no matter what his or her percentage of fault, and merely reduces the plaintiff's recovery by that fault. Here, Bob owed a duty to act as a reasonable person with both a helicopter and a monkey. He likely failed to do so in letting the monkey on the helicopter, especially in light of the state law specifically saying monkeys cannot be on helicopters. He is also likely negligent per se for violating the statute. Bob could argue that Steve parking in the no-parking zone was also negligent. If the court found Steve's actions negligent, he might be completely barred from recovery, but the more likely outcome is that his recovery would simply be reduced by the percentage of his negligence. Bob was also likely negligent in pointing the way to the hospital without actually knowing which was way it was. Consequently, Bob is likely liable for Steve's injuries in the crash and his later injuries caused by walking until he fell. Bob could argue that Steve was negligent himself in listening to the advice from a man who had just crashed into his car with a helicopter and a monkey, but such an argument would be unavailing.

2. Wheezy v. Kill'Em

Negligence consists of a duty owed to the plaintiff by the defendant to act reasonably, breach of that duty, causation between that breach and the injury, and damages. Under the common law, a manufacturer owes a duty of due care to all persons who may foreseeably be damaged by the manufacturer's negligence. Even if there is no direct evidence of negligence, it can be established by res ipsa loquiter. Res ipsa applies when the injury or the damage would not have occurred except for someone's negligence, the instrumentality causing the damage was in the control of the defendant, and the plaintiff did not contribute to the damages or injury. Here, it was foreseeable someone could be injured if sprayed with the adulterated poison. It is unlikely the poisons would have mixed together without someone's negligence, and the factory was under Kill'Em's control. Finally, the plaintiff had nothing to do with the poison. All of the intervening forces that led to Wheezy's death were likely foreseeable since this was intended to be a sprayed poison (the wind, floating off the field). Finally, defendants generally have to take plaintiffs as they find them, and while Wheezy's age might have had something to do his susceptibility, this would not relieve Kill'Em from liability. Consequently, Kill'Em could be liable under common law negligence.

Kill'Em could also be liable under strict liability. **Many states now extend strict liability to bystanders. If strict liability**

applies, it negates the requirement to show Kill'Em's negligence. Under strict liability, the manufacturer is strictly liable in tort for injuries caused to bystanders resulting in a defect in the product if the product was being used in the manner it was designed for. To show strict liability, the plaintiff must show absolute duty owed by a commercial supplier, production or sale of defective good, causation, and damages. Here, Kill'Em could likely be liable in strict liability for Wheezy's death since Wheezy was a bystander, the inclusion of the other poison in the product killed him, and the product was being used as intended. Here, the poison caused Wheezy's death, and Kill'Em was supplying defective goods. Consequently, Kill'Em is likely liable to Wheezy.

Wheezy v. Linus

The rule for negligence is stated above. Linus likely breached his duty to behave as a reasonable property owner when he decided to allow an elderly baseball game to go on next to fields he was spraying with a dangerous pesticide. As such, he likely breached the duty of care. A reasonable orchard owner would know that it was unreasonable to spray poison gas in the area when others were close by and there was every likelihood the gas would escape the property. Consequently, Linus is likely liable to Wheezy for his injuries.

BLANK SCHEDULE

	MONDAY	TUESDAY	WEDNESDAY	THURSDAY	FRIDAY	SATURDAY	SUNDAY
7:00–9:00							
9:10–10:10							
10:20–11:20							
11:30–12:30							
12:40–1:40							
2:00–3:00							
3:10–4:10							
4:20–5:20							
5:30–7:30							
7:30–9:00							
9:00–11:00							

INDEX

References are to Pages